REDISCOVER THE JOYS AND BEAUTY OF NATURE WITH TOM BROWN, JR.

At the age of eight, Tom Brown, Jr., began to learn tracking and hunting under the tutelage of the Apache elder Stalking Wolf. He has been a frequent contributor to *Sports Afield* magazine, *East/West Journal* and *Mother Earth News*. Featured in *People* magazine as the "Pine Barrens Tracker," Tom Brown disappeared at the height of his fame to spend a year in the wilderness with only a knife, honing the skills that he shares today at his famous survival school and in his unique series of books...

THE TRACKER
Tom Brown's classic true story—the most powerful and magical high spiritual adventure since *The Teachings of Don Juan*

THE SEARCH
The continuing story of *The Tracker*, exploring the ancient art of the new survival

THE QUEST
Tom Brown's profound search for peace and insight shows us all how to save our endangered planet...

ING

THE
VISION

TOM BROWN, JR.

BERKLEY BOOKS, NEW YORK

THE VISION

A Berkley Book / published by arrangement with
the author

PRINTING HISTORY
Berkley trade paperback edition / March 1988
Berkley mass market edition / July 1991

ISBN: 0-425-12911-X

A BERKLEY BOOK ® TM 757,375
Berkley Books are published by The Berkley Publishing Group,
200 Madison Avenue, New York, New York 10016.
The name "BERKLEY" and the "B" logo
are trademarks belonging to Berkley Publishing Corporation.

PRINTED IN THE UNITED STATES OF AMERICA

10 9 8 7 6 5 4 3 2 1

Thanks: to Tom Brown III for helping me decide to walk this Vision; to my kids, Kelly Ford and Paul Brown, who gave up themselves for the Vision; to Frank and Karen Sherwood, who stood by me, picked me up, and loved me unconditionally even in the darkest times; to Karlis (Bear) Povisils, who stood by me during all the ups and downs; to Frank and Lisa Rochelle, whose tireless efforts help in so many ways; and to Wanda Terhaar for her wisdom and love.

Special thanks: to the People of the Thunder Society, who have stood beside me through it all: Larry and Maxine Jones, Tom and Ellen Hanratty, David Mark Fletcher, Mina Viladas, Malcolm and Debbie Ringwalt, Chuck Goewey, Joyce Van Dyke, Jim Spina, Henry Combs, Ed Lombi, Scott Dewaard, Sal Lumetta, Wade Oliver, Bill Gryder, Bill Peacock, Pamela Stone, and Doc Vincent.

To Judy, my wife, my life, my Vision,
I dedicate this book with love

Contents

THE
VISION

Introduction

There is a world beyond that of our everyday physical, mental, and emotional experiences. It is a world beyond the five senses, and different than the realm of the imagination. It is the world of the unseen and eternal, the world of spirit and vision. It is a dimension of life that very few people of today seek, or perhaps care to know. Existence, for the most part, has become a rather two-dimensional affair; events deemed important unfold only within physical and intellectually logical parameters, leaving little or no room for belief in the spiritual. The demands of modern life—fulfilling obligations, making money, getting ahead—often mean that there's little time to slow down long enough to take a good, long look at life and its motivating forces, to contemplate one's current path or foreseeable destiny. Spirituality, for many, is merely something that happens for a few hours, once a week, only to be forgotten in the intervening rush of life. And for large numbers of other people there simply is no spiritual dimension. For them life happens only on a rather dull plane of physical existence. It amazes me that so many people rarely ask themselves if there is more to life than 8 to 5, television, games, and nightclubs.

In our technologically oriented society, the world of the spirit does not really exist for most, because they require scientific proof for their beliefs, and the spiritual scientific proof exists beyond the verifiable physical. They accept nothing that cannot be explained in modern tactile terms. Yet they accept the theory of the atom, even though atoms have never been seen, because they can be proven by inference, reproducible results, and data.

The world of the spirit might be compared to the enigma of the atom. The *results* of its inner workings are tangible, and we know that there are certain universal spiritual beliefs, like a common thread, linking all peoples together. But unlike the laws of atoms, spiritual laws and their manifestations are as different as each person who believes. The key to the spiritual realm is faith, and it is this faith factor that is common to all religions and philosophies. Because modern man so often cannot sense the world of the spirit in modern scientific terms, he concludes that it does not exist; at best it becomes a play thing. Yet, in his love of books, movies, and TV stories that contain characters of the mystical world, spiritual overtones, and battles between mythical good and evil is evidenced modern man's intrigue and fascination with the spiritual and the possibilities of the spiritual dimension.

Others in this modern society, feeling the void of material existence, want desperately to believe in the magical world of spirit. In a way, their searching adds a certain mystical existence to their lives, a fantasy world of demons, sorcerers, witches, and shamans. They search out endless religions, gurus, and philosophies. They play with crystals, meditation, songs, chants, ceremonies. They reach toward the customs and traditions of cultures other than their own, mixing and matching, hoping to create out of it some personal religion or philosophy. But in the modern era, where results are immediate, people are rarely willing to dedicate the concentrated amounts of time and energy to just one path. They get bored quickly with anything that requires time and dedication. They want to be instant gurus, shamans, and healers, without paying the price. They want it right away and quickly. "I want it now" is the disease of modern society. When their "quick fixes" do not pan out, they are abandoned or lost, and the people once again return to their desperate searching.

Part of what this book is about is breaking down the complications and the inaccurate conceptions that modern man has of the spiritual world. The common threads of truth that run through all religions and philosophies have always been distorted, but especially in modern times. The searcher in the modern world no longer has a clear and pure path to follow and finds in its stead only foggy, vague distortions of the original truths. And so the searcher never fully understands where he or she is going; the successes are few and far between, and the results questionable. The greatest teachers of the spiritual world are still out there, not to be found in dusty books or hidden temples, but in the temples of creation and through vision. What follows is not, in any sense, a "field guide" to the spiritual realm, but it will set forth, for all who read between the lines of these pages, a path. It is offered as a clarification of, or an introduction to, one of the greatest teachers of all—nature, the vision, the Creator.

For me, the spiritual world is truly the stuff of life. Once rooted on a spiritual path, I found that life loosened its shallow fleshiness, that I was able to transcend time and place, and enter a new, fuller dimension of life. The path of a spiritual seeker is one of the most difficult paths a man or woman can walk in life, and I urge it on no one unwilling to devote the time or take the risks involved. It takes a lifetime to understand and a zealous dedication to reach this higher plane of existence. The spiritual is a world to which the seeker comes slowly—first with the faith of a child and then with the patience and dedication of a sage. It requires one to let go of all beliefs, all prejudices, and all need for modern scientific methods of verification. One must abandon logical thinking and learn to deal in the abstract, learn to accept that each moment is an eternity and that each entity becomes, at once, a physical and spiritual teacher. It is here that I started, with the faith, openness, and curiosity of a child, that magical time of life when anything and everything was possible, where reality and fantasy mix, and where dream and flesh are fused into the eternity of mind.

I met Stalking Wolf, whom I have always called Grandfather, when I was seven. I called him Grandfather, not only out of respect for his age and knowledge, but also because, to me, he was, and remains, my spiritual Grandfather and guardian; for years he was both my teacher and my best friend. His spirit is the spirit of the wilderness, wild, ranging, comprehensive. He was always able to perceive things beyond what I could hear or feel. And it seemed there was nothing he did not know at least something about. What he knew, I wanted desperately to know.

For ten years, from the ages of seven to seventeen, I was taught by him the skills of survival in the woods: how to stalk, how to observe the flow of life, how to track and read signs, and how to heal with wild plants. Grandfather's lessons of survival were, however, only a small part of what he sought to teach me. For·him, the greatest teachings were of matters of the ancient spiritual world. True life was far greater than the existence of the physical and mental, logical or intellectual. It was not life outside of the self that mattered so much as the life beyond the self. And so life at its fullest was to be found, almost entirely, in the realm of spirit. Each and every lesson he taught led ultimately to a greater understanding of the guiding forces behind creation, of the Creator.

Because of this conviction, everything Grandfather taught had a deeper meaning than was immediately apparent. Some of these meanings would not become apparent until years after the lessons had been given and understanding reached only after all the proper, necessary, steps were lived through and the experiences assimilated into my heart. Some of these "steps" might take a lifetime to climb, and so, in many ways, even after his death, Grandfather is still teaching me.

Grandfather never forced any teaching on Rick, his blood grandson, or me. Teachings came only in response to our desire to know and our lessons were worked like a carefully wrought chess game, each move leading us, teasing us, toward a teaching until we became obsessed with wanting to know the answer. Our questions rarely elicited direct answers; instead he would respond with another question or lead us, carefully, indirectly, to the answer. This circuitous route was not capricious, but intended to show us that answers could be found within our own experiences. Whatever it was that we wanted to know, we had to work for it; we had to want and need that knowledge more than anything else. This kind of teaching, where questions brought more questions and where the best path to knowledge was not always the most direct, Grandfather called the teachings of the Coyote, or Coyote Teaching. It was a teaching that would grow in depth and meaning over the course of one's lifetime, revealing, as time and experience extended, answers far beyond the initial answers, and resonating at depths far greater than the physical realms from which they had originated. Most of all it taught us how to think, to look beyond the immediate and draw upon the knowledge we had inside ourselves. Thus each skill and technique Grandfather taught us had not only practical value but philosophical and spiritual import as well. That is why all my wilderness skills are so sacred to me; they are the physical symbols of many spiritual teachings.

Grandfather was as mystical as his past, an anachronism wandering in modern society. He was an Apache, raised by his great-grandfather in the mountains of the deep Southwest to be a warrior, a scout, and eventually a shaman and healer. It was his destiny, however, to be a wanderer, and for the better part of his lifetime he traveled from Canada to Mexico, Oregon to Virginia, always learning, always searching, living with the old ones— Native American, black, and white alike—learning all he could about the ancient ways, the ancient medicine, herbs, and shamanism. His origins became obscured along the path he walked, for he had lived and become many things. His life, ascetic and nomadic, was a continuous vision as he searched for common threads in all philosophies and religions he encountered. He sought what was pure in each rather than accept the distortions—through greed, prejudice or ego—that man had made of them. His vision, his quest, was a lifelong struggle to find the pure and the universal and pass these down untainted.

It was not the thunder on a clear night, the fire where there was no wood, the healings, or the miracles that surrounded Grandfather that brought me to my spiritual beliefs. Such things are really only incidentals. It was the example of Grandfather's life and the profound aura of mystery and reverence pervading his everyday words and actions that led me to the matters of spirit. It was the reproducible results of this attitude that kept me going— the sureness, the deftness, the agility and strength, the knowledge that infused his every coming and going. Faith is pure and needs no miracles to sustain it. Miracles might be a product of faith, but without an understanding of the faith that fuels them, miracles are simply empty tricks. The teachings of Grandfather did not hinder my biblical upbringing, but enhanced it and proved its validity. Today I still use the Bible, but purely, listening to its overall intentions and taking care not to get lost in picking apart the details. I feel that it is still the greatest work ever written, truly the Word of God. Its messages can be found in all religions and philosophies, and its lessons are part of a common thread to them all. No matter what approach, no matter which religion you choose, if you seek to discover the pure, it can only lead to the universal truths found in all things.

The spiritual teachings and miracles that Grandfather showed to me were not blasphemous. They were, instead, a manifestation of the reality of religion and spirituality, an undeniable proof that transcended the common laws and thoughts of modern man's religion of the here and now. He proved to me, and I to myself, that the age of miracles and spirituality is not over but is just beginning. With a new consciousness and understanding, modern man can reach out, search for this greater dimension. He can take the time to look at his life and goals and discover that these are not enough, that there must be more, much more. As starvation, hatred, prejudice, wars, terrorism, and the threat of ultimate destruction of nature become the rule, we must begin to search for a common vision, for all peoples, to save what we have left before it is too late. We are tired of the old ways that do not work; we see the emptiness in chasing the false gods of the flesh; and we can now hear the crying of our grandchildren in the dusty destruction of the future. The spiritual path then seems the only answer, for we have tried and failed with everything else.

To Grandfather, to me, and to many others, the world of the spirit, the unseen and eternal, is the grand reality of life and love. This book, then, is part of my path, or rather, a combination of the paths Grandfather and I have taken, fused together toward finding the absolute oneness of flesh and spirit. I do not intend for you to walk this exact path, for no two men can walk the same path to the sacred truths. Nor do I wish to force my path and beliefs on you. But the truths of this path are universal and may help you along your path, on your quest. It is written like the teachings of the coyote, deeper in meaning than just the veneer of words. The truths are there for those who seek them, for those who learn how to look deeper. This is my path as I have come to understand it thus far in my travels. I am still somewhere on that path, searching for greater truths. The search never ends until we take our final walk to the other side. Then, and only then, can we ever know all things.

The language in this book may be hard for some to understand, because mere words can never come close to describing the concepts of the spiritual world. The language used is that of the world of vision, of dreams, and symbols, and of spiritual reality. I have tried to express ancient concepts in more modern language, without diluting or polluting the intended lesson. Some parts may seem vague and abstract, subject to wide interpretation, for they are the teachings of the coyote—meaning different things to different people and best left undefined. This is a book to be reread. It is, in its own special way, intended as a field guide to the spiritual, and at each new sitting the reader should discern in the manner of the coyote new and greater meanings.

1

Grandfather

Grandfather was born into a small, nomadic clan of Lipan Apaches, sometime in the 1880's, before the Apache people had been fully relocated to the reservations. I can only guess at the specifics of his childhood, about which he was always very vague, from the stories he told. The first two years of his life, until the horror and butchering of war came from the south and killed most of his family and relatives, were spent in the American Southwest. He was then taken south by his great-grandfather, a revered shaman and warrior, to the seclusion of the trackless deserts and mountains. There, with a small group of elders and a few children, he was raised in the old ways. It was a nomadic and simple existence, hidden from the wars that beset the territory and from those who sought to destroy the centuries-old way of Native American life. The old ones, seeing the greed and destruction that the whites caused, would not permit anything of the outside world to be taught or used by their people. Theirs was a pure existence, of ancient skills and natural wisdoms to guide their lives and destiny as a people. When most tribes had fallen prey to the reservations and atrocities of white suppression, they lived free and unfettered. To all but the mountain spirits, it would seem that they did not exist.

Grandfather's people developed the skills of survival, stalking, and tracking to absolute perfection, for these skills were necessary to their survival. In their ability to escape detection they were almost invisible, and the acuity of their awareness kept them safe among the barren rocks and scrub they called home. They deftly moved from one camp to another, living free and wild, as their ancestors had. The power of their wisdom, worship, and medicine grew with the ascetic life they lived. The world of the spirit became the single guiding force and the vision of this small group. Their quest was to live in peace, to walk with the Creator, and to keep the old ways alive. It was a life characterized by an extreme simplicity on both a material and spiritual level. And out of the deepening of an understanding of the spiritual dimension came the ability to speak a different language; the ability to communicate with each other and the natural forces in a real, forceful, and essential way. Grandfather often spoke of his people, of their teaching and love. To this day their legacy remains a guiding force in my life.

Grandfather began his life, as all small children did, learning the ways of gathering herbs, cooking, mending, and making camp, as well as learning the philosophy and mythology behind each activity and skill. All things "of the camp" were of the domain of the women of the tribe, and it was in these matters that Grandfather was first schooled. These teachings were never thought of as being lesser but rather as necessary life skills for the hunter and scout. To his people, within their vision of the completeness of life, innate power or spiritual growth existed regardless of gender. All skills were necessary to keep the camp alive. So Grandfather was taught all the things of the camp. From the women he learned the compassion of healing, the mothering instinct, and the profound patience that would serve him throughout his life. The women of his people were always highly respected for their power and medicine. It was the women who gave him his first spiritual tutoring, which was the catalyst that started him on his spiritual path.

Grandfather was the youngest member of the small group of displaced Apaches and as such was somewhat of a child to all. But his great-grandfather, Coyote Thunder, was his foremost guardian and his most powerful teacher. Even while under the tutelage of the women of the tribe, Coyote Thunder still oversaw his education.

By tradition, Grandfather was, at age seven, officially given over to the care and teaching of Coyote Thunder and the other tribesmen, in order to learn the ways of the men. Now he began to learn the skills of the hunt. He learned to make bows, lances, clubs, arrowheads, and traps. As with the lessons of the camp, each lesson of the hunt—each new tool, each new skill—was accompanied by a story explaining the underlying spiritual implication. Later he learned to trap and track; he learned the honor of the hunt and the dignity of stalking. It was from his prowess as a stalker that Grandfather acquired the name Stalking Wolf. One day some of the elders watched him stalk and then touch a wolf—one of the most aware, cunning, and hence most difficult of animals to catch. Thus, in ceremony, Grandfather was renamed.

Stalking Wolf became one of the greatest hunters of the group, always providing meat as well as medicinal herbs. Always, when returning from a hunt, he would first feed the sick and weak or bring them the medicinal herbs he had collected from his hunting trip. By the time he had reached ten winters, he was leading his own hunting parties. But Grandfather preferred to hunt alone, and it was on such a hunt that he was given a vision, a powerful vision that would change his life and direct him toward a path of medicine. Certainly he had undertaken before ritual quests of the spirit, and with each quest he had gained insight and understanding. But the grand visions of life come infrequently, and then, only after long searching and many vision quests. This, however, was the first vision to address the questions of his path and purpose in life, a guiding force that would prepare the ground for future visions and quests.

He was hunting alone, far from his people. This hunt was for the mountain lion, an animal whose stealth awareness almost always required the hunter to be alone. He had been fasting for the entire hunt—four days in all—and had traveled without rest to the place where his father had once killed a white mountain lion, the skin of which Grandfather still used for his medicine bundle. Upon reaching his destination, he climbed a high ridge to sit and pray. A spirit in the guise of an ancient warrior and scout appeared before him. The spirit just stood there, looking at him. It was a searching look, searing through his flesh, looking straight through to Grandfather's heart and spirit. When Grandfather tried to communicate with the spirit, using both language and sign, he was ignored. And so, for a long time, they each stared at the other. Grandfather said that he was at once both fascinated and fearful. Instinctively, however, he knew that the ancient one was a messenger from the bright vision, not from darkness.

The spirit then approached Grandfather. In his right hand he held the ancient headband of the scout society and in his left hand he held the feathered staff of the shaman. Without word or ceremony he first handed Grandfather the scout headband, paused, then handed him the staff. Grandfather trembled inwardly with fear and excitement, unable to think or move. The spirit backed away and resumed his silent vigil, gazing at Grandfather as he held the gifts in his outstretched hands. Slowly, feeling the powerful force of the medicine items he held, Grandfather drew them in and clutched them to his chest. His motion was the symbol of accepted gift and spiritual possession. At this sign of acceptance the ancient one smiled, nodding slightly, then made the sign for ten winters, ten years, and faded from view. In his place stood a huge, white mountain lion. It growled at the sky, turned, and then slipped from white to gray and then to shadow.

Grandfather was shaken with what he had just experienced. The objects he held were very old and tattered but they were very real and extraordinarily beautiful. He was aware of the awesome power, the mystery they contained, and the honor of holding them. They were fascinating, compelling, as if containing the knowledge of the ages. He sat until dark, rethinking what he had witnessed, and the mystery of all that happened overwhelmed him. He had so many questions, and the answers that came were vague at best.

He arose from this place and walked down to the creek to wash. From the mists of dusk, the spirit reappeared, this time accompanied by the white mountain lion walking by his side. From across the creek, the spirit again stood facing him, watching. Again, after a long oppressive silence, he made the sign for sixty winters and gestured toward Grandfather. The mountain lion arose and leaped across the creek to Grandfather. With an uttered sound the lion passed to Grandfather the ancient medicine of the traveler, while across the riverbank the ancient one pointed the directions. Motioning to the east, the spirit and the lion faded into the shadows. Grandfather looked toward the eastern horizon where the spirit had last pointed, and there, in a cluster of pines stood a young white coyote. But it too faded from view, vanishing into the moonlight. Grandfather was even more shaken. Greater questions fell around him. Try as he might nothing seemed to make any sense.

Grandfather stayed in this sacred place for four more days, waiting for explanations, searching for answers. Perhaps there would be yet another vision, one that would dispel his confusion. When earth and spirit refused to speak, however, he headed back to the tribe, and to the wisdom of the elders. The ancient tradition was to seek out the guidance of the elders and tribal shamans, especially where a vision was concerned. The elders had always helped before, on all his quests and spiritual searchings, but he wondered if they could really help him now. He didn't even know if he should reveal any of what he had seen or, for that matter, show them the sacred staff and headband. Did his reluctance to share these matters stem simply from a feeling of possessiveness or could it possibly be that in the sharing he would be violating some sacred trust between himself and the spirit of the scout? He took his time with the journey back to the encampment so he would have plenty of time to search his heart for answers.

By the time camp came into view, he knew what he would have to do, and that was to ask the elders to help. He had searched his heart for this answer and it felt good; his heart was, he knew, the only thing he could truly trust for clear thinking. And so he asked the elders to give him a council fire, following the old tradition of presenting them all with gifts for their time, effort, and wisdom. That night, in a simple ceremony, Grandfather danced his vision, describing in detail its events and symbols. He displayed the sacred items, but sensing the sacredness and power within, none would touch or disturb them. Once the vision story was complete, the elders asked Grandfather a few questions for clarity, then sent him away. It was customary to leave the elders in silence, once the vision was told. This would give the elders time to discuss the vision, and the seeker time to meditate. It would also allow the elders time to prepare for any ceremony or ordeal that they felt the seeker should witness.

Four days later, Grandfather was called from the hills, his personal place of solitude and prayer, to sit before the elders. They met him in a big brushy lodge at the far edge of camp. The mood was somber and reverent. They sat in a semicircle before a small fire and the smoke of many sacred herbs hung heavy in the rafters. Opposite the semicircle, Grandfather sat alone before the fire, awaiting patiently the reply of the elders. Coyote Thunder spoke first, his voice weak with age, trembling with sadness. Yet the gleam in his eye held hope and pride. He told Grandfather that the vision and the spirit had guided him toward a path he must take. To follow his vision he must first spend ten winters training to become a scout, one of the most powerful positions in the tribe. He must then abandon this path for another ten winters and seek the path of a shaman and healer. And finally, Coyote told him, he would have to leave his people and wander alone for sixty more winters, seeking vision and knowledge, until his vision was reality.

Grandfather's spirit soared at the thought of becoming a scout and he felt greatly honored that he had been chosen for the path of the shaman. But his heart was sad at the prospect of having to leave his people and his homeland for so long a time. He asked Coyote if there was a way he could stay and still fulfill his vision, a way in which all could share with him his honor and he could honor his people. Coyote was adamant in his refusal. "A man not living his vision is living death. Unless there is a question that the vision was a trick of the mind, the vision should never be altered. But the sacred items I hold are real, and so the vision is real." Coyote went on to explain that Grandfather's calling was from the Creator and its undertaking was necessary for the overall vision of his people and of the earth: that although Coyote's heart would be sick and sad at Grandfather's eventual departure, the journey was essential, even critical. Coyote ended by saying, "You have been my hope for many years, my life, but at the end of the training, for the good of all things, you must go." The other elders, men and women, echoed the feelings of Coyote and encouraged Grandfather in his quest. There was no communal ceremony or feast at the finish of this council, for Grandfather had chosen the life of the scout, a path that would, throughout his training, separate him from the group. With this exile he would begin his journey. He would now sleep alone, eat alone, and live alone.

Grandfather then journeyed frequently, for weeks at a stretch and without any man-made tools, into the harshest lands. He honed his survival skills until they became instinctual. He came to look upon even the most violent and lonely of places as home, and found comfort and security where other men would only find death. He became an animal again, a shadow living on pure sunshine and air. Survival and the ability to face any environment without the need of any supplies, were skills essential to the scout. Thus, the many skills of survival and the philosophy behind them became Grandfather's first priority. It was only through survival that a scout learned to become one with the landscape, to find refuge in the most rugged terrains.

Survival practice took Grandfather far from his people for great periods of time and introduced him to many landscapes and environments. He learned how to survive easily in the hottest deserts, on the mesas, on the plains, in the coldest snows, and in the depths of the deepest forests. Each survival test the elders put him through he easily passed, oftentimes to the disbelief of the old ones. Where he should have been emaciated with starvation and exposure, he seemed to flourish. He could live where no one else could; he could travel at great speeds and over great distances where even the animals faltered. His skill was unparalleled by any tribal member and even the noted elders marveled at his ability.

Once the survival skills were mastered, he was then led to the arts of tracking, stalking, and awareness. Absolute proficiency in these skills—the ability to move, silent and unseen, across landscapes with little cover, the ability to read tracks quickly and accurately, and an uncanny ability to observe all things at a glance—were essential to a scout. Tracking, stalking, and awareness are never separated but rather viewed as a whole, a sort of continuum in which one is dependent on the others for absolute precision and perfection. These skills, coupled with the ability to survive, made of the scout a shadowy ghost, mystical and shrouded in an air of secrecy and legend, much like the ancient ninjas. Grandfather's lessons and ordeals were soon intensified in these areas. The tests of the elders pushed Grandfather to the limits of his ability and beyond.

Grandfather worked long and hard, pushing himself harder

than the elders pushed him, always holding his vision as a driving force, always trying to live up to and beyond the expectations of the elders. He stalked without ceasing, slipping unobserved in and out of camp. He tracked, stalked, and ultimately touched all manner of animals, moving as if composed more of spirit than of flesh. He added danger to his tests by stalking powerful animals, where one mistake could cost him his life. Finally he stalked and tracked the camps of others: hostile tribes, cavalry, and settlers. He pushed his skill to the limits of mortal man, traveling along open ground, never observed in form or in track by his enemies. There came a point where he could come across open desert, where no cover for even insects could be had, unobserved by even his fiercest and most aware tribal enemies. Truly he lived up to his name as the one who stalked wolves.

It was awareness lessons and tests, however, that were of paramount importance. For Grandfather, for the scout, awareness of all things, close and afar, was essential both to his own personal survival and to the survival of his people. It was the scout's awareness that kept his people safe. So Stalking Wolf pushed himself to observe at all levels, not only on the physical level but also on a deeper, more encompassing, spiritual level. Eventually his skills transcended the mere senses, and he began to reach beyond to the force of life itself. The confluence of physical sensing and spiritual awareness was eventually so complete that when asked how he knew that something was moving in the distance, he was often at a loss to explain. Complete awareness became for him a state of being. It was said of him that if a feather dropped from a bird several miles away, Grandfather would know about it. This keen awareness, surely and inexorably, began to break down the distraction between the inner and outer dimensions, creating a oneness of the self, where nothing happened that he could not feel.

Then came the training that Grandfather hated but had to learn—the kill. The mark of a good scout was the ability to become invisible, to be able to get in and get out of situations without being detected, but sometimes his life depended on his fighting ability. Grandfather abhorred warfare and the pain and slaughter that went with it, but he learned its skills just as well as he had those of absolute survival, tracking, stalking, and observation. He understood the necessity of the fight, but his heart would never agree with his ability, nor could he find any honor in it, and so during the tests of the fight and the kill he would never hurt an enemy, only take their weapons, tie them up, or mark part of their flesh in red to show how the kill would have taken place. Only a few times did he have to fight, but these fights ended quickly because of his agility and the strength acquired from his powerful life-style.

Sometimes Grandfather would lead bands of warriors to distant lands to check on neighbors to ensure the security of his tribe. Only once did he actually have to fight and that was when he rescued a young Lipan woman from her captors. Hair was removed from several enemy warriors but not with scalp. He left them alive, unharmed, and ashamed. He became a powerful force among his people, an excellent scout, and though he was very young, he was considered by many to be an elder, or Grandfather, meaning teacher. To nearby tribes and cavalry his prowess assumed mythic proportions. He was so feared by many that even a fleeting appearance by him at the edge of camp would send warriors into blind panic. To neighboring tribes every time something went wrong or was missing, the people would smile and blame it on Grandfather. When someone was walking alone and felt he was being watched, the common expression was that the "wolf" was doing the watching, or he was "wolf-watched," as it was sometimes called.

As Grandfather's skill as a scout neared perfection, the elders held a council with him again. It was just past five winters from the first major meeting, and they met as they had before, in the big lodge at the edge of the old village. Again he faced the elders, but this time the ambiance of the lodge and the mood of the old ones were different. The lodge itself had remained the same—the fire at its center was low, and the smoky scents of sacred herbs hung in the air. Now, however, the lodge was filled with the myriad sacred items of the tribe and the elders wore their most sacred attire. The attitude was one of reverential worship. A lone drum rang out softly from the dark recesses of the outer lodge poles, and there was a presence beyond that of the elders. It was a powerful feeling, a feeling that the spirit world stood with rapt attention, watching, waiting, guiding the words that the elders would speak. The old ones seemed to be listening, beyond the mortal sounds of the night, to voices that only the pure heart could hear.

Grandfather stayed in the lodge for six days of teaching from the elders. They all fasted; they all prayed. Sleep was rare. When one elder counseled Grandfather, the others would sleep. His mind and emotion, body and spirit, swooned with the fatigue and intensity of it all, but he held on. He knew that this was his initiation to an apprenticeship in the shamanic way of life. This had been his vision. This was his driving force, and he wanted to live this vision or not live at all.

The lessons imparted during this session in the lodge formed the essentials of a code of ethics by which the healer and shaman lived, a direction, and a path to greater spiritual power. Chant, song, and ceremony followed each of the major lessons. At these times the lodge would come alive with sound and motion, freeing Grandfather's spirits from the talons of fatigue. At the end of the sixth day Grandfather was sent away for his first test—he would wander the deserts for two moons. At the end of this time he would return to the elders, if he was still alive, for further counsel.

The desert felt like a furnace. His task was to face this emptiness purely, to live without tools, fire, or clothing. He could not trap, hunt, or kill. Instead he would have to forage the leaves of plants as did the deer and lick dew from the rocks and sand as did the mice. No shelter could be built, for he had to wander, wander to the limits of starvation, thirst, and fatigue. He was not permitted to speak or communicate in any way with any being, not even with the Creator. To all, he no longer existed, he was to walk as the dead. It was his first trial, a trial of one long waking, walking, vision quest, to show himself and the Creator that he was worthy of the path of the shaman, to show all of creation that he wished to walk this path more than he wished to live and that everything he owned, even himself, was sacrificed and dedicated to this path, this vision of visions.

In retrospect, Grandfather remembered only the first four days and the last seven. All else remained vague and dreamlike. Of the first four days he remembered vividly the fatigue, the thirst, the starkness of the landscape, and the intense heat of the sun, which seemingly burned holes into his soul. No one spoke to him; nothing yielded any sign or concern. Except for the perpetual pain and fear, he felt as if he had ceased to exist.

On the fourth day he remembered falling from a high ledge of rock, his body pounding into the sand below as if slammed onto a hot anvil. Then all reality was gone. Surreal images rushed to fill the void. Events and teachings, symbols and signs, ran by him at high speed, flooding his mind with a swirling mass of unconnected knowledge. He remembered long and short journeys of the imagination, he saw and spoke with spirit entities of animal, plant, rock, wind, and water. He heard the voices of many spirit people, and the symphony of the earth, that low vibration of all things. He remembered knowing all things and then nothing.

He awoke many miles from where he remembered falling from the ledge. He noticed the autumn colors and realized that the season had changed, that he was several weeks beyond the time of his fall. His body was undamaged; he felt no fatigue, hunger, pain, or thirst. His once parched and broken skin was as soft and resilient as the day he had first seen the world. But he could not piece together the past weeks of forgotten travel or of the lessons he knew he must have had learned along the way. And he realized that the hell of the barren desert could no longer affect him. He had been reborn, renewed, and had moved beyond the effects of comfort or pain. He now traveled easily, without the restrictions of flesh; his senses reached beyond human limits. He knew instinctively things of life and of creation that he had never consciously, wilfully learned. And he understood that with the fusion of inner and outer dimension came a release from the exigencies of survival. There was only the balance, the harmony of his thought and spirit with that of the universal mind force. He had arrived at the sacred "oneness."

On the morning of the appointed day, he returned to the camp. The elders were amazed, for Grandfather's life force seemed to glow from deep within. Here he stood, fresh, relaxed, and powerful, unscarred from his ordeal. It was as if the Creator had taken his life only to send him back more alive than he had ever been, full of knowledge and power. From that day and for the next five winters he was schooled by the elders and he flourished. His lessons were learned quickly and effectively, and his tests and trials were undertaken with ease.

His knowledge of the old ways grew daily. But as months passed Grandfather came to see that the old ones could teach him no more, that all they could offer was a physical reinforcement of what he had learned intuitively on his first quest in the desert. The desert quest had certainly been mysterious, shocking sometimes, yet he never questioned the truth of the spirit world or of the Creator. He knew that all things were possible; he did not need to know why; all he needed was absolute faith.

Nearing the end of his training, the elders began to address him as Grandfather, though he was still in his early twenties. At first Coyote Thunder called him Brother, but it wasn't long before he, as the others, called him Grandfather. He was given all the honors of an elder and he traveled frequently into the wilderness to quest and pray, or to heal a distant patient. The group quickly learned to depend on Grandfather's wisdom and power for guidance.

It was when he returned from a long trip one day that he discovered his people gone. Not a mark of foot, fire, or lodge could be found. It had been swept clean by the fiery winds of the desert, and even his keen eyes failed to find a sign. At the center of what was once camp, however, was his scout headband and the staff of the shaman. Hanging from the lance was the medicine of the traveler and scattered about the lance in a circle were sixty feathers. He knew that the time had come, as his long ago vision had declared, for him to wander—alone, far away from his people.

As Stalking Wolf pulled the lance from the ground, a coyote sounded from afar. He lifted his eyes, and there on a ridge in the misty distance stood Coyote Thunder. His great-grandfather waved a solemn good-bye, and Grandfather knew that this would probably be the last time he would see him. Coyote was very old, over 100 winters, and his health was failing. Suddenly there was the call of another coyote. The mists of the distant ridge cleared and where Coyote had stood there was a young boy, dressed in the clothes of the white man, collecting ancient stones, talking stones that spoke of ancient times. The boy stood and waved to Grandfather, as had Coyote; then he was gone.

Grandfather struggled to find the message of what he had seen. First there had been Coyote and then a boy—a white boy at that—playing with stones. It didn't make sense. But the land remained mute and unyielding, and a great loneliness filled him.

For over twenty years his small tribe had been his family. Now, because of his vision, he was forced into exile. This vision seemed to have no end, except perhaps in the wandering itself. Was there more? He knew that he would spend the rest of his life looking for the answer to this question. But for now he just sat at the old camp, searching his thoughts for a place to start his journey, his quest. He lost himself for a while in the work of setting up camp, for here he decided to stay until the path revealed itself. That night he dreamed of a white mountain lion calling him back to the place of the original quest.

Before the morning sun broke the horizon, Grandfather had broken camp and was heading back to the place of the original vision. He hadn't been back to that place since the vision, and now he yearned to drink of its purity and isolation once again. There he hoped he would find the answers, or at least a direction. He traveled quickly, as a scout, avoiding all the potential dangers, real and imagined. His mind was fixed on that sacred place where it all began for him, for his father, and for so many of his people. The trek lasted several days, across desert, over mountain, and through forest. The terrain was tough, but his training easily carried him. Like the eagles soaring the skies, his trip was an effortless flight. It was sunset as he approached the final ridge that looked over the sacred area. As he neared the top, the memories of his first trip flooded forth. His spirit soared, his body trembled with anticipation—until his longing eyes broke the horizon of the ridge and his stomach sickened at what lay below.

There below him was sprawled a miners' town. Huge holes gaped in the earth and the soil was torn by the deep swathes of roadway. All about lay garbage, broken machinery, and muddy water, where once the stream had flowed fast and clear. Buildings were tossed about the landscape in a careless, haphazard manner, and the smell of rotted sweat and liquor filled the air. On the winds drifted the drunken laughter, arguing, and turmoil of the inhabitants. People stumbled from building to building, throwing bottles to the ground, laughing, shoving, and shouting. This sacred place had been destroyed, butchered. Trees had been cut, rocks moved, and the solitude destroyed. To Grandfather's horror, nailed on the front of a building was the gorgeous hide of a white mountain lion. A coyote sounded near Grandfather, and the people began firing their guns blindly at the ridge where Grandfather sat. In a flurry of bullets, Grandfather slipped from the ridge and to the safety of the wilderness, his head spinning with disbelief, anger, and pain.

He wandered aimlessly for many suns, trying to understand these white people who had no regard or reverence for the natural things. Moreover, he did not know why the mountain lion spirit had called him back. Why? What reason could there possibly be in all that destruction and sacrilege? What reason could there be for him to be its witness? The more he thought about that sacred area, the more he knew that he had to go back and find the lesson in the destruction. Whatever the intent, he had to follow his dreams and visions, seeking their wisdom no matter how painful. It was an incomplete answer, but it was the only direction he had right then, and he knew that no more would be given until he followed the one at hand. What troubled him perhaps even more was that he should have known something was wrong miles before he got to the sacred area. Had the sacred scout skills failed him or did the spirits blind him to the warning? He would return again to this diseased town, only this time as a scout, to get a closer look.

He used the cover of night to slip back to the town. He knew that where there were villages, there would be men scattered throughout the surrounding area. The nuances of the night foretold of people coming and going all around him, but he could sense their apprehension, their inability to blend with the landscape, especially at night. He was secure in his skill and at home in the wilderness of darkness. His trip went easily; not a bird or beast sang of his arrival. To all concerned, he was invisible.

A few hours before sunrise, he arrived at the ridge overlooking the town. Below, everything was silent. Like a phantom, he slipped down to the street, passing the horses and dogs without a sound. Nothing stirred to his presence. The main street was thick with the smell of manure and the stench of unclean men. Garbage, rotted food, and broken bottles were strewn about, making travel slow and difficult. On the raised wooden side-walks, men slept the blind sleep of drunkenness. Some lay clutching bottles, others were clutching guns as if in subconscious battle with the night and all its imagined terrors. Grandfather easily passed through the town, searching every alley, peering into windows, and gazing into the open holes of the mines. He searched for answers to the questions of his heart, until the sky turned from black to the dark blue of approaching dawn, when he returned to the ridge, to a small fissured cave to sleep, escaping the eyes of man.

He awoke late in the afternoon, judging by the action of the birds. The sky was dark and overcast, the distant hills misty with rain. He slipped back to the edge of town, hiding momentarily in a dilapidated tool shack. From this vantage point he could see the comings and goings of the townspeople. Grandfather noticed how restricted their movements were, how square, boxlike houses and heavy clothing cut them off from the elements. It seemed they saw nothing of the natural world—eagles soared overhead unnoticed. They lived in a vacuum, separated from everything but themselves and the squalor they'd created.

These people seemed so strange. They didn't blend with the wilderness but feared it, holding it at a safe distance, like a man handling a deadly snake. They had no regard for the land, animals, plants, or even water. Litter was freely tossed. Live trees and brush were carelessly cut from around the dwellings, animals were callously beaten, and their water polluted by unnameable waste. These men were worse than their domesticated animals, living in their own filth, having no other purpose, it seemed, than to fatten and die. Laughter was usually drunken and at the expense of others, otherwise there was none. The faces of this village looked so pained and distorted with sadness that Grandfather wondered what directed these lives into this septic existence. So many questions filled his head. Why did they wear heavy clothes against the reality of living nature? Why did they cloister themselves in sterile houses, rush about so aimlessly, or take such great time and care with the simple processes of survival? Their lust for comfort, security, and safety seemed almost barbaric. It was foreign to Grandfather's thinking that anyone could consciously insulate themselves so lavishly from the wilderness and life itself.

Grandfather's attention was drawn to a young boy, a Native American but of uncertain origin. His hair was crudely chopped, and he was dressed in old ripped clothing of the white man that was far too big for him. His walk was labored and clumsy in the heavy boots, not at all the fluid and silent gait of his ancestors. He was stumbling around a wagon while unloading bundles onto a deck. One of the bundles burst and spilled onto the muddy street. A large white man that had been standing on the platform the whole time began screaming at the young man, finally kicking him in the chest, then throwing him facedown into the mud. Other people began laughing at the boy as the man beat him with a whip. As the boy collapsed in pain and humiliation, the group of men went inside the building. Grandfather stared on in horror, for they had treated that boy worse than they treated their animals.

Rain began falling hard, casting the village into the darkness of cloud and mist. The boy lay in the mud, as still as death. Grandfather could no longer contain the rage and anguish that flooded his heart. In a flash, he slipped from the shed, then under one of the buildings, finally to the deck beside the young man. He carried the young one back to the old toolshed and threw a blanket over him, nursing him back to consciousness. The young boy opened his eyes for a moment, trying to orient himself, then without a word, fell back to sleep. Grandfather waited for night, lashed together a travois and dragged the semiconscious boy to a distant cave, far away from town. He made a fire and a warm bed of debris. When he had made sure the boy was in a comfortable sleep, he slipped back out into the night to hunt food.

The next morning the boy awoke with a start, disoriented. His face and chest held old scars of past whippings and the fresh scars of yesterday's lashing. The boy was afraid that he would be hunted and killed, but Grandfather put his mind at ease. It took a while for the boy to relax enough and accept Grandfather's caring, but somewhere deep inside his forgotten heritage the boy instinctively trusted Grandfather's medicine and power. To Grandfather's horror, the boy related his story. He had been taken from his parents when he was very young by the man who had beaten him the day before. He had been treated like a slave, a beast of burden, and a whipping post. He was forced to sleep, with the animals and forage for rotten scraps of food. Escape would mean a certain death because the man would hunt him down and kill him as he had others before. The boy, having none of his ancestors' skills, also feared the prospect of survival in the wilderness. He had never been trained in the old ways, but deep inside he could feel the pull of the pure and natural world, an existence far from the insanity of what he was living.

Grandfather learned much from this young boy; all the horrors of the white suppression, all the restrictions of reservation life, the starvation, the disease, the drunkenness, and the child stealing. He learned that the old ones were not even allowed to practice their religion, nor could they hunt for food. Instead, they had to live imprisoned on lands that could not support them, where the winters were cold enough to kill elders and children, and the summers were full of thirst, scorching heat, and killing disease. White Indian agents grew fat and rich by hoarding the government food and clothing that was meant for the reservation. Disparate tribes were thrown together, warriors were tortured or killed, and quickly the old ways were being destroyed. The once proud tribes were disillusioned and broken; hopelessness and helplessness had become the rule.

The boy went on to describe the white man's religion and how no two whites could agree on what was right. They had forced their religion upon the people, and though this religion held many truths spoken, rarely did the whites live the truths they espoused. Their black robes might speak of peace and love, but their lives were struggles of greed, power, and war. This only confused the people more, and the elders who turned their backs on the teachings of the whites were cast aside, beaten, starved, and even killed. The young ones were sent away to distant schools to learn the white man's ways, only to find on their return that they were unable to live in either world. Treaties signed in good faith were met with lies and deceit and, in the end, the prison of reservation.

The whites were strong in numbers, as well as weapons, but proved enormously weak in their ability to live with the earth. And because they feared the earth, they called it wild and forbidden, something to be ruled and civilized. The young Native American begged Grandfather earnestly to train him in the old ways, so he could live away from the hell of the white world. Without hesitation Grandfather agreed.

At that moment a coyote howled from a distant ridge, thunder rolled across the sky, and Grandfather knew why he had been led back to this place. He had seen the insanity of people living against nature, and he had seen the cruelty that this isolation brings. He had seen the children of the earth lose their skills and beliefs to the suppression by the whites. He knew that someday the white man would have to pay for his sins.

The most immediate lesson Grandfather had drawn from his vision was that he should learn as much as he could physically and spiritually, then share it with all peoples. He knew also, deep in his heart, that someday all peoples would be open to what he had to teach, even if it took forever.

Grandfather took care of the young boy for more than a moon. He nursed him back to health and taught him simple survival and stalking skills and introduced him to the ancient spiritual truths. During that time they moved camp farther back into the hills for safety as encounters with people from the village were becoming frequent. Once the boy was strong enough to travel and had mastered the basics of escaping detection, Grandfather decided to move north and to the mountains. Before leaving, however, Grandfather went to the village one last time, saying only that he had to free the lion. That night he entered the village once again, stalked through town and climbed the building that held the white mountain lion captive. He cut the skin down, praying and making ritual offerings as he wrapped it carefully into a buckskin bag. He slipped from the village, leaving this once sacred place to the cancerous insanity of the whites. He felt the urge to stay and fight for the sanctity of the place, but he knew that fighting would not produce anything but pain and hatred. So with a reluctant heart, he looked now to the high purity of the mountains.

Grandfather spoke often of his years in the mountains, wandering up into the heart of Canada, then back again to the southern reaches. For a few years the young Indian stayed with Grandfather, learning the old ways until his skills were sufficient to keep him alive anywhere. He eventually took a young Indian wife and retired into the wild upper reaches of the Canadian Rockies. Grandfather visited them whenever he was near their home, until the young man was killed while bringing his baby to a mission for help. Some local farmers had mistaken him for a thief as they saw him running from the mission with a bundle in his arms. The bundle was his infant son and both father and child died in the same senseless flurry of bullets. Grandfather never understood how anyone could feel that any possession was worth a human life. Thief or no, the young Indian should not have had to die.

It was about the time of the young Indian's death that Grandfather left the sanctuary of the high, rugged Rocky Mountains and began living in the deserts. Like his life in the mountains, he pushed his skills to perfection, practiced the spiritual teachings, and vision-quested. Whenever possible he would seek out the elders of tribes in the area, learning whatever he could and sharing his knowledge. Some of these old ones became lifelong friends and guides, and he would visit them often in his travels. Many times he would sneak onto reservations and gather a group of children, teaching them the old ways of skill and spirit. Often, however, he was run off by the whites and sometimes even the Indian people themselves. So brainwashed were they about the taboos of the ancient ways and what the repercussions of learning them could bring that they kept their children from them. But more places than not, he and his teachings were welcomed.

Again and again, another calling, another vision would lead him to other lands. His spiritual quests led him to the West Coast, up to Alaska, down the center corridor of the Plains, to the Mississippi Valley, up the East Coast again, then back down through Mexico and into Central America. In his wanderings Grandfather crossed this country many times, and always he was learning, seeking the things of the spirit, and pushing himself beyond his limitations of yesterday. He would settle in and learn an area only until the next vision pushed him on. But even where he did settle, there was little rest, for he was always a scout, living secretly and undetected, fearful always that he would be caught by whites and sent to a reservation or worse. With few exceptions, he stayed away from the white people. And as he grew older, he sought only the company of the wilderness and the spirits, rarely visiting even the elders.

He wandered for the better part of his life. Everywhere he traveled he witnessed the senseless destruction of the earth and his people. Like an unchecked cancer, the devastation quickly grew out of control. No place seemed safe, untouched, not even the rugged, hidden areas, the places in which as a young man, he had always sought refuge. The more he witnessed, the more he despaired of fulfilling the calling of his vision, of becoming a great and inexhaustible teacher. Willing students, young or old, were increasingly difficult to find in this fast-changing society. And many of those who seemed willing were at best only curious and not willing to put in the work and sacrifice needed to learn the old ways properly. Modern society had produced people who thrived on instant gratification, on lightning-fast and easy learning. Their new values were foreign to the teachings of the earth. He was growing old and running out of time; his desperation, loneliness, and despair were intense. His vision had led him to a weariness beyond old age. There seemed to be no end in sight to the helter-skelter folly of modern life.

It was at this pinnacle of despair and old age, when his vision was fading, that Stalking Wolf decided to end his life. He felt as if the spirits had abandoned him, that he had not followed his vision properly, that all was lost. So he wandered back to his homeland to find his people and decided that if he found them vanished like so many others, he would end his existence. He wanted no longer to see the destruction of the earth; he would rather live out the remainder of his years with his people or not live at all.

His long path brought him back to the ancient sacred area where he had had his first vision—the place of the ancient scout, the white mountain lion, and the white coyote. As he crested the ridge, he expected to see the squalid village once again, but to his amazement it was gone. It had vanished from the face of the earth in the flames of fire, the drying winds, and the erosion of time. Hardly a scar was visible. Nature had reclaimed what was once hers. And his heart soared.

He set up camp near the same rocky outcropping where he had his vision. Here he felt safe, and here he wanted to stay until he died. As the sun set, a lone coyote moved to a distant ridge and released its long primal cry of loneliness, and thunder rolled across the clear sky. Grandfather stood trembling, knowing it was a calling from his great-grandfather. More coyotes and more thunder joined in until the night vibrated with their callings, then all fell absolutely silent. The ancient warrior appeared as he had many years before, vivid and strong, standing out from the blazing horizon like he was cast in stone. He motioned to Stalking Wolf. Then, as before, he motioned to the east, only this time with more power in his command. Coyote's body turned to shadow, then evaporated, leaving only the pointing hand. Grandfather gazed toward the east. A small boy collecting ancient talking stones turned and looked at Grandfather, then smiled and became a white coyote that finally lost itself in the final flicker of sunset. Grandfather headed east. By plan or design, I was collecting fossils that day by the river when I saw Grandfather. I smiled, feeling that I had known him forever, and in the distance I heard a coyote howl. Grandfather smiled with tears running down his cheeks, but I was too young then to know why.

2

▼▪▼▪▼▪▼

Awareness

From the start of my training, Grandfather stressed the importance of the physical skills of awareness and survival. To him, as to his elders, these skills were a doorway to the grander things of the spirit. Without these skills, the journey toward spirituality would be frustrating, incomplete, mediocre at best. There were no substitutes for these skills, no shortcuts, and until these skills were perfected, any search into the spiritual realm would be fruitless.

The path of all shamans was through a long period of wilderness asceticism and fasting from all worldly things. Only in the perfection of survival skills could a searcher fully detach himself from the world of man. Only the challenge of survival could teach him the basic, physical "oneness" with Creation. But it was the attainment of complete awareness that distinguished the true shaman. No one could pass through the doorways of spirit or understand those realms without absolute awareness on all levels. How could anyone be aware of all the complexities of the spiritual realms if he was not first aware of the physical realms. The one had to precede the other. Grandfather always said the power of a shaman was forged first in the depths of his asceticism—the perfection of living fully and as "one" with the earth, only secondarily in his awareness of the physical world about him.

To Rick and me it was essential to develop first the skills of survival and awareness. Then and only then could we begin to penetrate the vast domain of the spiritual world. Survival and awareness were never seen separately but rather as a continuous pair, each depending on and complementing the other. At first, we did not realize that Grandfather was leading us, through these arts, to the philosophical worlds. We were simply and fully caught up in the sense of excitement and great adventure. For each skill we learned there was always a story or philosophy behind it, so that as we learned the physical workings of something, we also learned its greater spiritual teachings. When we learned the skill of expanding our vision to take in the entire landscape, we also learned that it expanded our senses. Where the eyes went, the senses followed. We also understood the "silence" of the expanded vision that took us to our first steps of meditation. The fire-making apparatus was not only the physical spinning of wood to produce a coal and subsequent fire, but also the story of creation, man and woman, child and earth, the Great Spirit and his nurturing. Everything we learned had greater meaning; beyond the skill, beyond the physical action, we learned the truths of life.

Beyond even the sum total of all the skills, new ways of life began to emerge, more effective means to living with the earth on a grand physical level. Through the elements of survival and awareness we learned to avoid the mistakes that modern man had made. We learned to live every day with intensity, rapture, and adventure, creating a fuller life, one with more meaning than just the senseless rush of society. From wilderness we learned purity, learned to listen to the voices that could only be heard with the heart, not the ears. We understood things that were beyond normal human comprehension. Slowly and effectively, we were led from the physical skills to the more dynamic philosophies of life and nature. The transition away from the concerns of physical existence was a natural, unrestricted one as each skill led us to a basic truth of the spiritual world.

Survival, to Grandfather and to me, is a philosophy unto itself. With years of living close to the earth, without the umbilical cord of society, I understand a certain "oneness"—a "oneness" that only knowledge of survival can bring. When I think of modern man entering the wilderness, I see a scenario much like an astronaut landing on the moon: Man as an alien, part of his environment but never one with it. So also when man enters the woods. He carries with him his backpack full of provisions, a sort of lifeline back to society. Both the man on the moon and the man in the woods are severely dependent on that lifeline; life without it would mean certain death. There is also a further insulation from the earth by heavy clothing and shoes, outer garments and tents; all to "protect" man from the splendid forces of nature. Carrying with him all his insulation and protection, neither can ever fully understand the world around him. And their fears of being separated from the lifeline, whether conscious or not, keeps them close to the burdens of life. In all he tries, in all outdoor excursions, man can never know that "oneness" with the earth until he sheds his shields.

The deeper significance of survival extends far beyond the simple feat of knowing how to stay alive in the wilderness in the event you become separated from the lifeline. Survival is more than just an insurance policy. With the practice of survival one begins to relax into the earth, to learn its rhythms, to blend in balance and harmony with all things. Survival, as a way of life, removes man from the sterility of society and brings him to a hand-to-mouth existence with the earth. With this experience comes the realization that the only umbilical cord needed is the one that connects him to the earth in a real way. He begins to understand what the ancients understood: that earth is Mother, and we can never live without her. Because all things of the earth—people, animals, insects, plants—are from one Mother, we must realize that we are all brothers and sisters in a real way. Seen from this perspective reverence for the earth, her forces, and the one who created it all becomes a real and driving life force. Only through survival can man ever hope to realize the true reality of life, the "oneness" of all things and the reality of the spiritual world beyond common thoughts.

Grandfather taught us more than just the physical skills. He also taught us, with story and philosophy, the mental and emotional skills of survival, equal in depth to those skills of the physical. It was not enough just to have the skills perfected; attitude and thinking were just as important. One is unable to exist without the other. First and most important of the skills we learned in survival concerned our attitude toward the survival situation and the world around us. Essentially, it was our attitude that would decide whether a survival situation was going to be an exhilarating experience or a debilitating existence. Attitude was first and most important, and a more positive attitude developed as our skills developed. But even the learning of a new skill required a healthy, positive, and determined attitude in order to generate the patience and persistence to master that skill.

Grandfather, and living survival, taught us to separate our wants from our needs. We came to understand what was necessary and important in life and what was luxury. We learned to live fully in the span of a moment, for in survival, living in the future would only bring pain and take away the grandeur of the now. At first it was a hard lesson to learn because society taught us to plan for the future, save for the future, and try to live for the future. Survival taught us the stupidity of that concept, for one can only live fully in the now; no one can live the future. Any attempt at living the future would not be living at all. While society and our schools taught us to chase illusive goals, the wilderness taught us the raptures of life, fully lived.

As we penetrated deeper into the nuances of survival and our closeness to the earth, we began to learn the laws of creation. We blended our existence into a perfect harmony and balance with the wilderness, becoming a necessary part, then finally "one" with the force of nature and the spirit-that-moves-in-all-things. We learned to walk silently and in silence; each step was like a prayer, blessing the earth. Our movement became a dance that carried us deeper into the flow of nature, undisturbed. We learned that each entity we used for our survival was a gift of life, a life given up so we could live. Everything, too, was a gift from the Creator, and to honor him and the life we took, our skills were perfected to works of art. Certainly it was good survival sense to perfect these skills simply for the accuracy that their perfection brings, but we saw them in the deeper sense of honor and thanksgiving. We also learned to keep our bodies strong, for a strong body fits the world of survival. We believed, as nature dictates, that there is only survival of the fittest. Physical training became an everyday ritual.

We understood the awesome responsibility of the hunt, of killing our brothers and sisters among the plant and animal people. It was a sacred act, stemming from need, never for sport or cruelty. The animals and plants we killed became our flesh and forever moved within us, and we were forever thankful. We followed the ancient laws of the hunt, becoming an integral part of the land, part of the natural order of things, part of a natural system of checks and balances, accepting that we, too, someday, would fall to that same law. Only once did I feel above and aloof from Creation, as if my skills made me lord of the land. Grandfather then taught me a very profound lesson of survival—a lesson that taught me that although man was equal to all parts of creation he was also, in some instances, beneath it, frail by comparison. Without his tools—which were made from that which I thought beneath me—man could not survive.

Thick snow covered the Pine Barrens making travel difficult. It took us most of the morning to reach our campsite and all of the afternoon to build shelters, make a fire, and gather food. By dusk, our camp was built, dinner eaten, and we were relaxed, warm and comfortable. The skies had cleared and the moon shone down on the white landscape, turning the night to day. I felt proud of myself and the skills I had mastered. I'd entered this frozen landscape with just my clothing and had made such a splendid camp. Despite the below-freezing temperature and the biting wind, I was enormously content. As the conversation between Grandfather, Rick and me drifted from one subject to another (as I look back, I know that Grandfather was aware of my superior attitude, my overconfidence and arrogance), I caught sight of a fox at the edge of a distant field and told Rick to look. Grandfather, as always, knew it was there long before we had seen it.

In the frozen moonlight the fox looked so cold and frozen, so stiff, uncomfortable, and hungry. I watched it for a long time as it drifted about the frozen landscape, sniffing out bush and tufts of exposed grasses for food. I thought out loud, "I bet that fox wishes he were next to this fire right now," not realizing my mocking tone of voice. Grandfather answered that the fox would never give up its life for a life like ours. I only laughed a little at the thought. "Who wouldn't want to be sitting here, warm and comfortable, looking out on things and realizing how well off we are compared to that fox with the cold feet?" I mumbled, however, not wanting to argue with Grandfather and without another word we each got into our huts and went to sleep.

I awoke the next morning, stiff with cold. The temperature had dropped further during the night, and it was snowing again. My hut had collapsed under the snow, for in my haste to build it I had not anchored its ridge pole properly. I instinctively reached for my capote, but it was gone; fumbling further, I searched the leaves on the hut floor for my bow-drill, and it too was gone. Thinking that I had left them outside, I peered through the door, and to my horror the other huts were abandoned, the fire was out and there was no sign of Grandfather or Rick. In a panic I tried to make another bow-drill, but my hands were too cold to carve the wood. I raced around trying to gather more leaves for the hut, but everything was covered, and the snow only bit deeper into my hands. In a blind panic, I ran, hoping to make it back to the medicine cabin several miles away, thinking that running would warm me up along the way.

My energy dwindled as the cold and snow sapped my energy. I began to shiver uncontrollably, and my run became more of a stumbling walk. I fell frequently, each time getting colder, each time finding it more difficult to continue. I was still miles from the cabin, and my mind reeled unchecked, wondering where Rick and Grandfather had gone, fearing that I would die. I tried calling them, but my voice hardly penetrated the snowy winds. I pulled myself up once again, took a few stumbling steps, then fell again. I drifted in and out of consciousness for what seemed an eternity. With the snapping of a distant twig—that could have been from Rick—I lifted my head to call to him. There, right in front of me, sat a fox unaffected by the cold and snow about him. I felt like a fool. Here was this fox, comfortable and relaxed even in this violent storm. He needed nothing except his cunning to survive. I on the other hand needed my tools and protective clothing to survive. I knew then what Grandfather had meant. I knew then that man, without his tools, was a poor survival risk. I now wished I was where the fox was.

I awoke several hours later in the medicine cabin. A fire was raging and I felt warm and comfortable, though weak. Not a word was exchanged between Grandfather and me about the incident with the fox, but I knew that he had planned the entire lesson. It was a painful lesson, but it was the only lesson that would teach me about humility in the face of man's frailty.

Our survival lessons were many; we learned to build shelters and fires, to find water, and to gather food with ease. We learned how to hunt, stalk, and track, to blend with the wilderness and become "one" with life. But our lessons went far beyond just the survival and the mental attitude necessary to it. Certainly survival was important to our spiritual growth and the asceticism we needed, but what was more important was our awareness. Grandfather stressed awareness the most, for that was the doorway to the spirit world, and total awareness in the physical world led to total awareness in the spiritual realms. Grandfather taught me to see beyond the surface of superficial things, which makes up the bulk of what most people see. When Grandfather looked at a tree, for instance, he could find a wealth of information that would escape even the most careful observer. If he looked at a pitch pine, certainly he could tell the name of the tree, but from it he could tell me so much more—oftentimes information that bordered on the spiritual. He would precisely tell what the tree could yield, such as food, medicine, or utilitarian supplies. By the way the tree grew he could look deep into its past history, telling of past fires, prevailing winds, or where other trees had stood, casting it into shade when it was young. He could read the trunk for marks of insects, climbing animals, even the depth of disease, if there was any. By the slightest nuance of color and shape, he could tell what the soil was like, if it had adequate water year-round, and what kind of cone crop it would have next year or in years to come. He could also establish its relationship to the land, to the other plants, to the animals, and to the forest it grew in. Beyond these physical traits, he could penetrate the depths of its heartwood, understand its essence, and communicate with it in a real way. Many trees he would have named.

He could read all things this way in a glance at speeds that would put to shame modern computers. He could scan a landscape and in one sweep pick out all the types of vegetation, know what birds and animals were about, and listen to the voices of the overall forest. He would know where things were moving many miles away, where there was peace, and where the woods were sick. Within an area of just ten feet of forest, Grandfather could spend hours, days, even years searching out all the physical and spiritual meanings. His uncanny ability of observation and awareness bordered on the impossible. He never ceased to amaze me with what he saw and shock me with what I had missed. It took me years to look as deeply into things and with the same blinding speed as Grandfather had. The training for such an undertaking takes a lifetime to master and entails a way of looking at things entirely different from the ways used by most people.

Today, I find it very difficult to walk with people in the woods. What they miss is absolutely incredible. The way Grandfather taught me to look at things is so different from the way modern man looks. I see things beyond the normal consciousness of reality, penetrating to finer and finer detail, transcending finally into the reality of spiritual awareness and understanding. But it took years of effort and hard work to be able to read at a glance things that would take most people hours to see, never mind understand. It has become my unspoken code today to remain mute to all I see, even to my family and closest friends. From experience, I have learned that to expound on every little detail, pick out the various animals or plants or the grandeur of what most consider mundane landscapes, either intimidates others or makes me something of a star act in a three-ring circus. I have learned to play dumb. The people who do not really know me, who cannot look beyond the veneer of the superficial, believe I live in a fantasy world. What I can see is simply not visible to them. They have my deepest sympathy, for they will never really see the magnificence around them, never really understand.

Like survival skills, awareness and observation concern more than just the physical skills of stalking, fox-walking, expanded vision, and tracking. Awareness also encompasses highly developed mental and emotional skills. Grandfather found it very difficult to teach us the deeper mental attitudes of awareness because the values and teachings of modern society were in conflict with the values and teachings of the ancient ways of awareness. Where society was teaching one thing, Grandfather taught the opposite. Fortunately, the ancient teachings were borne out in the purity of nature.

Grandfather's first teaching aimed at slowing Rick and me down. Even at our young age, we had already become caught up in the unthinking rush of society, chasing irrelevant goals, gauging our actions by clocks, and living with our eyes focused on the future. By learning to appreciate the rapture of the moment, we abandoned the rush and met the slower heartbeat of Creation.

Grandfather broke us loose from our encapsulation or insulation from the wilderness. Society had taught us to live in houses, cut off from the natural world. Our artificial heating and air conditioners were buffers to the elements. Our clothing and shoes were heavy, cutting us off even as we ventured outside. We were constantly being told to stay warm, stay dry, stay out of the mud, put on a coat, and otherwise stay safe, secure, and comfortable. Grandfather showed us how these things were actually euphemisms for a kind of death. People cut off from the life-giving forces of nature could never really know life and could, therefore, never flourish. Whenever we went out into the pines, off came the protective shells, and we were baptized into the stimulating reality and rapture of life. When we learned to stop resisting nature and let it flow through us, we were never really uncomfortable in the elements again. We came to understand that the more man resisted the forces of nature, the more nature broke down his defenses. To resist was as senseless as standing firm against an ocean wave only to be smashed on the beach like a piece of broken driftwood. By giving in to that wave, the beach is reached easily and without pain.

By shedding society's restrictions and pushing the senses, these natural tools of sight, smell, touch, taste, and hearing became keen again. It seems that many people have allowed their senses to atrophy from lack of use, and it is only the exaggerated and extreme that leaves an impression. Grandfather planted us back into the soil. He knew that when man's feet are removed from the soil, he loses his sensitivity to the natural world. As he grows deaf to the earth, he no longer understands her language, and what he cannot understand, he destroys. Grandfather knew that the reason people destroyed the earth so freely was that they had lost the connection and no longer cared about living, growing things. Our awareness of living close to the earth and its creatures kept us safe among them, and we spoke a common tongue.

Grandfather led us away from modern society's delusive belief that experiencing something once or twice meant you knew that something well. With Grandfather, you *never truly knew* something; each time you experienced it, it would be different. He taught me this lesson once when I watched him gazing at a common robin. He looked captivated by it and spent the better part of an hour watching its every move, until it eventually flew off. I asked him what was so special about a common everyday robin, and I remember the pained expression on his face. He silently sketched the outline of a robin in the sand, handed me a stick, then told me to fill in all the black marks. I was flabbergasted. I had no idea where all the black marks were located or how many there were. He asked me the color of its claws, its eyes, the shape of the primary feathers, and the markings of its tail feathers. With every new question I grew more upset, totally unable to answer even the simplest question. With that one robin, Grandfather had shown me that nothing is commonplace, that we can never really know something fully. In fact, as our stalking skills increased, Grandfather would say, "You begin to understand an animal only after you can touch it." All things, common or not, are always a source of wonder and new understanding.

Grandfather also taught us not to rely on names as modern society does. Naming only removes the mystery, and all too often people think that because they know the name of something, they really *know* it. Naming is a dead end that deludes the namer into believing that there is nothing else to learn. Likewise we learned that no two experiences can ever be the same. He taught us never to think a feeling, to abstract it but to really feel it every time. Things change and grow as we change and grow, and with each passing moment we are changed, along with our understanding of things. All too often, instead of leaving our minds open to the possibilities of a situation, we anticipate adversity, thus prejudicing our mind against any new experiences. When we try hard to *live* the feeling rather than base it on the prejudice of past experiences, nothing will ever be the same.

Rick and I were taught to look close to the earth, to appreciate the little things and find the grand lessons in them. He often said that one could not know or appreciate the grand vistas of Creation unless you first knew her smaller works. He taught us to follow our heart when we wandered the wilderness, to go without time or destination, to abandon the grand goals and just appreciate everything along the way. He taught us the wisdom of sitting quietly, the timelessness of patience and its rewards. We saturated our flesh and souls in nature, fully and unrestrictedly to a point where there was no inner or outer dimension, no separation of self, where there was only the sacred "oneness." Then, and only then, could we begin to know the things of the spirit.

3

Fusion

Grandfather taught Rick and me to fuse the body, mind, emotion and spirit together as one, and to not regard them as separate, unrelated aspects of the self. Where one leads, the others follow. At its finest this synchronicity affords the seeker ultimate control of the self and allows optimum performance as a way of life. The absolute control of mind, body, and spirit is essential not just in the wilderness, but in all matters of living; like the mastery of survival and awareness, it is critical to functioning in the physical world, and ultimately in the spiritual. Once the fusion of self occurs, fusion of the self with the natural world soon follows, which in turn leads to the fusion of self to the worlds of the spirit, of the unseen and eternal.

There were no hard or fast lessons by which we came to this teaching, but only through a slow progress of experiences the cumulative effect of which was the creation of that ultimate fusion. This was the quest that accompanied our survival and awareness training. And over time, what we once thought to be insurmountable tasks became possibilities, as we saw Grandfather create examples in himself, or lead us to create our own examples. The proof of the power of this lesson came with ever reproducible results, and, most important, increasing faith.

Grandfather taught us first to control our bodies. It began by an example, macabre at first, but then fascinating. The lesson started quite by accident one day as I was carving a spindle for my bow-drill. I had been growing tired of the carving and had become quite careless, my slicing continuing along the drill and ending someplace in space far in front of me. As Grandfather walked by, the flailing knife sliced through his buckskin pants and slashed deep into the muscle just above the knee. He didn't flinch nor did he get upset. I, however, was upset enough for both of us, and worried because the blood was pouring out. I feared that he would bleed to death. Without rushing, he took off his pants, exposing a gaping wound that was over ten inches long, and deep, almost to the bone. I watched him in utter horror as he carefully looked at the wound but never rushed or showed any pain. I was sick with the thought of what I had done to Grandfather, and for my careless stupidity.

Gently he straightened his leg and pulled the wound together with his hands. Holding it firmly with one hand, he wiped off the blood with the other, never asking me to help, but holding an everyday conversation with me as he worked. He laughed, telling me I should be more careful with the knife. He gazed at the cut silently for a few moments, and to my astonishment, the blood stopped. He then wrapped the wound in a piece of clean buckskin, returning again to our conversation. He used no stitches and no medication; the only thing stitched was his badly sliced buckskin pants. He walked to the stream, washed some of the blood from his clothes, then continued with his work around camp. There was no limp, no restriction in his movement as he bent over or kneeled on the ground. It was almost as if he had never been cut.

The next day he removed the buckskin bandage, revealing a long scar that was now scabbed over, as if welded shut. There was no infection, no swelling, and no discoloration. I was more than amazed, to say the least. Over the period of the next week, the scab fell off and by the end of the month there was no scar. I finally got up enough guts to ask him how he could possibly heal so fast. Was it diet, medication, or a secret healing method? How could a gaping wound close so fast without stitches, and a scar disappear in less than a month, especially when I saw it cut almost to the bone with my own eyes? To my flood of questions, he only smiled. "I used the greatest healing tool of all," he said. "But," I said, "I didn't see you use anything on that cut." "I did," he said. "I used my mind." "How was that possible?" I asked. Grandfather smiled again and said, "You believe that wounds heal at a certain rate and in a certain way; I believe that wounds heal as fast as you believe they can, sometimes faster. It is the same with all things in all situations. For what the mind believes is true, is true." I spent many years perfecting this belief in self. It is only with this belief that the belief in the greater self will begin; only then will faith in the grander realms beyond the self become reality.

Out of so many lessons over the years in belief and faith, one stands out in my mind above all others. It was a lesson in the control of body and a fusion of all elements of self in order to perform a certain seemingly impossible task. I guess I remember it so well because it was one of the first lessons I had in belief after I had cut Grandfather. Since that time I had been particularly captivated by the power of belief, though I could not understand or internalize the whole process. Grandfather's subsequent lesson taught me the essence of mind and body control, and of belief. Though it was only the beginning of a long road, I could plainly see the connection belief had, not only to the physical self, but also to the spiritual self.

The branch I stood upon shook with my own trembling fear. Some forty feet below me the stream looked like a tiny ribbon winding under my tree and disappearing in the misty horizon. My legs felt like rubber and my heart pounded in my throat. Swallowing was impossible, for my mouth was dry and my neck tight. I clung to the limb above me with a grip so tight that it threatened to tear the flesh from the tree or snap the limb. The few minutes I had been up the tree felt like an eternity, the limb I had to jump to seemed so far away, and getting farther with each passing moment. Grandfather stood far below me. Not a word of encouragement had been spoken since I'd climbed the tree. Certainly I had jumped from one tree to another in our travels but never before so high or so far. Indeed, for this lesson, the distance I had to jump was farther than I was capable of jumping on the ground, and I felt the task impossible.

Grandfather quietly called up to me. He told me to relax and catch my breath and to visualize myself as if on the ground. As I calmed, he spoke. "It is not enough just to think you can do something," he said. "You must also have absolute faith, absolute belief that you can; just thinking you can is not enough." He also explained in no uncertain terms that I had to visualize the entire jump. I had to imagine it so well that I would actually feel every movement, every muscle action, and even the wind in my hair. I must pass out of my mind all thoughts of the impossible, any negativity or probability of failure. Again he told me that if I believed something to be impossible, then it became impossible, but with confidence and an absolute belief, anything became possible. Even with all those words of wisdom and all the encouragement, it took forever to calm down enough to think. I visualized the entire jump, picturing myself as a flying squirrel, feeling the whole process. I passed out of my mind all negativity and began to believe I could do it. My visualization grew stronger, along with my confidence. Suddenly, as if some magical spell were cast, I believed, without a doubt, and I made the jump effortlessly.

On that day of the jump, I learned the importance of belief. I learned that thinking you can is not enough, that there must be absolute confidence and belief to provide strength. I learned the importance of visualizing an action perfectly before it is attempted. This way the scenario goes well. I learned also the importance of a strong body, of physical strength and conditioning. But I learned much more than just the things that were obvious, for in those lessons was the beginning of the process of fusing together all processes of self. With only the proper physical conditioning and strength, the jump would have been impossible. Certainly there are finite limits to physical ability, but in the realm of spirit all is possible. Nonetheless, strengthening the body is important, for a strong and healthy body is essential to all things, physical and spiritual.

The training and strengthening of the body became an everyday ritual; we were always pushing beyond what we had thought were our limits. We ran continually, we sprinted in deep sand, hiked long distances, and carried heavy loads. We climbed trees until we shook with fatigue, and we also did a form of weight lifting using heavy rocks. We ran harder and longer distances until we dropped, then got up and ran again. We pushed our bodies through the most adverse weather and built up our endurance. We would sometimes travel without food or water, sometimes even taking winter hikes in just a loin cloth and moccasins. The more we worked our bodies, the better we knew them. We learned, through knowledge of ourselves and our thinking process, to control our heart rate and our metabolism, to send blood to our extremities during cold days, to stop bleeding, and to otherwise have absolute control over all our physical functions. With this training, we eventually fused the body and the mind together as one, where one could control the other and vice versa. We found that by just changing body posture we could control thinking and emotion, and by changing thinking we could control our bodies. This meshing, this fusion, enabled us to do things that most people would consider humanly impossible.

We practiced this control and the fusion of self frequently. We would create a situation that would need absolute control, then push ourselves beyond our expectations. We would go out on a cold winter day and sit on the ground, naked, pushing our minds until our bodies would sweat. We would swim in the winter and practice sending blood to our extremities and pushing our metabolism until we achieved comfort. We would walk across hot coals, knowing our bodies would not allow us to be burned. We walked endlessly on the hot "dog days" of August, controlling our sweat so we did not have to drink. The fusion of body and mind was practiced every day, and we constantly pushed ourselves past our last limits. In time we learned to control the duration of a common cold or to abandon sickness, and to find energy where there was only exhaustion and to flourish in the most difficult situations.

Our mental training went further than just the control of body. We began to learn the dynamics of life, of doing, and of action. Grandfather said that there were only two types of people in the world, critics and doers. Critics were people who sat around criticizing everything, all too lazy to make a change, too lethargic to live. He said that there would be many critics we would meet in life, from the critical know-it-alls, to the critical do-nothings. He said that there are only a few real doers in life. Doers are the people that the critics criticize, because they are the ones doing. With doing there is living. Doers are the people who make change, who never criticize, because they are too busy doing. He taught us to become doers, for being a doer is difficult; being a critic is all too easy. Critics are people who so often say that things are impossible, or who are basically skeptical. Because a critic hasn't ever tried something, that something thus becomes impossible to be done by anyone. A doer knows anything and everything is possible.

Grandfather also taught us that we create our own reality. Our mental attitude is the only thing that decides how we will feel about something, about some situation, or some person. Thus, lessons and trials that taught us a proper, positive mental attitude and how to create our own reality were frequent. Anytime I found myself upset about something or looking at something in a negative way, Grandfather would ask me why I chose to feel that way. That question would lead to a deep introspection, and I would find that my perceptions and understandings would change when I looked at them differently. Thus the first thing we learned about creating our own reality was the ability to be flexible and to change when necessary. It is flexibility and change in the world of nature that prevents extinction. I began to ask myself why I chose to feel a certain way whenever something negative was encountered. I then could change that feeling at will, thus controlling my mind and emotion.

I remember one of my first lessons in creating my own reality. It was during one of my first full survival camp outs, and my skills were not yet up to par. It was in the late fall; the winds were bitter cold and the rain heavy, soaking everything. I had spent all night and most of the next day in the debris hut. I was soaked to the bone, cold, and depressed about the conditions. I had been looking forward to exploring the lower swamps, and now the whole day was wasted, boring, and rather debilitating. I lacked energy and drive to do anything and chose to lie down and bemoan my imprisonment. All at once, I caught myself being a critic, and without another thought, I jumped out of the hut and built a fire. The fire began to warm me, and I felt good again. I began thinking about how I looked at this day and how I chose to feel about the situation. I decided to try to change my debilitating perception and to look at it as an adventure and a challenge.

I sprang into action. The challenge of making my camp the most warm and comfortable one ever filled me with a boundless energy. Within a few hours I had created a masterpiece in survival living. What I had learned about shelters and camp through that experimentation has lasted me a lifetime, things that I could not have learned if I had chosen to remain inactive and debilitated. Instead I chose happiness and energy, and though the day remained the same in external conditions, my internal representations had changed and my spirit soared. From these basic truths I began to reach out further, creating my own reality. I found that there was no such thing as a good or bad day; there is only the kind of day we choose to look at. If we learn something, even from what we consider bad or a failure, then it is good. It is always our choice.

From the wisdom of fusion, of mind and body control, we began to enter realms of the inner world, where separation between reality and dream, between the physical and the spiritual world, were dissolved. Once we became proficient in the fusion of self, we began to penetrate the primal world within ourselves. We learned, through the teachings of Grandfather and through survival, that we have within us a primitive self—a self that could be called upon for insight, or for power in a time of need. This is a basic self that all beings carry within; a primal self closest in kind to the spirit-that-moves-in-all-things. We learned that the only thing standing in the way of this inner primal self was logical thinking and the restrictions of the society we lived in. Grandfather taught us to reach through to this inner self, to tap its energy and resources in a real way.

One of the first lessons we were taught about the primal self was the necessity of releasing the animal, the more instinctual self, within. This is the ancient part of our being and it is through the animal that we are connected to our distant ancestors, to a time when there was no separation between man and animal. We learned also that there were two types of physical action: the action of the body controlled by the mind, and the action of the body controlled by the primal mind. Most of the time the body would be controlled by the mind, but there were times when this control was not powerful or fast enough. At these rare times, when the body had to be at peak strength and the interaction between body and mind was too slow, the animal within was called upon. Once the animal could be controlled and released at will, reaction replaced thought, creating a direct and fast link between the body and the primal mind. Thus reaction time was increased and strength, agility, and endurance transcended normal maximum levels. It is a power long forgotten by modern man but implicit in nature.

The animal within could be used for long or short periods of time, during times of crisis. However, because during its use the body is at peak levels, the animal has to be controlled or the body will burn out. Whenever the animal within was released, there had to be a recovery time, a longer period than would be needed for normal physical exertion. We learned to control the animal within and its power very slowly. At first it was very difficult to control, but with constant practice, we began to use it effectively. When the animal is released, the mind is let go, and the body takes over fully. There is no thought or analysis; instead the body just reacts to the situation with the ultimate power and speed of an animal. In certain situations the primal animal knows better what to do than the logical mind does, for there is no time for analysis, there is only time for reaction and action. During these times the mind virtually disappears, with only vague recollections of what is happening. The human then becomes animal, with animal actions and sounds. It can be a hideous beast unless controlled.

The first time I released the animal within was when I had an accident during an intense winter survival situation. It was bitter cold; temperatures were below zero and winds were nearing thirty miles per hour. I was making my way back to the medicine cabin when I decided to cut across a lake to make my trip shorter. Nearing the far end of the lake I suddenly plunged through the ice into water over my head. I had failed to see the nuances in the snow that foretold of a spring entrance and thin ice. Nevertheless, I plunged in over my head, my lower body lodging in the thick mud, to the waist. I struggled to get free for what seemed like an eternity. I quickly lost control of my body because of the freezing water, and I ran out of air fast. The mud still held me under, my mind faltered, my head pounded with the cold, and I could feel the life begin to slip from me.

At first, I lost all will to fight, then suddenly an anger welled up, and I could feel the fight begin to pound back into my veins. As my thoughts disappeared, I could feel the animal within emerging. All the training had taught me well. The primal mind took over all thought, and my body responded like a powerful beast. I vaguely remember blasting from the mud and over the lip of the ice, and running toward the medicine cabin, over a mile away. I remember the freezing of my hair and clothing, but I ran furiously, the growls from deep within echoing above the winds. By the time I reached the cabin, I was in a pour of sweat, exhausted from the extreme energy burn, but alive. No amount of human energy, thought, or adrenaline rush could have saved me back in that frozen mucky grave. For even with an adrenaline rush there would still have been thought, and with that thought, a restriction of power. The animal had saved me, and I slept for the next twenty hours.

Throughout my life I have called upon this animal within to save my life, or to help me in a dire situation. It dwells within me like an old friend, there to help build a debris hut quickly or a fire in the pouring rain, or to run from danger. It is also the basis for the scout wolverine fighting, which I consider one of the best fighting arts. Knowing that the animal exists within me puts me in touch with the spirits of the past, with the animal world we are part of, and with creation. It teaches our place in the scheme of things, and our connection to all things around us. Grandfather used this animal as a beginning, a doorway to our deeper past, to our instincts, our primal gut feeling and intuitions. From the animal within, we began to understand the wealth of natural gifts given to man by the Creator, and by life itself—gifts that everyone possesses no matter how hidden by our civilized, logical minds.

Through our lessons in nature, and by relentlessly watching animals, we learned the power of instincts. We could clearly see that each entity of the natural world was given an instinct to survive, to reproduce, and to thrive. It never occurred to us that we had similar instincts, that was, until Grandfather began showing us how to get in direct touch with that part of our primal self. Communicating with our instincts, in a real way, was the beginning. This communication with our inner selves would eventually lead to the communication with the world beyond the self and finally to the spirit-that-moves-in-all-things. For it is the primal self that dwells closest to the natural world and understands all the forces and truths that escape logical minds.

I once asked Grandfather how he knew the uses of so many plants from all over the country. He had no books to learn from and only infrequent teachers; most he had to learn in some other way. His answer was so simple, yet so complicated. "Simply," he said, "if you want to know the spirit of a plant and what it is used for, you must ask it." The statement was so profound, so intriguing, that I took a long time to ask the next obvious question. "And how does one ask a plant?" I said. Grandfather smiled with his usual coyote smile, a knowing smile that meant there would be a long path of learning needed to follow his answer. "You ask with the heart," he answered. In true coyote fashion, Grandfather began to unfold the secrets of the inner self and of instinct. He asked us if a fawn was given a field guide to all the plants he could eat or did the doe take him from bush to bush, showing him what to eat. How did a cat know how to hunt? How did a raccoon, or the hawk we had raised, so easily blend back into the natural world without training? "It was instinct," he said. "The same instinct that teaches an animal how to survive and live also teaches us. We already know what plants are edible and which are medicinal, because it is our basic instinct. The only problem is getting back to that instinct in a pure way, something that modern man can not easily do."

As the years passed, we began to slowly understand the basic animal instincts within us. We also realized how dangerous it was for modern man to try to use this instinct without the proper training. His logical mind had to be set aside and the flow of instinct recognized and correctly interpreted. Often the logical mind will interfere with this process and make instinct very difficult to understand, and it is very easy for us to make a deadly mistake when using plants. It took us years to master the awesome power of instincts, but with Grandfather's careful training, we began to understand the uses of plants we had never seen before. Our instincts for survival complemented our practical skills, to a point where one could not be separated from the other. We learned never to deny our instincts or that part of us that is the primal animal, as society tries to do. For to deny that part of self, one denies his entire self. Man cannot live by mind alone.

Far beyond the practical uses of the animal within and the instincts, we began to tap even deeper resources. We began to know things about the natural world around us that could not have been known by just using the senses. Because the primal self is close to the life force of nature, we began to tap into that force. That force, the spirit-that-moves-in-all-things, could tell us things that we would not physically or cognitively know. We began to call this inner force our connection, our gut feeling or intuition. It was a viable force in our lives, as keen as any of our senses. When our intuition spoke, we listened, for it was never wrong. I learned through results that to abandon or disregard that inner voice could be very dangerous. It gave us a knowledge beyond that of human understanding. But it took years of hard work to perfect it to a precise tool. Once mastered, however, we were well on our way to understanding the world of the shaman.

I remember vividly the first time I realized that Grandfather was using this intuition I had learned about. We were just beginning to vaguely understand the concepts of the inner vision, as Grandfather called it, and had no idea how powerful it could be. Grandfather, in a powerful yet subtle way, revealed to us just how dynamic the intuitions and the inner vision can be. We were heading to a distant camp area to meet Grandfather, who was coming from another direction. On the way, Rick and I decided to set some traps. Since we knew that it was going to be a full survival camp out, we could get a jump on things. Quite a few miles from camp, we found a good transition area and set our traps. I set a deadfall and Rick set a snare. We finished quickly and hurried to the camp area to meet Grandfather. As we finished our shelters, Grandfather finally got to camp.

As we greeted him, he told us that this was going to be a spiritual camp and there would be no hunting, only fasting. Rick and I glanced at each other and, without a word, continued with our work of building camp. Neither of us would dare tell Grandfather we had set traps, but we decided that after he was asleep, we would return to the trapping area and take them down. After dinner, we sat around the fire till well into the night, discussing spiritual things. Eventually the conversation trailed off, I worked on a talking stick, Rick beaded a pipe bag, and Grandfather leaned back against a tree, apparently asleep. Slowly, he leaned forward but did not open his eyes. "Grandson," he said, now looking at me. "A rabbit has sprung your deadfall, but it did not get him." Pausing for a moment he spoke again. Now looking at Rick, he said, "Your snare got him." He slumped back against the tree and went back to sleep, or whatever he does at night.

Rick and I were beside ourselves with confusion. How could he have known we had set traps? He was miles south of us when we set them, and neither of us had mentioned them. And how could he tell when the traps were sprung, and that it was the same rabbit? We had set them several miles away, across two swamps, and it would have taken quite a while for any emanating rings of movement to reach him. Rick marked the time on his pocket watch, and we slipped from camp and ran to the trap area. I reached mine first, and to my utter amazement the trap had been sprung by a rabbit. We followed his tracks, which ended at Rick's snare site. There, high above our heads, was the rabbit. At that time in our lives we could read a two-week-old track to within minutes of when it was made. These tracks were made at the precise time Grandfather had told us about the traps. It was impossible to have heard any concentric rings or nuances of the kill in that short a time.

Grandfather was awaiting us as we returned to camp. There was no need for explanation, for Grandfather had guessed the whole scenario. With great shame, I asked him how he had known exactly when the traps had sprung, what kind of traps they were, and that the same rabbit was involved in both. What he said, not only explained the world of inner vision but also touched on the "oneness" that he so often spoke of. He said, "If a rabbit moved upon your back, could you not feel it? There is no separation in the force of nature, no inner or outer dimension; we are at once part of nature and nature is part of us." It took me many years to understand that profound statement and many more years to be able to do what he had done. With each understanding comes new mysteries to be understood. I am only now beginning to understand the vast complexity of Grandfather, and of the force.

4

▼▼▼▼▼

The Trail

Heavy morning mist blanketed the Pine Barrens, reducing visibility to only a few yards. Bird song, what little there was, sounded muffled and distant, and insect voices had ended with the cold front that had come through last night. It was cool and damp, the air still and thick, and it was hard to believe it was only early fall. Here and there I could pick out the faint colors of autumn's advance, backdropped against the wall of green. Near me was the intense but soft glow of late summer wildflowers bowing toward the ground with their heavy burden of dew. All colors seemed so soft and vibrant, as if waxed with a glassy coat. Even the few insects, motionless with chill, appeared as jewels on the foliage as they awaited the morning sun. The whole forest seemed so mysterious, primal, yet so full of pulsating life and motion.

I had been sitting motionless for hours, watching as the mist grew opaque with the advancing dawn. I was practicing the inner stillness that Grandfather had taught me not so long ago, but it was hard for an eleven-year-old boy to remain still for very long. I knew that this time the stillness and quietude of body and mind were important, not just for practice but for the necessity of food,

Grandfather's food, for winter survival. The earth beneath me was dry, but my clothing, hair, and skin were soaked with the dew-ladened mists, and I felt a deep chill to my core. My mind wandered in and out of reality, in and out of dream and thought, as I fought the lack of sleep and boredom of endless waiting, the fatigue of anticipation. Grandfather's whisper broke the silence: "Boredom is only for people who do not know themselves or the wonders of life."

My mind feasted on his words, for they were the only words spoken for many hours. I searched their meaning but I had been there before, bored beyond all thought and reason. I knew that the moment boredom arises, it is a teacher. It is our mind and spirit's way of communicating to us that we are not looking deep enough into the things around us, nor are we living fully in the span of a moment and understanding eternity. I realized then the source of my boredom. I had lost touch with reality and allowed my mind to rush, wandering aimlessly over all the things I should be doing rather than enjoying fully what was. I let go the distracted thought and nature rushed in to fill the void, carrying me back to the world of silence and beauty that enveloped me. At once I felt connected to the earth again, and the internal clock slipped slowly back to the expansion of eternity.

The snap of a twig in the distance brought my body to full alert, though there was no external or internal movement. Many hours of watching animals had taught me not to show any movement or allow the trembling of anticipation to take over. I knew also to not think but to meditate so as not to give my position away to the oncoming animal. With experience I learned the lessons of how the tides of spirit can be picked up easily by the animal and plant worlds. I gave no thought to the oncoming animal but disappeared into the reality of my body, becoming an old weathered stump. All excited thoughts were erased—my body, mind, and spirit rooted to the landscape as if I had sat there for ages. I could feel my breathing slow, my lower body extend beneath the earth like roots, and my skin become weathered bark.

Another soft snap of a twig and a small gray fox came into view, deftly passed by, then evaporated into a misty bush.

Before the fox had left my mind, there was another rustle and snap—not the soft snap of a paw, but a sharp crack, most likely made by a hard hoof. I thought, no doubt a deer, a small one, judging by the size of the crackle it made. Sound is an experience imprinted upon the subconscious and deciphered by intuition. Unlike the more scientific, cognitive way in which I remember the nuances of tracks, sound is remembered through the inner self. Through repetition and association sound simply becomes something that is known. Though you don't know why, or how to explain it to anyone the knowledge becomes an integral part of who you are. In the purity of wilderness I learned to give myself over to the intuitive, the instinct, and the inner voice that remembers without thinking. The intuitive is as important to survival and understanding as common thought. The small deer, still faintly spotted with its old fawn coat, drifted by as did the fox.

The inner voice grew stronger. I knew that another deer was on its way, not far behind, though I did not hear or see anything. Yes, the passing of the small deer could have alerted me to others in the area, but again this was something internally known but not mentally realized. There was more sharp snapping, this time heavier and more powerful. There was no hesitation in the oncoming movement, though there should have been. Grandfather and I had made no attempt to camouflage our bodies or scents, and this should have put the animal on alert, especially with the air barely moving. I had wondered about this hunt and its success. Grandfather had always been so careful of these things in the past, but this time there were no pre-hunt preparations, except the prayers. I could not believe that the deer would come close enough for Grandfather to get a clean shot, especially since he would not kill anything farther away than ten feet. To him the prowess of a hunter came from how close one came to the animal and how quick the kill. I thought that the haphazard way we had prepared for the hunt could not possibly produce any success.

A big doe slipped from the cover, drifting along a well-worn deer trail. I had seen this trail and many like it, worn deep into the earth, winding through the landscape, creating the labyrinth of roadways throughout the pines and scrub oaks. She walked with a determination, obviously heading back to her day bed. There was no uneasiness in her step or hesitation as would have been normal for a deer. Instead she paid no attention to her surroundings or to the light brushy area along the trail where we sat. I wondered for a moment if this deer had any senses at all, especially to have entered an area like this, where human scent was heavy and where there were now "stumps" that never had been there before. She walked past Rick, within a few feet of his shoulder, to stop momentarily to urinate, before going on.

She moved forward; there was a blur of motion that I caught out of the corner of my eye but no sound of brush, only the thud and crunch of Grandfather's arrow hitting flesh. The deer took a few stumbling steps, half twisted around as if to change direction, then collapsed in front of me. A sound rushed forward like a concentric ring from where she lay, emanating outward to the local crows sounding their warning as they flew off. The little deer took flight from a distant bush, other birds gave their alarm, then as suddenly as it began, there was complete silence again. Grandfather slowly arose from his place and walked to the deer. Kneeling beside her and stroking her face, he fell into silent prayer. I could feel the sense of loss he felt, but I also knew and felt the necessity of the hunt, its place in the celebration of thanksgiving for life.

My mind was full of why's. Questions of all sorts filled my head, and I wanted to burst out with them all at once. Most of all I could not understand why the kill and the hunt had been so easy, especially with all the elements of the hunt going against us. We had not made proper preparations, the air wafted our scent in all directions, and in my mind we had chosen a poor place to sit and wait. With all this going against us, we should not have even seen a deer, far less had one come so close to us as to almost rub against Rick and to allow Grandfather such a clean and quick kill. In my mind, I went through all the possible reasons why it worked so well, but none seemed even close to logical. As Grandfather gutted the deer, I asked him why it had been such an easy hunt, and if the tracks told him that there was something wrong with the deer's senses when he had found them the previous day.

Grandfather answered very slowly, taking care to choose the proper words. I knew that whenever Grandfather spoke in this manner the lessons were important for both our physical and spiritual development. Beyond his words, I could sense a deep emotion in his voice, a sense of sorrow and pity about which he spoke. "Animals, like humans, make in life the mistakes that will ultimately lead to their death, either physically or on a spiritual and emotional level, as with this deer. People and animals that stay on the same paths in life will eventually wear themselves into ruts—a complacency to life born of the false security, comfort, and monotony of that path. Soon the ruts become so deep that they can no longer see over the sides. They see neither danger nor beauty, only the path before them, nor do they abandon that path so often traveled, for fear of losing their security and entering the land of the unknown."

I was stunned at what he said. The words cut like a knife deep into my world. I thought of all my friends at school, how they take the same routes to school and how they follow the same paths and routines in their everyday lives, how I knew exactly where each friend would be by the time of day. I even saw it in the adult world, only with more routines, some oppressive and overbearing, like taskmasters driving them blindly toward some elusive goal along the same overtraveled pathways that everyone else was on. That is why it had been so easy for me to watch them unobserved, even though many times I had stood in the open. I realized that new people in town were harder to watch than the natives were because they had not yet established a routine. I saw how many things people really missed, things going on all about them, life itself, unobserved and unlived. I could understand the pity in Grandfather's voice, and felt remorse for the people who would never really know the treasures of life because of their ruts.

I looked into my own life and found there too many patterns and ruts. I thought myself through a typical day and discovered the many things I did in the same way at the same time so often as to become unconscious of them. I regretted all the lost time and everything I had failed to see or feel and knew that I had, in a very real sense, lost a bit of my life. I knew also that I had come to this loss lured by the security and comfort that such a routine offered. My quest had been driven by an impersonal goal dictated by society's external shoulds—my path had become a rut worn in by the masses in their search for conformity. In keeping to the rut, I had become numb to the possibilities of life; when I had wandered I was dead to the vitality around me. I saw with fear that such a mindless, unaware existence would only lead to the sensory and spiritual destruction of humankind. I vowed then to break every rut and routine in my life. I was not going to end up like that deer, or for that matter anyone else. I wanted desperately to savor every moment, every nuance, of life. I could not afford to give myself over, even for a moment, to the deadening routine.

I was so determined to break all routines that I went even further than just changing things that were obvious, like the way I walked to school, got up in the morning, or hiked into the Pine Barrens. I began to change the little things, like the way I sat, my position while observing things, and the way I listened or touched. I continually made things new and different, sensing the same things in different ways. Unfortunately, I developed a routine for avoiding routine and eventually had to change that, striving to make of the whole process a spontaneous adventure rather than another routine path. It turned out to be a lot of hard work and constant self-monitoring, but in breaking bad habits there is always struggle, and the end result always justifies the effort.

Grandfather also helped us with our quest to break the routine of everyday living. He taught us how to look at the world in a new way. Instead of the usual practice of focusing on one point in the landscape, we learned how to take in the entire picture while remaining aware of all its elements. This technique of extending our visual reach to the limits of our peripheral vision opened up the sensory world. Being the very sight-oriented animal that the human is, our senses follow our vision. If we pinpoint our vision we do likewise to our senses but expanding the vision expands the senses. We learned that by taking in the grand picture, our ability to pick up movement increases. This is the vision of animals and people attuned to the earth, and accounts for why they see us before we see them. Using the grand vision picture at night also opens a better night vision. We learned that, by changing from the ruts of human vision, we could see more and feel more of our place on earth.

We also learned about the danger of a kind of automatic vision that plagues most people. When a landscape is scanned by the eyes for the first time, they take a series of pictures. Every time the landscape is looked at again, the eyes automatically bring into focus the areas focused on before. The areas between these focus points become blind spots and are the areas where the secretive Apache scouts would dwell. We learned to get out of these ruts of automatic vision by always forcing our eyes to look all around, even to the obscure areas. Grandfather said, "Always look at life as if you have never seen it before, using all your senses as if for the first time." Many of the ruts and routines become habits that are hard to break, but I learned that half the battle was being aware of them.

Not many days after the deer hunt I was sitting quietly in the bushes watching some men in a pickup truck dumping garbage along one of the larger sand trails. Tears filled my eyes, and I found I hated them to the core, wishing that I was bigger so I could beat them senseless. Grandfather's silent approach went unnoticed until he sat down beside me and gazed toward the two men and the truck. Without looking at me he said, "Thinking and emotions take pathways too and can become ruts just as deadly as physical ruts." Just as silently as he had come, he slipped away, leaving me with my thoughts, my anger, and my mental ruts. As I watched the men unloading the truck, I thought for a long time, desperately trying to work through the anger and find a different way of seeing and understanding things.

The anger was so entrenched that it was hard to let it go, but slowly the anger faded. I was no longer angry at these men but rather pitied them for their ignorance. So many times I heard Grandfather say, "There is always some other answer rather than anger," and for the first time I knew what he meant. The pity led to an action that I had never thought I would make. I walked silently up to the truck and begged the men to stop throwing their garbage in one of my favorite areas. Money was hard to come by in those days, but I had a quarter and I offered it to them for gas to drive to the dump, which was free, and asked if they would want me to unload the truck for them there. They were so surprised by my offer and intensity that they stood as if shocked. I guess that they were not only shocked by my silent appearance but also by the pleading of a small boy.

They began to apologize profusely and sincerely as they packed up the truck. They promised to take the load the few extra miles to the dump. I helped them pack the truck and explained to them that there had been a lot of the same type of dumping farther up the sand road. Without hesitation they asked me where and I led them to a pile of rubble larger than the one they had intended to leave. As I left them, I glanced back and watched them loading the other pile of garbage on their truck, collecting even the scraps of paper that had blown into the trees.

Grandfather had been watching me all the time, and as I got back to my sitting area, he sat beside me. "Anger would not have solved this problem," he said. "Pity and teaching were the only answers. These men would have learned nothing if you had approached them with anger in your heart. Instead you thought of a different way and found the answers. Now your thinking and emotions of sorrow are transformed into growth, all because you strayed from the trail and thought and felt in a new way." I carry the lessons of the men in the truck to this day. I now know, because of what happened so many years ago, that ignorance is one of the primary causes of the destruction of the earth. Re-education and getting man's feet back in the soil are some of the answers to the saving of the earth.

Many months later I had just finished an important Vision Quest, a ritual of fasting and reflection lasting from one to forty days in the wilderness. I had prepared myself and my place for months so that this spring quest would bear fruit. I entered Grandfather's camp quietly and in a sullen mood, feeling as if the four days I had spent in seclusion had failed. Grandfather looked at me for a long time with that gaze of his that felt as if he were looking right through me and pondering my spirit. He smiled. "There are paths and ruts in the spirit world, as there are in the physical and mental world. One must take the tools of the spirit world and make one's own path rather than exactly follow the paths of those who once were. You expected this Vision to be like that of the grandfathers and grandmothers, with the same symbols, dreams, and understandings as they had. You must not seek their path and their understanding, but you must seek your own. The ruts of the spirit are trying to follow others and it can not be done."

I was shocked at what he said, for he had continually told us to follow the teachings of the old ones. He had stressed the use of the old customs, traditions, and ceremonies, and stressed following them precisely. Now he was contradicting himself. I asked him how he could tell me one thing at one time, then change it completely. He smiled again, making me feel a little foolish for asking. "Custom, tradition, and ceremony are but tools for a spiritual path. Once learned they are used to make your own path. The only danger would be for those who did not learn the use of the tools fully and tried to walk a spiritual path. They would be thrashing aimlessly in the dark and eventually hurt themselves and others. That is the trouble with this modern world; everyone wants things too fast without taking the time to learn the tools before setting out on his or her journeys. Anyone who has the tools and follows the paths of others will only meet a dead end and pain. It's like trying to make a long journey in someone else's shoes. You have learned all the tools of the Vision Quest. Undertake and interpret your Vision in your own way, without taking someone else's trail. You must learn not to create a rut."

Through the years, those words have been a guide to the spiritual realms; I have always taken the utmost care to know all my tools well. It is important to escape not only the ruts of body, mind, and emotion, but also the ruts of spirit. For the overall good of the earth what is needed are people who are guided by the old ways but who use them to push forward into new spiritual territories. That way each new generation gains from those who have come before and in its openness toward present and future furthers the consciousness of the earth to new heights of spiritual oneness. Modern religion and philosophy must continuously forge new trails, otherwise mankind will stagnate in the ruts of yesterday. Reading many years later in a Chinese text, I came across a parable: "Seek not to follow in the footsteps of the men of old; seek instead what they sought." I thought of Grandfather.

5

■▼■▼■▼■

The Center Skull

I lay on my belly, nestled in a thicket at the edge of a field, watching the advancing dawn. The blackness of the night slowly diffused to a soft yellow-white light silhouetting the horizon trees at the edge of the field into strange contorted shapes. Soon distance and perspective returned. Darkness always has a way of distorting time and distance and casts deep shadows of mystery through the land. As I lay there watching, I understood why east has always been associated with wisdom: cutting through the darkness and distortion of night comes the wisdom of the sun, a purity of thought and vision. Mist patches that clung to the low places quickly evaporated as the sun broke the horizon like a soft yellow-gold ball. Trails of sunlight washed across the earth, splashing here and there with warmth, drying the dew, and emblazoning the landscape with color. The pine trees were now etched in a deep gold, creating a haloed effect, as if these were the special trees of the Creator.

The advance of dawn was so powerful. I could feel the sun warming my back, reaching deep into the very marrow of my bones. Birds began to call and sing from the edges of the fields and were soon joined by the chorus of insects, blending into a grand symphony. All around came the sound of fluttering wings, the drone of bees, and the rustling of feeding animals. This morning trembled with the flow of life and motion. I too could feel the ancient callings, sensing the excitement deep within. Soft balmy breezes began wafting across the fields, carrying with them the rich fragrances of pine-drenched loam and countless wildflowers. The scents became so thick and intoxicating that my mind could trace each scent to its source. The heat of the sun finally warmed the fields, creating visible columns of ascending, wavering heat. The air grew thick and heavy, hot and humid, but still I lay as if dead, waiting.

Rick lay not far from me, only several feet away, but I could not see him, and like me, he lay absolutely motionless. A cottontail, his tracks actually, had brought us to this place, and we awaited his arrival patiently. It wasn't just any cottontail but a big—no, a *gigantic*—rabbit for this area. His size rivaled that of a New England cottontail, and his prints were much bigger than any we had yet seen in the Pine Barrens. For months the tracks had fascinated us. His trails indicated he was always cautious, elusive, and secretive, leaving nothing to chance. It was as if each move had been carefully calculated to evade risk and all dangers and that this ability had made it possible for him to grow to tremendous size. Other rabbits were not nearly as stealthy, which had probably resulted in their high mortality rate and smaller size. But this huge rabbit broke all laws and traditions, ranging over large areas and rotating feeding places.

This constant changing of feeding areas and habits, as well as his huge size, was the lure that started our quest to find that rabbit. For weeks we plotted his travels, running down his trails to find how they flowed with the landscape so as to be unobserved by predators. We carefully reviewed all our information and found that in his seemingly erratic movements there was an overall pattern. We found that every few days he would come to this field in which Rick and I now waited to feed, though we could not determine the day or time of day precisely. This was our second day. All that was needed was for us to lie absolutely still and have the patience of a rock.

The close silence of midmorning was broken by a faint compressing of dried grasses. There was a long pause, a gentle rustle, another faint compressing of crackling grasses, a soft rustling and movement of the grasses, another compressed crack, and a huge rabbit head peered out of a grass clump just a few feet in front of me. He nibbled slowly on a succulent stem of grass, froze a moment and listened. With one tremendous hop he was free of his hiding place and fully out in the open. His body shifted in and out of shadows, stopping frequently in a frozen position to observe what was around. I was paralyzed with excitement, afraid even to breathe. I never saw a rabbit that big or well fed, nor had I seen one so observant and skillful at the use of brush and shadow to conceal his movement and position.

I noticed that his fur glistened in the sun, though not enough to stand out from the brush. His body was heavy but strong, showing no fat, just bandlike muscles visible through the soft outline of his fur. He moved about slowly and carefully, taking turns between nibbling succulents and watching in his frozen pose. A squirrel sounded a warning and without hesitation the rabbit dove for the heavy brush and grass, zigzagging a few times. Then there was absolute silence. I could hear my excited breathing and tried desperately to control it, regaining my composure and fighting the trembling that had drifted visibly to my body. With a long wait and no danger about, the rabbit stealthily returned, watching more cautiously as he fed.

He fed close to us at the edge of the field for a long time, longer than I could hold my body absolutely still and control my breathing. I wanted desperately to change my position and get more comfortable. The grasses, bushes, and earth beneath seemed so soft and comfortable when I had first lain down several hours earlier, but now the grass stalks were poking me, and my body felt bruised by each dent and rise of the earth. To make matters worse, some red ants were biting me on the elbow, since I was too close to their home. I hung tough as long as I could and tried to relax deeper into the earth, hoping that the discomfort would pass through my body. I'd learned that only by accepting discomfort or pain and allowing it to pass through, would it lessen and disappear. To try to fight the discomfort would only increase its power, for the sheer act of trying anything will always negate itself. There was, of course, the purely pride-oriented reason for bearing the discomfort—so as not to tarnish my image—though I was sure Rick was going through the same torture. Each of us desperately wanted the other to break the long silence.

Suddenly the rabbit froze. I caught a flash from above, and a shadow of wings momentarily covered me. The next instant a huge red-tailed hawk pounced on the rabbit. There was a thrashing and the dying scream of the rabbit, then all was silent again except for the scolding of the local birds and the sentinel red squirrel. As I watched the hawk remove and reset his deadly talons my pain and discomfort of my position disappeared. (I've always found it amazing how the energy of excitement can make the most intense pain and discomfort disappear, how the mind can control the comfort or discomfort of the body. With the proper thought and/or stimulation, even the most harsh conditions can become bearable—and even comfortable.)

The hawk reset his talons again, then again. With slow, labored wing beats, he began to lift from the ground, trailing away from the death scene in a slow ascending diagonal, reaching toward the distant trees and waiting young. The kill area was bloody. Bits of hair were strewn about and the earth was scarred deep with the thrashing of the rabbit. Blood had splattered up to the standing grasses and over to where Rick had lain. His face also had a few stray spots of the blood. A thin trail of blood spattered across the ground followed the flight path of the hawk until it finally disappeared in the deeper grasses, leaving us little hope of following. We were amazed, energized, so excited and trembling that we could not utter a sound. We were both awed by the power and sureness of the hawk's kill and overcome by a sense of loss at the fall of such a magnificent rabbit. He had evaded danger for so many seasons and yet right in front of us, so very close to us, in one brief, fatal moment, it had fallen prey to the hawk. Our quaking seemed to last an eternity, and it was quite some time before we could talk.

Once we regained our voices our talk began to drift into argument, then gradually into a yelling match that threatened violence. Instead of reveling in what we had just experienced, the awe of it all and the proximity, we were arguing fine points and details. Rick maintained that the hawk had hit the rabbit near the neck with one of his feet, the other missing its mark. That was why, he said, the hawk had to readjust his talons before flying off and the reason the rabbit let out the scream and thrashed. I, on the other hand, said that the hawk had hit the rabbit with full talons, one on the neck and the other in the back. The hawk was merely adjusting the talons for a better grip for flight and probably to insure the kill. We then argued about who was closer and who had the better view. Rick's blood-splattered face was his evidence that he was closer—a source of even greater disagreement.

Little did we realize that Grandfather had been standing at the far end of the field and was a silent witness to the whole adventure, including the argument that followed. He approached us silently, listening to our yelling and threats, then finally appeared near where we sat. In respect for him we immediately quit arguing and fell to an angry silence as he walked up. Without a word, he reached into his old buckskin bag and pulled out an old and weathered deer skull. He carefully placed it between us and asked us to sit down. Still upset with Rick but not willing to miss anything Grandfather had to teach, I sat down. Rick reluctantly squatted near the far side of the skull. I thought at first that Grandfather was angry at us for disgracing the woods and the death of the rabbit with our bickering, but his voice was as soft and easy as always.

He asked me to look at the skull and tell him what I saw. I

knew that he wanted much more than just what it was—a deer skull—so I went into a lengthy description. Spurred on by my anger at Rick, I wanted to tell what I saw in greatest detail, so I began describing the spider that lived in the nose cavity. I went on to describe the mouse nibbles around the eyes and the places where it was missing teeth on one side. Just as I was fully getting into the description, Grandfather waved his hand for silence. I thought I must have failed some secret test. He then asked Rick to describe what he saw. Rick responded with the same enthusiasm and showing-off that I had. He described the back of the head, the spinal opening, and the huge crack and hole in the back of the skull that must have killed the deer. Grandfather again waved his hand for silence.

In a matter-of-fact way, he asked, "What is it that you both are looking at?" Almost instantly, we both answered, "A deer skull," searching for the real meaning of his question. Grandfather then said, "You both look at a deer skull, but by your position in space relative to it, you both see it differently, yet you both are looking at the same skull. Is this not the same with all people and all things?" Sullenly, I answered, "Yes, Grandfather." He continued, "Each thing can do something that you cannot. Each spirit experiences all things differently, and like tracks, no two can be exactly alike. Each has his own spirit, his own prejudices and understanding, and each filters all things through his unique soul. Then, grandchildren, you must understand that all people and all things are teachers, no matter how much experience we think they have or have not. Each can teach something if we know how to listen."

"How do I listen?" Rick asked.

"You first must realize that everything is a teacher," Grandfather said. "Good or bad, each thing, all people, and all of Creation's creatures, have something to teach us. Because each is unique. That is the power of their medicine, and we must seek out and learn from that uniqueness, that medicine."

"But how do we listen?" I asked.

"You must learn to listen in purity so as not to pollute the teachings with your prejudices. You must forget you have a past, forget all you have ever learned, and who you are, then you will be empty and ready to listen purely. After the teaching is finished, then you can judge, but only after it is completely finished. This could take years. We must always remember: every person, every prophecy, and every religion is a teacher, but we must seek out all people and search for teachings, for some are buried deep. Nothing is bad or good, right or wrong; it all depends on how we judge with our prejudice. Listening in purity and emptiness judges not, only learns."

I felt like a fool—many times over—not only for refusing to listen to what Rick had seen, but also, I realized, for passing up so many teachers that were around me every day. Because of my prejudice for who I was and where I was going, I never took the time to listen and learn from anyone. I understood now that whether it be good or bad, everything is a teacher. I should learn not only from people's successes but also from their failures so I would not repeat the same mistakes.

Grandfather's lesson, which I have come to refer to as the lesson of the center skull, was a profound one. Its teachings were far reaching and have affected my life and my understanding of life to this day. It has broadened my natural curiosity and reached into realms that I never thought I would ever go. It has taught me to be a careful observer not only of all the things of the natural world but of people too.

There were many teachers that followed my introduction to the teachings of the "center skull," but two teachers encountered that same year stood out in my mind. Each was found at the same location; one was a child, the other an old man. (Children and the old ones are very much alike; they are closer to the vitality of life because they live life one moment at a time.) A few days after the profound lessons of the "center skull," I was cutting through a local playground at the edge of the Pine Barrens, heading to one of our camp areas. By the stream that cut through the lower end of the woods a small child played, his mother sitting close by reading. I stopped and stood by the edge of the water, a little downstream from them, watching them. When I realized how much the mother was missing, I vowed never to read in the woods; this was an activity better accomplished within the confines of four walls. Important as this lesson was, the child playing by the stream was to pass on the more profound teaching. He played at the water's edge with a fallen leaf. For the longest time I watched as he sailed his little leaf from one place to another, squealing with delight and laughter as it chased the water bugs over the surface.

The child looked up from the leaf at each nuance and surge of the woods; nothing seemed to escape him. Each thing was new and delighted him, sometimes to laughter and sometimes to awe. I could sense a timelessness about him, an unconditional play and curiosity, as he seemed to relish each moment. I could feel a longing deep inside me for that quest for play and joy, for being like a child again. Even though I was only a few years older than he, I had stuffed the child deep within me for fear that someone would think I was childish.

I began to imitate the child, using my own leaf. I soon lost myself to that child within, letting go with spontaneous laughter whenever the urge hit me. I let go of the restrictions I had placed on myself and began to feel fully alive. I decided that if society could not separate being childish from being childlike, then that was its concern. That child taught me a great lesson: to be a child again, to let go of time, and to keep the purity of play and curiosity alive, no matter how old I was.

A few months later, on my way home from the woods, I passed by the same stream. The child was long gone, but there, exactly where the child had been, was an old man, hunched over and gazing into the water. Normally, I would have slipped by, but the "skull" surged into my thought. Even though I was late for dinner, I decided to see what I could learn from him. I approached him slowly, but loud enough so as not to startle him.

He watched me coming closer but soon went back to what he was doing, until I said, "Hello." At first he was a little startled that I spoke to him, and I could sense a little anger at violating his space and thought. I asked him what he was doing, with all the sincerity I could muster. Being new to this game of finding teachers, I was a bit shaky and unsure of myself, and I could sense that he was too. It seemed as if no one had spoken to him in a very long time.

It turned out that he was watching the fingerlings catching mosquito larvae. He explained that he could tell a lot about fish by watching the little ones, and he could guess how good the fishing would become in seasons to come. He also told me about the stones in the river, how they were formed and eroded, and that he was once a worker at a local gravel pit. We talked well into the darkness. I was very taken by his wisdom of rocks and fish, and he was glad to have someone to share it with. He invited me to his house the following night to see his fossil collection, which he had amassed during his years at the gravel pit.

That was the beginning of what became a strong friendship. Over the years I often turned to him to decipher local fossils I've found in the course of my wanderings. In light of this experience, what I've gained and what I've been able to give, I feel great sorrow for all the old ones that society casts aside. Native Americans have always valued the wisdom of the old ones; modern society tends to dismiss these men and women after retirement, leaving them lonely and us losers—losers in that we will never be privy to the wisdom of their lives. I've learned from many old ones, things that would have taken me, on my own, many lifetimes to learn.

Certainly the death of the rabbit and the power of the hawk were great teachers on the day of the "center skull." From the start, Grandfather had always stressed nature as one of the most powerful teachers, and looking deeper into nature had become second nature to me. The "center skull" took me beyond the teachings of nature to other teachers, teachers that I had overlooked, and opened my mind to ever greater understandings and lessons. Once I realized that all people can be teachers, there was no longer any room for prejudice. Living by this premise one can't help but become a humanitarian. As you come to recognize the value of the self, of others, of the natural world, respect and preservation become the logical next steps. Each entity carries teachings of great value. To dismiss anyone as valueless, especially the old ones, is to throw away the wisdom of a life; it robs some of learning and others of purpose—and runs contrary to the underlying oneness of the natural order, which tells us that every part of nature has a reason, a purpose, for being.

6

▼▼▼▼▼

The Hunt

Most people view survivalists as being not unlike a swarm of locusts that swoop down upon the unsuspecting landscape and devour everything, leaving the landscape in total destruction. Unfortunately, this may have been the way our white ancestors treated the natural world but never was it the way of the Native American. To the ancient ones, man was an important part of the natural order of things and necessary to balance the landscape. If the Great Spirit did not want us here to be an integral part of Creation, then we would not be here. We, or our greed, decided to destroy that balance and break the laws of Creation, raping and polluting the land as if it had been placed here solely for us to abuse. Since the time this land was taken over by our immigrant ancestors, we have been a society of people that kills our grandchildren to feed our children. We believed that nature was an endless resource, that whenever the land no longer produced crops or became polluted and diseased, we would simply move on to another place. This attitude continues today, even as society faces a possible global breakdown of the earth. We defy the laws of nature. We feel we are above all primal codes, exempt from them as if gods. There is hardly a landscape that is left in balance, and we are and will continue to pay for the sins of our grandfathers. Fortunately, a true survivalist can set the balance of things again, possibly even turn things around.

Grandfather's attitude toward survival and the land was one of extreme reverence. At first our reverence was only a reflection of the respect we had for Grandfather, but in time, and with the practice of survival, we understood that reverence for ourselves. Certainly the skills of survival were sacred; they held not only the key to the preservation of human life, but, through their attendant, dynamic parables and stories, provided a vital connection between mankind and the earth. The skills of survival were a source of understanding for children and a way of life for the elders. But it was not only the skills that were sacred; survival itself demanded reverence, for survival was an important part of the natural order of things. Man was a gardener, a caretaker of the earth, and with the tools of survival he could keep things in balance. It was this attitude and the skills of the caretaker that Grandfather stressed as we perfected each new skill. Without that attitude, the skills could become tools of destruction.

Our ancestors' approach to Creation and the Native American consciousness of Earth Mother were extremely different. Where the native peoples viewed the earth with a sense of reverence and respect, the white man viewed the land as something frightening that had to be conquered. Where the ancient ones regarded the earth as owned by the Creator and put here for them to take care of, white men looked at it as an inexhaustible resource to be owned and exploited. The Native Americans never believed that they owned the land; the land was owned by the Creator, while the white man tried desperately to conquer the land and make it his own.

Grandfather explained the differences in attitude and thinking of the two cultures in his stories about how the white man used the landscape as compared to the ways of the Native American. If a pioneer or mountain man needed to make a bow, he would collect any sapling that was straight and tall. Usually he would take the biggest and best, with no thought as to what effect its removal would have on the landscape—or on future generations. To his way of thinking, the sapling was his for the taking. Sometimes he would collect several, use one, then discard the rest. He overharvested the trees, much as he overslaughtered buffalo for sport, in his search for that perfect sapling. Sadly, he would more often than not not know what perfect was and he would select trees that were growing in the open, little realizing that the trees that had such an easy life and hence regular growth rings would produce a bow with very little snap or cast.

He saw nothing in the entities of the landscape but the superficial. He saw none of the lessons and spiritual teachings that the Native Americans did. To him and his lopsided way of thinking, there was nothing more than the physical. The ancient Native American would explain that, like people, saplings that had an easy life would have no snap, cast, or strength. Those saplings that had to fight for the sun would have tight growth rings, giving them considerable strength, cast, and snap. It was obvious to the Native American that people were much like the saplings. Those who knew struggle were stronger and better able to survive the storms of existence than those who had an easy life, but the lessons did not end there. By obeying the laws and allowing the bow to create itself, the gnarled bow showed the maker how to follow the grain and the flow of nature. Straight bows had very little to teach.

When the Native Americans needed to take a sapling for a bow, their approach was far different than the pioneers'. First, an extreme need for that bow had to be established. They would not take the life of anything unnecessarily; to do so would mean very bad medicine. Nothing in the natural world was taken or killed senselessly. There was always a natural order, a need, and a balance, where nothing was wasted. The need would be followed by prayers, fasting, and sometimes a sweatlodge. These were customary to allow time for the Native American to think clearly and to prepare himself for taking a life. Prayers flowed to the

Creator, asking for guidance and giving thanks for the bow-making skills and the bow. Prayers were also sent to all the saplings. A deep gratitude was felt for the sapling that would make the ultimate sacrifice—giving up its life and spirit so that the hunter and his people could live.

Only then would the native bow-maker begin his search of the landscape. His wanderings were guided more by his heart than his head, and he would pass many fine saplings before he chose the one he needed. He did not seek those that had an easy life, growing at the edge of the fields straight and tall. He instead was looking for a grove of saplings that were in competition, fighting for the sun. He knew that these saplings would have tight and strong growth rings and fibers. Once a grove was located, he might search it for days, looking for just the right sapling. Kept in mind also was the fact that he wanted a stave that could be removed to the overall good of the landscape. Once chosen, prayers were sent to the Creator and the tree. He would explain to the little sapling what it would be used for and how his people were honored at its sacrifice. The sapling was told that it would be made well and cherished. It would become an extension of the hunter, the catalyst that would provide meat. Like the pioneer, the ancient ones considered the bow a tool, but unlike the pioneer who saw a tool as separate from the self, as an inanimate means, the ancient ones knew that the bow was part of themselves. The spirit of the bow would dwell within them.

The Native American harvested the bow as a gardener or caretaker harvests certain plants to make room for others to grow strong. The bow-maker knew that the sapling would eventually die in its struggle for the sun. He knew that too many saplings would damage each other and make the whole grove weak and susceptible to disease. By removing that sapling, he insured the strength of the grove. By taking the right one, it would benefit nature, and by helping to ensure existence of the grove, his action would benefit future generations of his people. Nothing was ever taken from the landscape without the prayers of thanksgiving.

Nothing was ever taken without first considering what it would do to the world of nature and future generations. Thus the ancient ones would benefit the natural world immediately and in the future. This care and the concern for their grandchildren kept the ancient ones in balance with the earth, fulfilling their destiny as a natural part of things.

When we heard Grandfather talk about killing things in this way, deciding what should live or die, we felt like we were playing God, and this should not be. No man should play God. Grandfather had a quick answer to our concern, and I could sense the urgency and commitment in what he was saying. He told us that we had to take lives of things, whether it be plant or animal, for our survival. We had to pay for the sins of our grandfathers and begin to take things from the earth in the right way. In the past, our ancestors gave no thought to the future, and their greed threw the world out of balance. By taking things the right way, as caretakers, we could begin to undo the damage that had been done. We were not to play God, but rather follow the natural order of things. In this way, living the natural way, our impact would have positive effects on all things of the earth.

I took this attitude of killing to heart and at first came away with a distorted sense of things. I had misunderstood the full concept of what Grandfather was saying and so I became more of a pioneer than one who lives with the earth. I began, in my mind, to create a hierarchy of spirits, feeling that rocks, water, and soil were lesser spirits than the plants, and plants were lesser spirits than animals. I began to treat things differently according to my concept of that spiritual ladder. This spiritual hierarchy of things that I'd created was, of course, in direct opposition to the spirit of the Native teachings. Grandfather, like all people of the earth, believed that all spirits were equal, no matter what form they took. All deserved the same respect and consideration. It was during the height of this misconception that I learned one of the most valuable lessons of my life, a lesson that would change my thoughts and my reality forever.

It was shortly after I turned twelve that Grandfather told me that I had to hunt my first big game. For all the early years I had lived in the forests, we killed only small game to eat by trap, bow and arrow, or throwing stick. We were removed from all the kills. We had merely thrown the weapon or set the trap that had been involved in the actual kill. We did not really know death because we were separated from that fateful moment where animal and death became one. We understood as best we could the precious gift of life given up so that we could live, and we understood the awesome and sacred responsibility of the hunt, of need, and of survival, but we were still removed, somewhat, from it all. Certainly we knew and loved animals, and we learned great lessons from them, but our connection and the full impact of the hunt's responsibilities were not realized fully until we had experienced the kill first-hand. This would be my passage into manhood.

Grandfather had said that when a young brave was between twelve and thirteen winters old, he would have to follow the rituals of his ancestors and take a large animal at close range. This would teach a young man many lessons—lessons about the hunt, the natural order of things, and about the spirit-that-moves-in-all-things. I did not know whether this hunt was part of Grandfather's clan ritual or if it was something he had learned in his travels. Wherever it came from, whatever its origins, I was readily excited about the process of completing both the ritual task and my rite of passage into manhood. Most important to Grandfather was that I take the animal with a short and primitive lance. This would put me close enough to the animal that I would be present when the animal spirit departed the body. He said that being present at that moment of departure would teach me more than any words ever could.

I was first told about my quest in the early spring, even though I would not be on the hunt until the fall. This would give me the necessary time to prepare myself and understand that which I was to undertake and why it was necessary. For the next several months, I prepared for the hunt on all levels of my existence. At times the quest permeated my every thought and action. I conditioned my body, making it faster and stronger than ever. I knew that it would take great strength and endurance to take a deer—the only accessible big game in the Pine Barrens—and so I conditioned my body, making it faster and stronger than ever before. I prepared my mind by envisioning the hunt—the swift kill, the use of the animal—and the tremendous gift of life. I fasted and prayed often. I wandered for days alone or sought out the purification of the sweatlodge. Every step of preparation had to be done in the proper manner. After all, I was passing into manhood, and the hunt was forever sacred, forever the deepest responsibility. I had to fully understand and respect what I was doing.

Great care was taken in preparing the lance I would use to kill the deer. I took the strongest oak sapling for the shaft. I searched for many days to find just the right tree—one that had been killed and hardened by the fires of the pines. The chipped flint tip was made from the choicest flint I had collected from the northern part of the state. And the bindings were from the rawhide of groundhog, one of the toughest hides of the smaller animals. I spent hours putting it together. Everything had to be perfect for a sure and swift kill. Everything had to be collected and assembled with the greatest care and thanksgiving. Each step had to be savored to fully appreciate and understand the deepest aspects and mysteries of the quest.

As spring drifted to summer and the landscape grew full, rich, and fruitful, I began to track deer. I searched many areas, looking for just the right conditions, just the right deer. I followed the ancient laws of survival; predators prey on the weaker or sick. This was the natural order of things, and I had to follow that order. I was too slow and weak to take a big animal so, following the laws, I searched for just the right deer, one that was sick and injured, one that would not survive the winter—indeed, death by my lance would be quick, less painful than the slow, lingering pain of starvation. It would be a small deer, one that I could handle, one with just the right amount of meat that would carry us through the lean times of winter without excess or waste. Always, I followed the laws of Creation, the universal laws of nature.

By late summer I had found the deer that would become my prey. It was a small deer, a little buck, born that spring. Sometime during the early summer he had injured his hip, either by being struck by a car or by a bad fall. The injury left him with a bad limp, unable to run, and certainly unable to keep up with his mother on her feeding circuit. This lack of agility would hinder and perhaps kill him in the winter months when deer would have to travel great distances to find browse adequate for sustenance. Even now, he was small in size and weight, a growth stunted by inadequate diet and, possibly, genetics, for his mother was also small. The deer would be an excellent choice; he was precisely what I was looking for. His condition would make him a prime target for any predator, starvation, or disease, and taking him would be within the universal laws.

I followed that deer frequently for the remainder of the summer and into early fall. His condition never improved and actually worsened as the cooler weather set in. It became more and more difficult for him to arise from his day bed and at times the pain must have been unbearable. I practically lived with that little deer and his mother. I knew his every move, his pattern of painful play, his failures, and his triumphs. I watched him falter and collapse under the strain of walking or keeping up with his mother. Yet the mother never abandoned him, and she stayed close by when he rested. She too was growing thin from the ordeal. I could feel the sense of panic in her at times, especially on the cold mornings.

After a while the deer began to accept my presence. At first they would slip through the heavy brush and swamps to avoid me, but after many weeks, they no longer tried. In fact, they hardly paid any attention to me, rather accepting me as a benign part of the landscape, a nonthreatening observer. At times they would walk right past me, never showing any fear or care. Eventually I could approach within a few yards of their bed or walk past them as they fed at the field's edge. I watched their habits, especially the little buck. I knew everything about him: where he slept, where he ate, the trails he traveled and when, and all his little quirks. For an injured deer he had a tremendous personal strength. He would fight the pain to play, rising above his affliction to enjoy life as other young deer do. His ability to hide was better than most, a compensation for his inability to run. He seemed to sense things farther off than his mother could, and he was very aware of all moods of the forest.

Then came the time, in early fall, when Grandfather sent me out to undertake that sacred hunt. I had fasted for four days so that I would purify my body and know hunger. I took of the sweatlodge and prayed frequently, asking the Creator to guide my lance and giving thanks for the gift of life. All things had to be right inside me before they could be right outside. I had to fully understand that which I was about to do. I had to know the awesome responsibility of the hunt, the tremendous sacrifice of the animal's life for me, and I had to justify that death as the ancients did. It was not enough to need the meat but I also had to need the spirit and to fully understand the effects that the deer's death would have on the land and for generations to come. Nothing was left to chance, all things had to be realized and understood.

Excitement welled up from deep inside me as I walked from camp to the hunting grounds. I felt like a great warrior and hunter, honored to be granted the duty of feeding my people. My body felt strong, my mind cunning. My body reacted to the land like a seasoned predator. I could feel the power rise up from within, and I was proud of my ability and of the weapon I had fashioned. I allowed the animal within and the primal mind to guide much of my action. I followed my instincts mostly, allowing my greater inner self to take over. I knew that in a close-range hunt there could be no room for error. Every move had to be rehearsed time and time again until it became instinct rather than thought. I knew exactly how I was going to hunt the little buck, and I fused that scenario to my consciousness until I could feel it manifest in the movement of my muscles.

I did not hunt the little deer right away. Instead, I chose to watch him again for a few days to make sure his patterns had not changed. Whenever one season flows into another there is always a chance that routine will vary. The weather was anything but fall-like, it was rather like mid-August. The land was dry, and the air chokingly hot and humid. I sweated profusely even while sitting quietly watching the buck, which forced me to take frequent swims to wash away all scent and to revive my faltering consciousness. The deer had broken their fall pattern and had gone back to the pattern of summer. They awoke late and retired early, staying close to the shadowy brush and swamps so as to stay cool. I knew the pattern well, and with a slight variation of thought I meshed the hunt to fit their patterns.

I climbed a small pine tree at the edge of the field. I knew that every morning the deer would come to this field to eat before retiring for the day. The little buck always paused beneath this tree for a few moments as he scanned the field for danger. His mother passed through the field at the upper edge and would not be close to him at that moment. The little pine would conceal my body as well as my scent and afford me excellent opportunity to watch as the buck approached. Fused into my body was the hunt. I would wait in that tree for him to pass beneath, then drop from the branch onto his back and run the short lance through the back of his neck and sever both arteries. Death would be quick and virtually painless. I rehearsed this all day, then into the night, remaining motionless in the branches the entire time.

The day grew hot fast, and I could see the wavering lines of heat boiling up from the parched field that lay before me. Sweat began to pour from my body, and I could feel it dripping to the ground. I worried that the little buck would catch scent of me, and I hoped that the thick bed of pine needles would mask what had fallen. My head swooned with the heat; my body ached from lack of sleep and holding my position all night in the tree. My mind wandered over all the events that led up to this time and place, to this hunt. I rehearsed again the hunt in my mind and felt confident that it would be easy, the killing swift. My mind wandered over many things; the heat grew even more intense and my thoughts foggy. Mirages of water began to take shape in the fields, only to dissipate as quickly as they appeared. I heard noises where there was none, my heart pounding as the surge of thoughts came and went.

My consciousness was snapped back into reality by the crackling of dead twigs under tiny hoofs. I turned abruptly toward the sound, momentarily forgetting I was hunting. The little buck had broken cover a few yards from me and stood staring at me for a long moment. He looked so frail, shaking for a moment in bewilderment at seeing me in the tree. Recognizing that it was me in the tree, he did not hesitate but came toward me, trusting, as he had so many times before. I never had shown him aggression in the past and never posed a threat, so there was no fear in his stumbling walk. I had no thought other than to watch him coming closer. There was no analysis, no time or place, just me, the little deer, and the hunt. Slowly he slipped beneath the tree and paused to look around as he had done so many times before. He never even looked upward, for I was no danger.

There is a point in any hunt where the mind is let go and the body reacts on its own. There is not conscious thought, just a deft obedience to instinct and reaction. I dropped from the tree, crashed the little deer to the ground and ran my short lance through the rear of his neck. In the violence of action my lance broke and severed only one artery and part of his windpipe. He thrashed in pain. The horror in his eyes penetrated my soul, but the animal within me grasped his neck, and I began to choke the life from him. Blood from the severed artery covered the ground, my face, and much of my body. I hammered his head into the ground, growling like an animal. My body trembled with a sick excitement as the profuse sweat and blood dripped from every limb. The little deer struggled again, then fell silent and still. I looked into his eyes and I could feel the horror as his spirit, his life, slipped through my fingers.

As his eyes veiled with death, I let go my grip and the silent rage within dissipated. I could hear the alarm calls of birds from all over the fields and forest ringing in my ears and the little buck's mother crashing through the distant brush. Suddenly, tremendous emotion washed over me, and I felt sick and dirty. Tears flowed from my eyes and heart as I stared at my bloody hands and the deer beneath me. I felt as if my hands did not belong to me but to some horribly vicious beast. The act of death was the most horrible destruction I could have ever imagined. I had known that little deer for many weeks. I had followed him, slept by him, and watched him eat, drink, and play. I knew him personally, as a brother and friend, and now he lay dead before me. I had destroyed something that trusted me, all for the passage into manhood, and I could no longer justify the hunt. If this was the mark of being a hunter and a man, then I wanted nothing to do with it ever again.

Rage filled me, saturating my every fiber and clouding any rational thought. I despised myself for what I had done, but most of all I despised Grandfather for glorifying this hunt and causing me to kill. Certainly, now, I could see why he wanted me close to the point of death. It had taught me how horrible death was and that I had been too removed and insulated from it before. But to teach it in this way was one of the most horrible lessons I had ever had in my life. I was sickened by the whole ordeal and retched bile from my empty contorted stomach until I ached deep within. I could barely walk, and I struggled to throw the little deer across my shoulders. He was so light and frail that I could hardly feel him. The remaining blood that dripped from his neck felt hot and heavy as it ran down my chest and back. I hated Grandfather and I felt bitter.

I wandered back to camp, my mind twisted with rage, and I knew what I had to do. I was going to walk back into camp, drop the little deer at Grandfather's feet, and walk out of the woods forever. If this was what survival, what being a man, and what the doorway to the spiritual world were all about, then I wanted nothing to do with them. As I approached the camp, I noticed Grandfather leaning against a tree and watching me. A wry smile was held motionless on his face and penetrated my soul, causing me to despise him even more. As I neared him, he lost the smile and his face went blank, except for his piercing eyes. His look made me feel like he had been where I was once before, and his words shook my foundations and broke the back of my hatred. Before I could utter a word, he pointed that old gnarled finger at me and spoke. "Grandson, when you can feel the same way about a blade of grass plucked from the ground as you do for that little deer, then and only then will you be 'one' with all things."

His words rocked me back on my heels, and I felt empty, ashamed. The hunt had taught me many more things than I had realized. I had pompously created a hierarchy of animal spirits, feeling that there were some lives more important than others. My ignorance had blinded me to the other spirits of Creation and I had been deaf to the screams and pains of plants and smaller animals. Because I could not hear them cry, I felt as if they were less important than the deer and the larger animals. But they weren't and they had just every bit as much right to live as anything else and their pain was as intense as ours. I made the mistake of comparing the way things felt and reacted to the way humans and larger animals react. There could be no comparison, for life is life, spirit is spirit, and pain is pain, no matter what the body it is housed in. As I cleaned and gutted the deer, I plucked grasses to soak up the blood, and I heard the grasses scream.

That evening after the hunt I went down to the water's edge to pray. All things appeared differently than they ever had before, all of Creation seemed to speak. Cool breezes replaced the heat of the day and washed my soul. My mind and spirit felt at peace, refreshed with the quietude of the darkening landscape, lulled by the symphony of insect voices. My consciousness drifted in and out of sleep, from dream to hazy reality and back again. I felt a deep understanding of the earth and Creation, something moving deep inside that I could not quite put to words—a realization, not of the rational mind but of the heart and emotions, something intangible yet very real. It was not long before I slipped off into a deep and dreamless sleep.

The crackle of brush and the sound of digging awakened me abruptly. My heart pounded with excitement as I heard the sound of a shovel penetrating again into the dirt. I was torn between the worlds of running and fighting, between listening and finding the origins of the noise. It was daybreak, though the sun was not up above the horizon and the landscape was cast in a misty veil. My mind surged with a rash of questions. How could someone be back this far? What was he digging and why? I thought for a moment that someone might be burying a body and I could be in danger, my mind swooning with a surge of that fear-laced thought. Again the shoveling sounds sliced through the air, then silence fell once again, and the sounds did not start again. I had been taught to face my fear and conquer its effects anytime it reared its ugly head. Fear negated clear thought and action and was not a good emotion to carry into any battle. I walked off in the direction from where I had first heard the shoveling sounds, though now the forest was silent.

Pressing through the brush cautiously and searching the landscape, I saw no one. The smell of fresh dirt filled the air and I followed it to its source. There before me was a hole dug deep into the ground. I suspected, then, that someone had come to this area to dig up a laurel or blueberry bush for their garden. I looked toward the hole to search for tracks, and the hole began to fill with liquid and to overflow. At first I thought that the digger had hit a spring, but the liquid was flowing too thick to be water. I drew closer and to my horror, I found that it wasn't water at all but fresh blood oozing from the hole. Yes, I thought, someone must have tried to bury an animal and never finished the job. Searching the hole with a stick I could not find any animal or, for that matter, anything else, but blood continued to seep from the earth. In the wind I could hear the faint cry of pain.

I sickened, for I realized that the earth was bleeding, and I desperately tried to stop the flow. I worked furiously, scooping and pushing dirt back into the wound with my hands, but the flow only continued and at times seemed to worsen. In desperation, I began to cover the bleeding mound with sticks and leaves that were strewn nearby, but still it continued. Growing desperate and out of my mind with panic, I tried everything, from planting small grasses to burying acorns in the blood-soaked earth. I was covered in blood and dirt; the vile smell of an infected wound filled my head; and the cry of pain circled in on me, growing louder and more intense. As the bleeding increased, like a fountain gushing and throbbing uncontrollably, I threw myself atop the mound and began to pray. In the distance I could see a man walking off, carrying a freshly dug tree and laughing to himself, oblivious to the bleeding earth and my screams for help.

I awoke to my own screams echoing from the swamps, still in the same spot I had sat down earlier that evening. As my head cleared, I peered through the darkness to see if the earth was bleeding, but the ground spread out before me clean and unblemished. It all had been a bad dream, and I could feel the mellow chill of relief soothe my sweating and knotted body. I knew that many dreams were important and should be searched for meaning, but I was still too exhausted to think clearly, and my head reeled with surges of unrelated thoughts. Any real thinking became painful, almost impossible, and I quickly fell back to sleep.

Again I found myself sitting in a strange part of the woods and again the sounds of shoveling cut through the air. This time, however, it wasn't only the sound of one shovel but many, possibly hundreds. I ran toward the sounds. As I rounded a bend, I saw groups of people digging up plants and excavating the earth. Blood was pouring from the ground profusely, and I could hear the groans of pain coming from the very soil. The people,— men, women, and children, stood around talking and laughing, totally oblivious to the blood spewing all around them, deaf to the cries of pain coming from beneath their feet. I began running toward the crowd screaming, begging them to stop digging and trying to draw their attention to the earth. No one listened, they paid no attention to me at all, and it was as if I wasn't there at all. I screamed louder and louder but to no avail; the laughter and digging continued, the blood and screams growing deeper and louder.

I ran furiously to get away from the carnage, the stench of rotted flesh, and the cry of pain. The complacency and the ignorance of the people sickened me. They had no idea of what they were doing. They paid no attention to anything but themselves and their greed to steal trees and tear up the earth. They had no concept of what they were doing; they couldn't even see the blood or hear the crying screams. I felt helpless; my pleading was falling on deaf ears; and I tried desperately to outrun them and their ignorance. I crashed through a distant tree line and traveled deep into the forest, but still the crying continued. As I ran, a different wailing filled the air, not like the crying of the earth but a multitude of different sobs, as if coming from many adults and children.

I ran toward the new sounds, feeling that people were desperately in need of help. A loud scream of terror and the deep crack of breaking wood halted me in my tracks. A huge tree crashed to the earth just a few feet in front of me. From the depths of the trunk a horrible groan of pain emerged and combined with a thousand other voices crying in pain. As I looked around, I saw adults and children cutting trees for firewood. As the axes bit into the trees, chunks of bark flew off in all directions like bloody flesh. Limbs that had been cut bled profusely and all around the pain of the trees could be heard above all else. As before, the people laughed and talked, while they carried bloody trunks to the carts or cut deep gaping wounds into the trees. The people were again totally oblivious to the crying and bleeding, paying no attention to my screaming.

Other people in the outer clearing broke open rocks, and the rocks too bled and sobbed. No attention was paid to them either. All around me people tore the flesh of the wilderness, blood flowed heavily, and painful screams became more intense, deafening. I ran again, this time into a desolate land of cut stumps and evulted earth. The air smelled of dead flesh, and nothing grew. The skies were thick with a heavy smoke that choked my breathing. Scattered about were groups of emaciated people, sobbing, crying, and dying. They ambled toward the lush wilderness I had just run from. They spoke of killing trees and digging the earth, all the while complaining of the people who had sickened the land they were now in.

I listened to their concern over the conditions and knew that they were learning a valuable lesson. The lessons of the laws of Creation, lessons clearly showing mankind that he is not above the laws of Creation but must abide by them or perish, lessons that foretold the future, for when the animals and plants die, man will soon follow. There was hope in my heart, and I prayed that these people would teach the others when they got to the forests. I collapsed to the ground when I saw them enter the distant forest, for instead of entering in reverence, they began cutting and digging, oblivious to the blood and pain. I screamed at the top of my lungs, "NO," and awoke to Grandfather shaking me.

Sobbing, I told Grandfather the entire dream. It was so real, so vivid, that it took me a long time to regain my composure. Grandfather comforted me, then spoke. "I too have lived this dream, in sleep and in reality." I was horrified that this could occur in any world outside that of nightmares and imagination. Grandfather answered, "This dream is reality, for man does not hear the crying and bleeding of the earth, trees, and rocks, any more than he hears the crying of dying animals. He is too removed from the soils of Creation to communicate with that

Creation, thus the pain of what he is doing goes unnoticed. He does not live by the laws of the universe, but feels he is above them, separated from all other things. He has lost touch with what is real, and in the ignorance of his reality he does not know he is doing wrong. To man, all things not like him are beneath him, and he is all that can know pain. To him, if it does not bleed or make a noise, then it has no spirit and knows no pain." Grandfather ended, saying, "It is not that all things do not feel pain, but that man can not hear it, nor will he listen to the prophets who can."

That dream would live with me always, as would Grandfather's words. It reoccurs any time I try to teach people or stop senseless destruction, any time my words fall on deaf ears. Man feels that he is above the laws of Creation, that he can invent his way out of any life-threatening situation, and that he doesn't really need the natural world. Because he can not hear the voices of the earth, sky, and nature, they do not exist, and as long as man remains insulated from the earth, he never will. He will continue to believe that he is all that matters, that he is the only one who can feel pain or has a spirit. Man believes that he is a god, and the dream reoccurs.

7

Grandfather and the Fisherman

Sometimes one must look at old things anew, changing his perspective and vision, and abandon the old ruts of thinking and experiencing. Grandfather was my greatest teacher; he taught me things on every level. In every part of his life, I found so many lessons, many without words, reaching far beyond the physical realms. One day Grandfather taught me a powerful lesson by just being himself, going about his life as he always did. I don't suspect that even he knew what a profound effect his actions had on my life. All I did was to look at him in a new way, with the purity he so often spoke of. Sometimes teachers come when you least expect them, bearing precious gifts of knowledge that somehow tie all things together. These gifts can come as a failure or a negativity, though there are no failures, or negatives, only teachers. So it was with me and an old fisherman. Unbeknownst to him, he became, also, one of my greatest teachers. In my life, these two events connect to each other and stand out above so many others. I call them "the wisdom of Grandfather and the fisherman."

The story of Grandfather and the fisherman is the story of two separate worlds, a contrast of separate realities. One has shown me the essence of the other, and they both have shown me how to live, one in very positive terms and the other in the negative. Little did I know that the differences they possessed could be fused into my consciousness as one harmonious teacher. But that is the natural order of things, if one knows how to learn without prejudice but with purity. There form associations, similarities, and a fusion where there could be none before. A balancing occurs, one world complementing the other, all in sharper focus than if viewed separately. Here, in what follows, and though the teachings occur many years apart, is the essence of living, taught jointly by two very different people.

I was sitting on an old cedar stump, watching the dawn advance across the swamp. The morning was so thick with mist, especially close to the stream that cut through the boggy cedar swamps. The trunks of the huge old cedar trees faded from sight as they reached to the pale skies, plunging through the dense sheet of mist that clung to their upper crowns. The cedar forest appeared as a mystical temple, something of vision or dream rather than reality. Its beauty was breathtaking; the overall feeling of reverence for this place saturated my soul. Shafts of angled sunlight cut through the lower forest with a hazy yellow-orange light that cast shadows into strange shapes and mists into flowing apparitions. Dew clung to every leaf and furrowed trunk, dripping here and there, mingling with the symphony of awaking birds and the gentle surging flow of the stream. I felt as if I sat on the edge of some primordial forest at the dawn of Creation.

I was deep in prayer, consciously and unconsciously, losing myself in meditation and in the deeper recesses of the misty shadows. I know of no one who could have sat in this place, at the edge of misty sun and shadowy forest, who could not have been in prayer, at peace with Creation and flooded with unspeakable awe. This kind of morning always tears away all cares and duties, all fleshly wants, and bares the soul to the elements to be washed and purified. The thrashings of the mind evaporate like the mists of dawn and real thoughts come into ever-sharpening focus. Adding their own mystique to this magical morning, deer drifted in and out of the mists, disappearing momentarily behind brush or fusing their color with that of distant trees. Everywhere animals moved, blending their motion to the flow of forest.

Another flow entered that morning. Grandfather drifted slowly down the trail to the stream. I was excited to see him, because he had been away in another part of the forest. I wanted to go to him, but the intrigue of sitting there watching him held me in place. I know that he knew that I was there, for there was little he missed in the woods, and I am sure the nuances and disturbances easily gave away my location. Whether he knew I was there or not, he showed no interest and continued walking slowly toward the stream. He stood for a long time, gazing at the water, as if distance would put it into perspective. He glanced up and down the stream, leisurely and methodically, as if searching for something. His eyes rested on the cathedral of cedars for a longing moment, and I caught the glisten of a tear on his cheek. To me, he appeared as if he were about to enter a temple, about to see God.

As I sat and watched, my mind took a strange turn, changing reality and dropping the self. All analysis ceased, and I began to look at Grandfather as if I were watching some stranger. It was a nebulous feeling, a thinking with no perimeters or consciousness of time or place. Watching him was like watching a surrealistic dance or play, with unnamed characters and dreamlike landscapes. The whole relationship between Grandfather and me was viewed like a fantasy, a distant reality not of this place. I was fascinated and intrigued by his actions. I saw each move as if I had never seen it before. Though I had known Grandfather for over eight years, his movements overwhelmed me now. Sometimes one gets so close to something that he can only see it in parts, separate from the whole. Sometimes, too, one gets so familiar with something that the commonplace, the awe, the everyday teachings fade from view, like trying to see a flower by holding it against the eye. That is essentially what I had done to Grandfather, turned the power of his everyday teachings into a faded commonplace event.

He approached close to the water's edge and stood with his arms raised in an attitude of worship. Again looking upstream and downstream as if searching, pausing at every glistening riff and misty hollow with his gaze. I could see clearly the streams of tears on his cheeks glistening in the sun and the contented smile on his face. He kneeled down solemnly and touched the water, ever so gently, as he watched his own concentric rings ripple and mix with those of the waterstrider. He began to stroke the water as if it were a living being, looking deep into its color and to the mosaic of sand-mixed pebbles at the bottom. He drew his face close to smell the water, then took a light sip. He sat back with the water in his mouth and swished it back and forth. His actions would have put the most experienced wine taster to shame. Reaching deeper into the water with cupped hands, he raised the water to the Creator in thanksgiving. Then and only then did he drink. Standing erect, once again, he dropped his blanket and entered the water. I could see his entire body trembling with excitement and the smile on his face. As he lay back in the water, he was one of total rapture.

Rapture, something I never see in society's world, except as a word, but not an emotion. Society does not seem to know what rapture is, far less what it feels like. Just like rapture is to society, water is something for them to guzzle, put here for their use or misuse, and never given a second thought. To Grandfather, water was Earth Mother's blood, a precious gift of life for all things living and growing, not just for man. My mind raced back over the events of what took place, searching them for meaning. I should not have been shocked at all, for he had done nothing new. He always approached water that way, solemnly, in reverence, and like a child. Even though he swam in thousands of different waters, stood at the foot of the most magnificent waterfalls, and drank the purest waters of the earth, all his life he still entered water this way. No, it should not have shocked me, for this was the way he was with everything, the whole of Creation. That day I had backed away and seen for the first time what had always been there.

Grandfather savored everything in life as he savored the water, fully and with all his senses, to a state of utter rapture. He would walk through the forests fondling leaves, touching flowers, hugging trees, and lifting loam in cupped hands to smell. He would observe even the most common things for long periods of time, extracting every nuance from them. Life was always new and fresh to him, an adventure packed with excitement. He was a child, always at play, always searching, tasting, touching, smelling, hearing, and seeing the world and life fully. To him, every entity of earth was an object of worship, his life a constant prayer of thanksgiving, and his quest was always for rapture. In watching him live that day, I learned how to live and the true meaning of life. But then there was the fisherman, who taught me how not to live.

Many years after Grandfather's physical death, I was seated on another beach awaiting the sunrise. The ocean was still black, the waves were accented by the pale glow of dawn, and the silhouettes of gulls appeared at the edge of dawn and darkness. Lonely cries of gulls, the soft wind moving the sand in a gentle hissing, and the light clap of waves created a soothing music for the soul. Prayers seemed to reach to the skies, penetrating the scant cloud cover, now etched in the liquid gold of dawn. The beach was deserted except for a lone fisherman who sat on a beach chair a dozen yards from me. He was gray and weathered, his skin showed overexposure to the sun and surf, and his clothes looked like those of styles long forgotten. He stared intently at the tip of his rod, watching it bob and shift with the rise and fall of wave and wind. He seemed to solely concentrate on that rod tip, looking away only to his watch, probably out of habit.

In time, I moved closer to him. The sun now fully broke the horizon, bringing with it a deep warmth. Gull voices increased, and the old fisherman and I slipped into a light conversation. We talked of fishing and tides, weather and fishing beaches, but mostly about him. He said that he had been fishing these beaches for over thirty years, and since his retirement, a few years ago, he bought a house near the beach. Now he fishes every day without fail. The only time he said he didn't fish was when the beaches were crowded, during cold winter days, or when storms made it impossible. Our conversation soon trailed off. I went back to my sunrise and he to his rod tip.

As my thoughts drifted with the tides, I unconsciously picked up a handful of beach sand and began studying its texture and color. I smelled it awhile, then held it up to the sunlight, watching it sparkle and change color. I always love beach sand and how it changes its size, color, shape, and texture with each new beach. I guess that I was so caught up in what I was doing that I didn't notice the fisherman staring at me. He must have thought I was holding some sort of shell when he asked, "What you got there?" Astonished at his inquiry I answered, matter-of-factly, "Beach sand!" "Beach sand?!" he said. "What's so interesting about beach sand! It's all the same, white and gray, sticks to everything." I wouldn't have paid this statement even a second thought except for the fact that it was said in a mocking way. "White and gray?" I said. "Old man, please, pick up some beach sand and look." He grumbled something and went back to watching his pole.

I had got up and walked a few steps away when some feeding terns caught my eye, and I sat back down to watch. I was watching them hovering and diving near the edge of the jetty when I happened to glance back at the fisherman. In his weathered hand he held a handful of beach sand, stirring it around with his finger and holding it close to his face. I heard him talking, half out loud and half to himself. "My God," he exclaimed, his voice bitter and breaking, "my God, I never realized." As I left the area I glanced back at the old man to wave good-bye, but he wasn't watching me. In his outstretched hands he held a bluefish to the sun. I could see the colors glistening in the sun, and I could see the tears glisten on the old man's cheeks. His hands trembled. Dropping the fish, he hunched over, sobbing silently to himself. I wanted to go to him so very badly, but there was nothing I could do.

"The horror," I thought. Here was a man who had spent the better part of his lifetime fishing these beaches but did not know what beach sand looked like. Here was an old man, who in the twilight of his life had seen a bluefish for the first time, a fish that he loved so much to catch but never really knew. The words of Marcus Aurelius thundered in my brain. "It is not dying that a man should fear, but a man should fear never having lived at all." This is what had broken the fisherman down to tears: realizing at this late time in life all the things he missed; all the things he would never see, all the wasted time; time that has been spent, never to be made up; the horror of it all, the absolute senseless waste of life, the living dead. I learned from that old man, more than he could ever know. I learned not to waste my life living to die, but rather to live a life of rapture.

I never saw that old man again, though I have been back to that beach many times. He will always be with me, however, and I think of him often. I carry him in my heart as one of my greatest teachers, and I wonder how many more people are out there just like him. I wonder how many people will never really see a sunrise or sunset. How many will never know the sands or the sparkle of bluefish. How many will never know how to savor water, to touch, really touch, someone they love, or to know the rapture of life. I wonder how many people are rushing through life blindly, never really sensing what living is all about. Several times every day I ask myself, Am I being Grandfather or am I being the fisherman? The choice is always up to me, and everyone has to make that choice, sooner or later, hopefully, not too late in life, as did the fisherman. And so it went, tears on the cheeks of two different old men, tears of sadness and tears of rapture.

8

The Veils

I sat naked and alone, atop a small hillock, watching the late summer rains hissing through the pines and splashing on the lake, casting the surface into a misty frame. Not a breeze stirred the lower oaks, only the constant trembling of leathery leaves in sync with the raindrops. Birds were silent, except for some lone, forlorn calls telling their friends of a good roost for the night. As the skies grew a deeper gray, a small spacious chorus of frogs drifted on the thickening misty air, foretelling of oncoming darkness. Most animals seemed to be hiding, awaiting the storm to pass rather than venturing out into the relentless rush of water. I felt bitter, left out of the natural order of things, as I sat unprotected, wet, and chilled by the oncoming night air. I fought back the small shivers that ran down my spine as I remained absolutely motionless. I was as silent and still as an old tree stump, at least to all outward appearances.

My inner rhythms and thoughts, however, were in a turmoil, fighting to mark time with my body and seeking that same inner stillness. My mind surged to fight the cold, to rise above stray thoughts, and to remember the reasons I was there. I had mastered the outward silencing of my body through many months of watching animals, but it was the inner silencing and stillness that Grandfather now wanted me to master. Consciously, it was easy to minimize the movement of the body, to control breathing and heartbeat and to flow with all the discomforts, allowing the elements to flow through me rather than fighting against them. But the inner stillness, the silencing of all thought, and the passing into the void of nothingness of oneness now seemed so impossible.

Grandfather called this inner silencing "passing into the veil," and to him it was the most important training Rick and I had yet received. To him the mastery of this skill was a kind of doorway, a rite of passage into the spiritual realms. Even though I was not yet nine years old, he thought it time enough for me to understand the veils of the spirit and their grander lessons and uses. I had found difficulty in controlling my body at first, and even in the process of fusion and inner voice, but they were easy compared to what I was trying to achieve here and now. I could see the reasons for most things that he taught, but for the veils, this profound silencing, he gave me no clear or understandable explanation. With some explanation I thought I would do much better, but I had no idea that these things could not be explained until I personally, actually touched the veil and understood what it was. All Grandfather said was that the silencing was what happened to the body when the stillness of the veil was touched. It was a perfect balance and equilibrium of nothingness, an absolute pure and fertile ground from which spiritual things would grow.

I remember, vividly, the conversation around the fire the night before I went to the hill. Grandfather was trying to explain the world of the spirit and how it was entered, but it could not be understood logically; it could only be understood by listening with the heart and abandoning the mind altogether. Grandfather lived in a world far different from the superficial world that most people existed in. He always seemed to be listening to voices far away, to things we could not hear or understand. His vision penetrated deeply into life, into levels we could only dream of. There was an aura he walked within that could not be experienced with the physical senses, and Rick and I desperately wanted to live in his world. He could read beyond the physical landscapes into the past or future and communicate with the spirits of nature in a real way. There was something about his every action that made us understand that he never walked alone but lived in a world far deeper than we knew. In his manner of speech and action, we knew that there must be much more than just the physical realms. We instinctively knew that there was a grander scheme of things, a force, a time, and a space beyond anything we could yet comprehend.

Grandfather had often described what he perceived as the plight of modern society, a society deceived by its shallowness into confusing material acquisition with fulfillment and yet in turn frustrated by its haunting sense of lack. There is a spiritual world beyond the fleshly existence of modern man, a world of the unseen and the eternal, a world that most people never really understand or seek to know. Certainly, he said, there were the meager attempts by modern man to reach this spiritual world, but at best, they were superficial, all too complicated with customs and traditions that no longer seemed to work. Most of modern society has lost its ability to see beyond the flesh and the logical thinking, which is its guiding force. Yet society so desperately seeks fulfillment outside the realms of that superficial flesh. It seemed to Grandfather that after man acquired the comforts of flesh and the heights of learning, he is then left lost and searching for more to life. He acquires more and more of the false gods of the flesh and mind, and he soon finds that the acquisitions of the flesh can give him no more. He seeks wilder forms of entertainment and toys, and nothing fulfills his most desperate yearnings or the emptiness inside of him.

In desperation he searches for a deeper meaning to life, but there are no answers. In frustration, he turns to drugs, alcohol, or sins of the flesh to quench his pain. Some end with killing themselves. Others realize that there must be more but do not know where to find it. Religions spring up, and philosophies that are only but a Band-Aid. Nothing really works for him. Modern man then grasps for straws, following anyone or anything that points the way to enlightenment, or playing with any spiritual toy that brings relief. In the end, none of these things will ever quench his inner fires of searching and loneliness. Even his children at an early age are realizing the futility of it all, feeling that there must be more for them than theoretical knowledge and owning. He is lost, desperate, and destined to live out his existence in exile from what life is all about, marking time and awaiting death to free him.

Grandfather felt that somewhere in man's ancient history society lost its communication with the spiritual world and with the spirit-that-moves-in-all-things, the life force. Grandfather knew that man was a duality, part logical and physical, but mostly spiritual. The problem is that man has concentrated on developing the logical mind, while allowing the spiritual consciousness to atrophy. Grandfather felt that man found it difficult to deal in the realms of the spirit and sought the logical, as it was more provable, probable, and less work. This pursuit of the logical then followed mankind through the centuries and into modern times, where now he believes only in things manifest in science and knows nothing based on faith. Thus logical man began to persecute and eradicate all who dealt in the spiritual, considering them pagans, insane, or lunatics. The spiritual way of life interfered with man's science and explanation, and showed the shallowness of society's meager attempts at being religious.

Grandfather clearly showed us how society today has become lopsidedly strong in logical thinking but weak and ineffective in the matters of the spirit. Modern man, then, is but half a person, unable to comprehend the spiritual world, or the intensity of real faith. His world has become shallow and unfulfilling. His desperation, now, has brought him to the brink of destruction. His thirst for fulfillment through logic, science, and technology has made the earth a graveyard for his grandchildren. He has removed himself from the earth and has become an alien on his own planet. Without the connection to the earth and her laws, he can never know fully the spiritual worlds. And so Grandfather began to guide us away from the superficial world of society and to the greater world of the spirit and the life force, guiding me to that hill where I now sat, so desperately trying to break free of the shackles of society's demands.

To modern man what I was attempting to do would be called meditation, but it was far greater than what he considered meditation. Grandfather had taught me to meditate many months before. First he had taught meditation through movement. The combination of fox-walking and wide-angle vision, plus the easy-flowing motion and absolute concentration on nature would produce a wondrous meditation. Other times he would have us sit and watch a track very carefully, until there was nothing but us and the track, until there was no consciousness of outer dimension. The track in essence had become our mandala and the closeness to the earth produced an absolute meditation. These meditations we knew very well, for they were at the seat of our power, the power of inner vision, of primal mind, and of absolute body control. But what Grandfather now wanted was far greater than any meditation. It was the absence of all thought, of consciousness of time, place, gravity, or body. It was an absolute nothingness, an equilibrium, and a limitless void. The veil was the absence of self, totally, an absolute purity of existence and nonexistence.

It was in this void, this veil, that Grandfather said all things of the spirit would be found. It was there that we would have total understanding and transcend the physical planes of man's existence. It was there that the primal self could be found; it was the abiding place of the life force, the spirit-that-moves-in-all-things, and all the spirits that inhabit our worlds. It was also where we could find all knowledge, create realities, and touch the Creator. In this veil was the apex of the power and the world of the shaman. Here was the world we should live in, for it is the grandest and greatest part of man's existence. Here and only here can man find absolute peace and the deepest meanings of life.

I so desperately wanted to penetrate that veil as I sat shivering on that hill. I could feel myself slip in and out of reality, but my mind would never fully let go. There was always something there, something left to stand in my way and yank me back from the brink of nothingness. With each surge back to reality, I tried harder to break into the veil, and the harder I tried, the more difficult it became. As the night skies closed in fully, I completely lost control of my body and began to shiver uncontrollably. There was no turning back into myself, and I was cast off the hill. Walking back toward camp, I was heartbroken and felt like an absolute failure. Despite the failure, I felt deep inside that I had come close to something, but it was more feeling than thought, something I could not explain. I felt more connected to the wilderness than I ever had before, but my feeling of defeat overrode any further analysis.

I walked back into camp and saw Grandfather sitting quietly, gazing into the camp fire. Without looking up, he said, "Trying creates impossibilities, letting go creates what is desired." I was not surprised by Grandfather's knowledge of what was bothering me. I had known him long enough now that nothing he did or said surprised me. He continued, "You believe that penetrating the veil is impossible, because that is what you have been told to believe. You have created that reality based on other people's beliefs that there can be no world of spirit. Somehow, you think that it must be difficult to enter this realm and that you must suffer and try hard to get there. This then is what you have created. But when you have absolute faith, learn to let go completely and purely, then, and only then, will you touch the veil." Without a word, I left camp and headed back to the hillock, if for nothing else than to try and digest Grandfather's words.

I thought deeply about what Grandfather had said. As I concentrated and searched out each apparent and deeper meaning, I lost consciousness of my body and my place. There was nothing in my world other than his words and my thoughts about them. Even these things slipped away, and I found myself floating in a void, an absolute darkness, having no awareness of time or place, or even of an existence outside that world. Though it was only for a moment, it felt like an eternity that I was there, where time had stood still. As I opened my eyes to the night, I felt a deep sense of relaxation wash over me. I felt pure, my mind free and absolutely clear. I was there physically, but, then again, I wasn't there, at least not how I normally felt. As I gazed across the piney landscape toward the lake, I understood many things, things I could have never known by just the physical senses. I saw rhythms and cycles, the nuances of nature combining and creating a splendid force. I became part of that force. I could feel myself move within wilderness and wilderness move within me. At once I knew where all things were, physical and spiritual, form and space, action and reaction. I was really here, now, and conscious of the spirit-that-moves-in-all-things in a real way for the first time.

I slowly wandered back to camp, feeling my essence flowing with that of the landscape. I felt a certain inner "oneness," a connection to all things. The forest seemed crowded with spirits, though none were visible. I sensed them there watching, waiting, and guiding, and I could feel Grandfather watching me from afar, as if from a tall tree. As I approached camp, it was empty; only the glow of coals marked where the fire had been. Without looking up, I called to Grandfather in the big tree at the edge of camp. He laughed wholeheartedly, and I feared that he would lose his balance and fall from the tree. It was then that I realized that I had known he was in the tree long before I had gotten to camp, and I too burst out into the uncontrollable laughter of delight. It was then I heard Grandfather say, "Welcome to my world, grandson." And I felt so alive.

It was from that point of understanding on that Grandfather began to diligently teach the things of the spiritual world along with all the other practical, physical skills. He began to teach the power of the spiritual world, that there were no tools other than pure thoughts that would penetrate this world. It was with the purity of thought and action that I learned to create a certain reality in the spiritual world first, then allow it to transcend into a physical reality. I learned to use the power of the life force and to harness its mystery. I eventually learned to communicate with the world of spirit and to tap into the purity of the absolute knowledge. All of this took so many years, so much asceticism and aloneness unencumbered by the distractions of man. I learned quickly the vast difference between man's simple meditation and the powers of the veil. It is within the power of the veil that Grandfather found his power as a shaman. This power rested not, however, solely in Grandfather's person, but in his ability to use himself as a bridge between two worlds.

9

The Silence

It wasn't very long after I first penetrated into the veil that I learned it had many more uses than I ever imagined. At first I had to sit and relax, going into a state of perfect meditation before I could get to the veil. This technique was very time consuming, and a sedentary meditation would not fill my needs. I knew that Grandfather was able to slip in and out of the veil at will, and I wanted to be able to do the same. It was Grandfather who encouraged this "switching," as he called it, for he knew that there would not always be time to visit the veil slowly and without distraction. I had to learn to dwell in two worlds almost simultaneously, otherwise there would always be a separation. It was not enough to get there, but I had to get there quickly, so that time did not become a barrier.

Over the next year I grew more and more adept at entering the void of the veil until I could "switch" instantly at will. At once I could view the world from a logical and physical standpoint, then in a heartbeat, understand it through my spiritual self. My life became simplified, yet so very complicated, a paradox, for there was always a duality to my perception and understanding. However, there was a point in time where there was no longer any separation of the two realities. The realities fused into a greater self, and I realized the duality of man for the first time. Every action then had a spiritual reaction, and every spiritual action had a reaction in the physical world. At first, however, it was quite difficult to enter the veil without the peace, solitude, and relaxation that had to precede the "switch." Though I continuously practiced and could slip into that state with just a little preparation, it wasn't until a day my life was in danger that I finally transcended to that void instantly.

It was a cold and bitter winter day, the winds gusting strong from the north, chilling the landscape and freezing the waters. The Pine Barrens were exceptionally dry and dusty for that time of year. The ground cover was brittle and cracked easily beneath the step, no matter how carefully I walked. Body scents were trailed off in all directions with each swirl of wind, casting the deer into a blind panic whenever they caught the scent. Windy days in general kept animals on edge, but when the wind swirled, it was worse. The scents of danger ebbed and flowed with the wind, coming from all areas of the landscape to a point where even the foxes were skittish. The hissing and roaring of the wind made the conditions even worse. Animals had to depend solely on their vision, now that the sound and wind were not dependable. I too could feel a certain nervousness, probably a reaction from deep within me, originating somewhere in my genes' primal past. The cold winds were far more exhilarating and energizing to me than they were a menace. But my senses reached out, watching for danger as did the animals.

In the natural world it is good practice to follow the example set by the animals, their every nuance and motion. This day was so beautiful that I paid no attention to the flow of life but created my own flow, actions contrary to what the woods and animals were telling me. I wandered for hours, listening to the music of the wind, the groaning of trees under strain, and the sounds of animals running through the brush for cover. Somehow, wrongly, I felt separated from the whole frenzy of sound and motion, as if I were an outside observer. This was very careless on my part, contrary to the philosophy of the wilderness and what Grandfather had taught me. This was especially true as I was passing through the woods at the lower end of the dump, where dogs were a very real danger. I felt a false sense of security in the winds, figuring that the dogs would not be out and about when the game were so fidgety. I would have been more careful on a still day.

As I slipped into the lower cedar swamp, a sound caught my ears. It was a distant sound, hard to place above the hiss of the wind in the cedars. I listened intently, trying to blot out the immediate noises around me. Another sound broke above the hiss and whirl of cedars, a howling of some sort, like the wind makes when rushing through bare oak branches. My insides wouldn't accept that explanation. I grew cautious, following now the flow of animals, reacting as they reacted. I heard a rustle in the distance, something I would not have picked up if I had stayed in my previous consciousness. It wasn't the rustle of dried leaves but of soft pads compressing and shuffling them. Dogs, I thought, many of them heading toward the swamp, toward me! I panicked at first and began to fumble for trees to climb, but the panic covered the sound of dogs and hindered clarity of action.

I sat down for a moment on a fallen cedar trunk to compose my reaction and to still myself so I could hear better. They caught my eye immediately; they were walking on the upper edge of the swamp but still on dry land. They looked as if they were gathering forces before they plunged into the swamp for the hunt. Some sniffed the air, others cocked their ears to listen, and others just awaited some unseen command to charge. I felt, by their actions, that they had not spotted me yet, nor did they know I was there. Most of the wind was blowing off me at an angle away from the dogs. Suddenly the wind shifted and blew toward the dogs. They froze in their tracks, all ears pointed toward me, all noses cocked toward my direction, and I froze all motion. I fought back the panic, for I knew that I was cornered. A wall of thick brush and briars rose up behind me to the highland side, and there were no close climbable trees. The ones I could get to were farther away than I could reach, if the dogs decided to charge.

It all happened so fast that I can only look back in retrospect and remember what transpired. I was planning my action and my escape when I remembered what Grandfather had told me about the void of the veils. He had said, "Being in the void is being invisible to all in the physical world." Whether he meant physically or spiritually invisible, I did not know, and with a blind leap of faith I let go completely as the dogs charged toward me. It wasn't as difficult as I had thought, even surrounded by all that fear and distraction. I went easily; all panic was abandoned, all thought and all self. I entered the veil easily, completely, remembering nothing about what was taking place or my place in time.

The next event I remember was waking up, looking desperately for the dogs on the edge of the swamp, but they had vanished. As I arose, I felt weak and stiff, as if I had been sitting for a long time. Even the winds had changed and were dying off. Not a sound of the dogs could be heard, only the soft singing of breeze in cedar boughs and the light talking of birds. I was amazed. Questions flooded my mind as I tried to remember what had happened. I even checked myself for scars or blood, but I felt whole and unhurt. It was then that I noticed all the dog tracks that wound around me. They were everywhere. The type of tracks a dog pack makes when it has treed something but can't get to it or find what tree it's in. They flowed around me in curious curves, some passing close to my legs and back, but none taking notice of my presence on the log. I was more than amazed, full of questions, and relieved that I had not become dog food.

Without thought or hesitation, I ran back to camp to find Grandfather and tell him what I had experienced. I told him the entire story, my feelings and actions before, during, and after, the whole experience. I told him of the dogs, their tracks, and how they did not know I was seated on the log. Grandfather patiently listened in silence, never asking a question. After a long and thoughtful pause, he finally spoke. "As I had told you before, being in the veil makes you invisible. You learned to immediately live within the protection of the veil, and the dogs did not know how to find you or see you. It is the same with the ancient scouts. They too became the veil and thus became invisible to keep themselves safe. The important lesson, however, is that you learned to touch the veil immediately, especially in the distraction of danger. You also learned the wisdom of real invisibility."

From that day's lessons, I learned much more about invisibility. I learned, first, how to walk in the physical world while living within the veil. I also learned to fuse that walking with stalking, to a point where there was no sound to any step, even in the most difficult terrain. "Silent walking" became more than just stalking, more like floating invisibly, allowing me to go places I had never gone before, allowing me to penetrate landscapes that had been impossible to stalk through in the past. Most of all, it allowed me to spend a great deal of time in the realms of animals, close and unobserved. It also gave me an advantage of protection only known to the ancient scouts. But I soon found that this was only the beginning of the veil and the absolute silence of invisibility.

With every moment of every day, Rick and I learned something more wondrous about the magic of the veil. Just as I thought there could be nothing more to learn, some marvelously impossible lesson and understanding emerged, amazing me completely. Grandfather had told me that the veil would unlock the secrets of the universe. In the veil there was no time, place, or space, only the purity of all things. I remember once having trouble with the use of a particular hunting weapon and how it was used. I asked Grandfather to show me how it worked, but he simply said, "If you want to know how a skill was used, go and watch the ancient ones use it, then you will know firsthand." "But how do I watch the old ones use something?" I said. He laughed saying, "Why, through the veil, of course. It knows no time."

I was amazed at what he was implying. Could it be that we could time-travel by using the veil, or was that one of Grandfather's coyote lessons? Rick and I discussed the possibilities of looking at the past, not with absolute belief, but in a rather joking way. We hoped it was true, but it was too farfetched for absolute belief. We fantasized for many hours, talking of dinosaurs, ancient man, atlatls, and all manner of forgotten histories. Actually, what we ended up doing was talking ourselves into faith, washing away many of our doubts by talking about what we believed. We decided to pick a date in the past and go out and meditate on that date before entering the veil. We wanted to pick the same date so there could be a chance we would end up at the same place at the same time. We chose May 15, 1500, when the woods would be full of native peoples, before white intervention.

We chose a likely place and sat down several feet from each other, overlooking a small swamp. For several hours, we tried to enter the veil, or think about the date, but absolutely nothing happened to either of us. We tried desperately to carry the date with us to the veil, but every time we passed through, the date would disappear with all other thought. Feeling a little angry with my failure, I went to ask Grandfather why it hadn't worked. "First," he said, "there must be absolute faith, and second, you must not try to carry the time or place back with you. You can not pass into the veil carrying any baggage. Instead, tell it where and when you would like to go and allow the 'all-knowing' veil to do the rest." Rick and I were excited about what he said, remembering how difficult it had been to concentrate on the date. We decided to try again the next day, after a good night's sleep.

Near the end of the same day, just before sunset, I went out to pray. I noticed that not far from me, Rick was also doing his evening devotions and prayer. I sat back for a while and thought about what Grandfather had said, digesting every last detail in my heart so it would become forever part of me. I prayed for a while, then slipped into a period of absolute thoughtlessness to meditate and rest. I awoke to the sound of voices coming through the woods. The sound startled me because it was nothing I could understand. As I opened my eyes to look, the entire landscape had transformed into a place I could barely recognize. There were huge pines where there had been none before. The vegetation was thicker, but the roll of the earth remained the same as it had been. Just several yards in front of me was a narrow and worn path that I had never seen before.

I heard the voices again, coming closer, and I began to distinguish footfalls, much like the sound of Grandfather's walk, though many more. From the thick brush that was growing by the edge of the swamp, there emerged an Indian, young, strong, and sinewy. He carried a club in his hand and across his back was an unstrung longbow. Others deftly followed, smiling and carefully watching the landscape as they went. Many carried bundles in their arms or on their backs. Near the end of the line an old man appeared, walking quieter than the rest, listening to the deeper voices of wilderness. I instinctively knew that this was a man of power, and as he passed by me on the trail, he nodded and smiled. The rest of his party had paid me no attention.

A few other people followed the old man, and at the end of the long line was a young girl. She carried a bundle in her arms and a larger bundle on her back. Loosely strung from the backpack was a small stone berrymasher attached to a sapling handle. As she turned at the edge of the trail to look at a large tree, the berrymasher fell to the ground, landing by the edge of the trail. She was not aware of it falling and continued walking. I instinctively yelled to her, pointing to the berrymasher, but no one paid attention. That is, except for the old man, who abruptly turned around and smiled at me. I looked toward the part of the trail where the masher had fallen, and as soon as I began to move, I felt the landscape surge. It was as if the whole scene flickered, went out of focus, then fell to blackness.

I opened my eyes only to find myself back in my original position, Rick not far away, and the landscape the same as I had always known it. I was amazed at the intensity of my imagination and subsequent daydream, it all seemed so real, so vivid. I walked over to where Rick was sitting, but he didn't move at my approach. Instead, he sat there staring at a large tree in the distance. I laughed and said, "Looking for Indians?" He looked at me coldly and said, "Berrymasher." His words silenced my laugh and shook me in my tracks. We sat for a long time discussing what each of us had seen. It wasn't long before we realized that we had both witnessed the same thing, or had the same daydream, anyway. It wasn't odd for us to tap into the same thought, since we spent so much time together, and practiced, frequently, a form of telepathy that Grandfather had taught us. We decided to tell Grandfather about our experience anyway.

Each of us told Grandfather our stories in great detail, giving the description of the landscape, the Indians, their clothing, the old man, and even the dropping of the berrymasher. We also told him that the whole thing was some kind of daydream we both shared and that we were very excited that we could communicate that well. I expected Grandfather to tell us how delighted he was with our shared thoughts, but instead he said, "Go dig up the berrymasher." Rick and I looked at each other, very startled at his reply. Without question, and with great speed because of oncoming dark, we went to the area we thought the berrymasher was dropped. We soon found a long, troughlike depression in the ground. I drew a line from where I sat to the place of the masher and did the same from Rick's original position. Where the two lines crossed, we began to dig.

In our experience with what we had seen, there were no trees close to the path. But next to where we wanted to dig now grew a huge old pine. We dug feverishly until full dark but found no berrymasher. Just as we were about to give up, I decided to dig beneath a large dead top root of the grandfather pine. My stick clicked, then slid off something just beneath the root with a thump. It was a sound much like hitting a snapping-turtle shell beneath the mud with a probing sapling staff. It was also the sound of solid rock. I quickly cleared around the area of the root and out fell a berrymasher head. It was cleanly pecked from a smooth river rock, the type found along the Delaware River. It was clearly identical to the ones used by the Indian people indigenous to this area and frequently carried on their migration routes to the bay and seashore area.

I was astonished, not only that I had never found such a large artifact before, but also at how I had found it, and where. Because of topography, I knew that there were no ancient camps in the area. Here was a celt head, many miles from any known campsite. We ran back to Grandfather carrying the head and dropped it in his lap. He smiled and said, "Why do you look so surprised? Has what you have seen changed your beliefs?" Rick and I talked until dawn, taking turns fondling the artifact, while trying to recall every detail of what we had seen. The energy and elation we felt would not allow sleep. As our conversation trailed off with the rising sun, we both made solemn promises never to tell anyone how we found the head. No one would understand or believe us anyway, for everyone outside the temples of the woods lived their own reality of disbelief.

For most of the next year we collected all manner of artifacts this way, our rooms growing full with storage boxes and cartons. It was on one of these collecting trips that I first learned the lesson of energy, and for the first time I saw and felt the real aura of energy Grandfather so often spoke of. It all began when I saw a pipe bowl fall to the ground during my entry into a veil. The pipe fell like a comet, with a long golden tail that mushroomed into intense white light as it hit the earth. As I watched, it glowed and pulsated with light, then disappeared into the earth. I awakened from the void and walked to the area I saw the pipe drop. It wasn't difficult to find, because it had dropped by a sandstone outcropping that was still visible now.

As I dug down, a strange feeling came over me, the type of

feeling I got when Grandfather was doing a ritual, or chanting. I was immediately humbled, afraid to dig any farther. I could not remember who dropped the pipe or any of the circumstances surrounding it, but that was a quite common occurrence during a veil meditation. Sometimes I would only remember certain parts of the experience. Instinctively, however, I knew that this pipe should not be touched, so I went to find Grandfather for help.

I told the story to Grandfather, especially explaining the reasons that I had not completed the dig. He explained, "All things have an energy, but some things have energy added onto them by a shaman, or through use. You have been wise not to touch this pipe, for there is good energy, then there is bad energy, and you must learn the difference." Without another word, he arose from the ground and began to walk out into the woods, and I followed. He found the location of the pipe without my having to tell him where it was. Slowly and carefully he dug it up, praying through the whole procedure. He examined the bowl carefully, and I could see that it was made from some sort of stone, not at all like Grandfather's pipes. It was very old, and I could feel some unseen and awesome power coming from its depths. Grandfather told me that it was a wise man's medicine pipe, one of great power. It was probably owned by one who healed. It should be taken care of as powerful medicine and kept safe.

Upon returning to camp, Grandfather carefully cleaned the pipe and set it on the top of a stump near the edge of the fire. As I watched the pipe, I was intrigued at how it looked when viewed from spiritual eyes. The aura of light that surrounded it was intense white and very soothing, and when Grandfather touched it, his light blended with it, fusing into a perfect oneness. Grandfather lifted his hand from the pipe and touched my shoulder. Immediately I felt very peaceful and relaxed, very whole, clear, and healthy. I could feel the pipe move within me and become part of me. Grandfather handed me the pipe and said, "Take care of this pipe until you can find the owner, then return it to him." I was deeply touched and honored, but more amazed at the pipe's power.

In the years to follow, I learned to see the power in all things, the power of the spirit-that-moves-in-all-things. I learned that each entity has this force, and that more energy can be added to things. I learned to understand this power, this force, and bend it to create. I began to use it in understanding the unity of all things, the "oneness" of it all. Through the spiritual veil, one can see the bands of power, one can touch the power and be made whole. To walk as "one" with Creation is to walk within the veil of power. It is to touch the Creator.

10

▼■▼■▼■▼

Vision

Grandfather stressed the Vision Quest as being as equal in importance to our survival path as survival training, awareness, and asceticism. The Vision Quest was held in the highest reverence as the ultimate sacrifice of self. Indeed, the quest was more important than any other spiritual practice, but it could not stand alone. Nevertheless, the Vision Quest did what could not be done with asceticism alone. It answered the deepest spiritual questions, directed our lives, and helped us transcend the realms of the flesh to the purity of spirit. The quest was the ultimate self-denial, requiring us to fast from all things familiar, including rational thought. It was a "little death" that sacrificed the self for the wisdom of the grander things of life and spirit. All outside distractions were cast aside, and a purity of thought and spirit was thus attained. It was only through the quest that we could ever hope to touch spiritual wisdom free from all outside influences. It penetrated into our deepest selves, preparing fertile ground for the seeds of the spirit world to grow in purity.

I remember, vividly, when Grandfather began to explain the Vision Quest. Rick and I were very young and had known Grandfather only a year or so. We had heard many stories about

Visions—of both his own and those of other people—and we knew that the Vision Quest was Grandfather's guiding force, not only in matters of the spirit, but also throughout everyday life. Whenever he spoke of the quest, it was with the highest reverence and humility. The quest seemed so abstract and yet so real, a vivid connection to the things beyond the senses, beyond the material, beyond what was to him the superficial nature of life outside of the wilderness. The quest seemed to hold all the answers to all the questions of life. We wanted to quest, desperately, but we were terribly afraid what would happen, of the power it apparently held—not to mention of the long periods of aloneness that would be required in our search. The woods still frightened us, or perhaps it was the unknown that was so terrifying. And we still had much to learn about the wilderness—and the self.

The camp fire flickered against the thick walls of mist shrouding the Pine Barrens. Wafts of smoke blended with the mists and cast them into weird forms that drifted about the camp on unseen breaths of air. Grandfather's voice was hushed, speaking almost in a whisper. His low tones combined with the soft wavering chorus of distant frogs, adding punctuation to his words. We sat silently drinking in every word. He spoke of many things, many Vision Quests, and things just outside our world of comprehension. "The Vision Quest," he said, "provides all the answers to life, to spirit. It is far more powerful than the asceticism of wandering alone in wilderness, for it is pure, untainted by the feasting mind. For even in the aloneness of asceticism, there are still things for the mind to feast upon. In the Vision Quest there is nothing but monotony for the mind. There the mind falters, then sleeps, allowing the real self, the self directed by the heart, to speak. Then and only then, during the sleep of the logical mind, do all the external shoulds that govern our mind slip away. Reality is then pure.

"The Vision Quest, then, is beyond the reality of asceticism and aloneness, for it brings forth the pure self untainted by any and all outside distractions. Once you sacrifice yourself and enter that confined circle, whether for four days, or forty, you make a commitment to self, and to the Creator. The denial of self, the sacrifice of all comforts and all distractions, proves the quester worthy of the Vision." We were spellbound at his words and by the power of the Vision Quest. Here we could reach a certain purity of thought, without any distractions. The mind could not feed on the beautiful things of nature nor be kept busy by the things of man. All the external shoulds that govern people's lives could be washed away, and the essence of the real self would flourish. Here we could learn who we really are, what our direction should be, a direction governed by our hearts and not by the outside worlds.

Grandfather continued, "What is understood first is the pure self—the self outside what you have been taught to think and believe, the self free of all restrictions, that deep inner self that is at the apex of all reality, and that self that is always trying to realize itself. Once the thought is pure, the true self is released, and the deepest yearnings and feelings become reality. But," Grandfather said, "there is much more to the quest than just self-realization. For once the true self is realized, it prepares the soul for communication and understanding with the spirit world. There, comes the voices of Creation and the wisdom of the Creator. It is then that the quest gives us a Vision, a command from the Creator, and a grand purpose to life. So, the quest satisfies a duality, the duality of knowing the pure self and its connection and 'oneness' to all things, and the direction given to us from the Creator. When the communication and contact between self and the Creator become pure, then this we call Vision."

We were too young to understand fully what Grandfather was teaching us. We had no experience with the Vision Quest, no references to help us understand his teaching, other than periods of aloneness and silence that we had while waiting for animals. Yet his words were so intriguing, so compelling that they diminished the fear of the extended period of aloneness that would be required for a quest. As always, when Grandfather taught us something, it was something that we desperately needed to know, to experience, immediately. He never attempted to force anything upon us, but rather he waited for us to beg to learn that skill. He constantly manipulated his teachings to lead us to greater things, leaving us thirsting for the next lesson. He knew that to teach anything there had to be a deep interest, a need, and a yearning, otherwise the lessons would fall on deaf ears. He also made each lesson exciting, almost mystical, so unlike the teachings we had to sit through in school.

As he spoke, the night closed in around us and our imaginations went wild. With each word, our yearnings grew stronger, and we lusted to live the Vision Quest. To us, it was the only way to reach the intimacy we wanted to achieve with self, and with Creation. We wanted to live the life of the ancients, the warrior scouts, and all the heroes we held in our hearts. The Vision Quest would be a powerful doorway to that life, a ritual to the rites of passage into the spirit world. It would bring us so close to the Native Americans and to Grandfather's way of living, of understanding. We wanted to do all the things that had been done by the ancients, for we knew that would be our only reality. Reality in the outside world was too superficial, too shallow to be real, and we desperately wanted the pure reality of Grandfather's world. We both decided silently that we would live the quest later that summer. However, Grandfather had his own time schedule and plan for our Vision Quest.

Grandfather's words drifted off and dissipated into the thickness of the night mists, followed by a long and intense period of absolute silence. He closed his eyes, as if to give us time to ponder what he had said. The silence penetrated my soul, and his words grew like wildfire through my consciousness. There was no longer any fear, but there was a yearning to find myself and to understand, if even in a small way, the wisdom of the words he spoke. His eyes opened, and he looked directly at me for a long time, as if to assess my heart. When he watched me this way, I could feel his stare burning holes in my reality, searching. Like the invisible radar of bats penetrates the darkness, his eyes penetrated the outer realm of what I truly understood and felt. Without warning, he said, "You will meet the morning sun in your Vision Quest area. Tomorrow you will die your little death. Tonight you will find your quest area, and prepare yourself." My mind swooned with fear, laced with excitement. I was numb with disbelief and shock from his words. I visibly shook from deep within.

It was still dark when I left camp and headed out to my Vision Quest area. Fatigue from being up all night clouded my thoughts with surrealistic images cast by the shadows woven by starlight and mists. Choruses of frogs and insects surged from the night, filling my senses with a dimension of spaciousness enlivened by the stereo of sound. The dampness of the air clung to my flesh, and I felt clammy and chilled, though the night air was warm. The darkness seemed alive with movement as animals drifted through the landscape. Pockets of absolute quietude and stillness were quickly replaced by areas of intense motion. Ancient pines thrust upward to the night skies, silhouetted by the stars into contorted shapes and apparitions. I felt so frail, a part of but separated from the intensity of this awesome wilderness. The fatigue welled up from within, causing me to vibrate with fear and anticipation. Part of me wanted a Vision more than anything else, and part of me wanted to run, terrified, back to the security of camp.

The events of the night seemed but a distant dream, vague and obscure, as if I were a witness rather than a participant. I remembered choosing the Vision Quest area—a special place to me in the heavy brush near the cedar swamp. I had used this place many times before to watch birds or when I needed to practice my silencing. The events that followed the selection of the area were fuzzy, especially after the long sweatlodge and the subsequent swim for spiritual and physical cleansing. We prayed for many hours, silently and aloud, offering the pipe periodically through the night. During the periods of prolonged and agonizing silence, I kept drifting off to sleep as the fatigue overpowered me. A few hours before dawn, I was sent from camp to go to the Vision arena, and the sudden fear of departure shook me awake. I departed to Grandfather's chanting, which slowly decreased as the distance between me and the camp increased. As I drew near the Vision area, night sounds replaced the chant, and fatigue became my nemesis.

I fumbled through the thick wall of brush that framed my chosen area. The briars tore at my flesh, and broken sticks punctured my legs. Fatigue caused me to stumble and become careless, and I fell into the area I had chosen for my grave. As I shook myself back to consciousness, I felt like a fool. A grand entrance into my first Vision Quest was now a stumble and fall. It shattered all the imagery that I had of my first baptism into that sacred area. Once inside the shell of brush, the small area where I was to spend the next four days seemed smaller and more suffocating than it had seemed when I had chosen it. Grandfather had told me to choose a close area, with no view, but this bordered on being a closet. I could barely stretch out when I lay down, but lying down was not permitted; neither was sleep. The area was certainly confined, perfect for taking away all distractions of sight and distance so that the mind had nothing to feed on.

I carried nothing with me except for a jug of water. I was to remove my clothing and place them out of sight, outside the area, along with the water. It was said that when we approach the Creator, we should have nothing but ourselves, for trinkets and clothing had no place in the purity of the visionary area. We are meant to approach, unadorned, as pure and unencumbered as the day we were born. Clothing and water stowed, I sat and awaited the rising of the sun, fighting sleep and rethinking all the reasons I was there. This little death, I thought, was a sacrifice of self, the ultimate sacrifice, giving up all I was for the Vision. The fear had departed now that I was safe in my area. Excitement surged through every fiber of my existence as I eagerly anticipated the adventure of it all.

I watched the dawn come, beginning as a small sliver of light on the horizon and ending with a gorgeous sunrise. It filled the sky with its golden fire, quickly warming the landscape even before it was fully up. Birds put on a grand show, fluttering and singing from every branch and bush. Insects joined in with a rapturous, almost deafening chorus, while animals slipped through the brush, setting the whole area into a tremendous flowing motion. My mind and senses feasted on the events of dawn and the tremendous surge of life. But as the sun rose, the activity and sound diminished to a few calling birds and the relentless, mocking chorus of insects. By midmorning, the sun was already beginning to burn holes in my flesh, my mind faltered with an extreme fatigue, and my body shook with exhaustion. I fought sleep by watching the brush around me very closely, savoring it for every detail. The appearance of a bird, mouse, or even an insect was enough to bring me back to consciousness.

By high noon, my head pounded from the heat of the sun, and my flesh felt as if it were on fire. The landscape seemed so dull. Even the goings and comings of animals seemed boring and mundane. My mind faltered over all manner of thoughts, worries, and personal inadequacies. Little things produced an intense anxiety, almost a panic. Even my most cherished thoughts grew hideous. My mind began to penetrate realms of the insane, self-doubt frequently welled from within, and a thousand voices tried to drive me from the area and back to camp. I thought of many excuses and reasons why I should leave, but still I hung on, determined to complete the quest at all costs, even at the cost of my sanity. If for no other reason, I wanted to prove to Grandfather, to the Creator, and to all else who were looking upon me that I was worthy, that I was strong.

Midafternoon produced a period of sleep, a tormented sleep

full of nightmares and pain. Each time I snapped back to a place just short of awake, my body jumped, only to fall back to sleep again. I vaguely remember falling over a few times. I suddenly awoke fully, hearing a distant laughter, but listening carefully, there was no laughter, just the laughter of the wilderness mocking my weakness. My thirst was intense, but I had to conserve water. I allowed my parched lips to barely touch the mouth of the jug, an act which was a tremendous relief. My head pounded with pain, and my mind could no longer think clearly. Thoughts ran together and made no sense at all. I tried to stand, but the fatigue was just too great, the sun was too hot, and the pain in my head kept me close to the ground. Periods of clear thought would come, followed by weird thoughts and dreamlike images, then sleep again.

I was jolted awake by the nearby alarm call of a crow. I was disoriented, out of touch with time, place, and reality. I had no idea how long I had been asleep. It could have been a few moments or a few hours. The sun had moved farther down in the sky, and the afternoon seemed cooler, my mind fresher. I flew into a self-contained rage over my weakness, cursing myself for allowing sleep. The rage dissipated and my mind seemed clear and sharp, my body strong and comfortable again. I was more determined than ever to do well, to prove myself, to know myself. I didn't like the self I had known so far into this quest, and I was determined to destroy that self that so eagerly sought defeat. The sleep, no matter how much, did me a lot of good. I faced the remainder of the daylight with new vitality. All things became clearer, and I could see so many things around me that had escaped my attention before. My mind fed on the images around me like a hungry child.

Sunset was spectacular, accented behind ever-thickening clouds that foretold an oncoming storm. Darkness came quickly, the rumblings of thunder grew louder, and the sunset was replaced by flashes of distant lightning. Light rain began to fall, chilling the burning of my sunburn. Lightning and thunder began to rage across the sky, fusing the landscape into flashes of windy motion with every spear of light. Trees bent and twisted in the wind, the brush surged and flowed like an angry sea, limbs fell all around, and drenching rains stung my body. I sat firm and unafraid, viewing the storm as a test of my worthiness sent from the Creator. The beauty of it all was that the storm's violent energy filled me and I was strong. The storm had taught me to tap into its wisdom, to fuse my consciousness with its power rather than cower in the abyss of an unknown and untouching fear.

Suddenly the storm was silent, passing as quickly as it had come, and I was left alone, abandoned, and in a sea of silent darkness. Thoughts began to come and go as the relentless fatigue began to quickly overtake me again. I fought hard most of the night. Thoughts went wilder than before, personal inadequacies and excuses seemed more powerful, demons of mind replaced all reality, and I felt as if I were drowning in my own flesh. I fought sleep by catching drops of rain dripping from the plants, but I could no longer hold on, crashing to the ground and into a deep sleep. Dreams and nightmares flooded me again, contorting my body in pain, and twisting my mind with hideous creatures. It was a tortured sleep that was anything but restful. I was in and out of this sleep most of the night, rocked awake by a horrifying dream only to fall instantly back to sleep, unable to come to full consciousness.

I awoke to a flood of bird song, singing praises to the rising sun. I was stiff and sore, angry at myself for giving into sleep again. Disorientation was worse than it had ever been, and I felt so terrified at the thought of being there for three more days. It already seemed like I had been here for an eternity, and my mind quickly faltered in desperation. All day I slipped in and out of reality, as my mind searched for something to feast upon. My consciousness resided someplace between awake and nightmare, my body trembled out of control even in the hot sun. With each passing moment the pain of mind and body felt more and more out of control. Thoughts grew stranger, my mind fluttering like a wounded butterfly on hot ground. Nothing I did could remove the pain or the crashing, disoriented thoughts in my skull. I felt on the verge of death, unable to return to the reality of life. I could hold on no more. I was physically broken, mentally disoriented, and emotionally dead. I gave up. I gave in.

I vaguely remember passing through the next day, though I could not remember any clear thoughts. I remember vividly feeling so defeated, so helpless, as if the whole of Creation were mocking my fleshy mortality and my thoughts. All pain was gone, or at least, not remembered. Sitting still and in absolute silence became easier, more effective, and the only thing I could do that made sense. I felt a certain knowing deep within me but vague and unclear at first. With each passing event, things became clearer, questions about myself were answered, and I felt a deep connection to that self. I suddenly knew who I was, where I was going, and what I really wanted to do in life. There was no more pain or discomfort, my mind no longer fought the imprisonment of the quest, but rather it expanded to become that quest, that wilderness.

The remaining day was like a vivid dream, connected with self and all things around me. I felt as if I could sit in this place unafraid for the rest of my life. I realized that all fear was of my own making, all events were of my own choosing, and my path was a series of choices. I knew then that I had to choose to live a spiritual life close to nature and nature's ruler, rather than the empty and dead-end existence of fleshly society. I needed to choose a pure reality filled with excitement, adventure, and intensity—a life of rapture rather than a life of comfort, security, and boredom like everyone else was choosing. I knew exactly what I wanted and how to get there. I would fly in the face of criticism and outside shoulds, or die trying, for I would not give in to a life I did not want to lead. I walked from the woods with the rising sun on the fourth day, never looking back. Back in that grave a part of me had died, the part that was full of fear and guided by external shoulds, rather than the heart.

As I walked back to camp, I felt far different than I had before. I felt purged of my old self and pure. The Pine Barrens felt so real, so alive, like each entity was trying to reach out and touch me, or communicate to me some sublime truth. I felt expansive, balanced, and part of the whole universe. I no longer felt helpless or like an alien, but I felt rooted to the land in a new way. I knew things instinctively, and I could feel the flow of life around me like never before. The inner sense of knowing had not abandoned me at the Vision Quest area but had grown stronger and more powerful. It was an inner knowing, feelings I could not put into words. I felt a sense of equilibrium and reality as I had never known it before. Most of all I felt a sense of deep relief from knowing who I was and where I was going. I had developed a tremendous commitment to living life, and to living my own personal truth. I was concerned, however, that I hadn't received the type of Vision that I so often heard of, a Vision of power, of tremendous spiritual entities, of color, and of grandeur.

As I approached camp, I could see Grandfather sitting by the fire. I slowed my pace because I was afraid to face him. The fear of not having a grand Vision was playing on my mind, and I felt ashamed. I did not want to disappoint Grandfather. I felt that he expected a grand Vision of me, and I had in some way let him down. I felt that I had not been found worthy enough by the Creator to receive a grand Vision, and Grandfather, seeing that I wasn't worthy, would find another student. The worry and inadequacies overwhelmed me as I entered camp. How could I possibly tell Grandfather that I was unworthy or a failure? I trembled as I approached him. His stare and half smile burned right through my soul, and I felt so naked, so helpless.

He smiled fully as I sat down. It was a proud smile, not at all mocking as I had feared. Before I could say a word, he spoke. "The grandest Visions," he said, "are of knowing the self first. The most powerful Visions come in little nuances, rarely in the grand dimension." How could he have known? I thought. Could it have been because he could read my mind, or was it because he too had been there before, or was it a combination of both? Whatever the reasons, I felt relieved, and all the grandeur of knowing myself filled me again. Before we went on with the discussion, we prayed to the Creator, thanking him for the Vision, and thanking all of Creation for its participation. The prayers, for the first time, felt real, and I knew that for once the words were in direct communication with all things. Grandfather seemed very proud of me, our communication felt much deeper than ever before, and I knew that I was beginning to share his world in a real way.

After the prayers, a good meal, and a short nap, Grandfather spoke of my Vision Quest again. "The Vision Quest is not a one-time event, but a continuing process," he said, "a process that you should seek throughout life. One quest is good for most people, but those who seek a spiritual path, apart from the workings of man, need to seek counseling from the quest several times a year, for the rest of their physical lives. The first Vision gives us tremendous insight into who we are, into the meaning of life, and into knowing that other self, that true self. It also brings us in touch with a greater Vision, and in touch with the Creator and Creation. But this is only a building block, a step, toward the grander Visions of self and direct communications with the Creator. Certainly, if this first Vision Quest was the beginning and the ending of all your quests, it would be very powerful and a guiding force for the rest of your life, but you must remember that this is only a beginning, never an end."

Grandfather finished his teachings, and I went to sleep for the night. The dreams that came to me were peaceful, clear and vivid, reinforcing what I had learned during the quest and providing insights into aspects that had passed me by during its process. They fused what I had learned in the quest to my soul. I sometimes awoke with the punctuation of each dream, and the sounds of the night hammered home all that I had dreamed. It was at these times of semiconsciousness that the grand lessons and connections to life flooded me, filling me with their magic. I felt so close, so intuned with this world, that I never wanted to leave the woods again. From that night on, the wilderness would always be my home, my inspiration, and my Vision. Here I would be safe.

Grandfather awakened me at sunrise for my morning prayers at the river. His words followed me that morning, as I prayed and contemplated all the events of the past four days and my dreams. He had said, "Dreams are important, but are for clarifying a Vision, or as an indicator that a Vision Quest must be undertaken. Dreams are for those who will not take the time or sacrifice for Vision Quest, or for those who do not know how to listen to their soul. Dreams are a way for the inner self to contact your mind but are not necessary for those who are 'one' with themselves and all things. Dreams are important, but only for warning the recipient that the Vision time is near. At best, dreams are unclear and only partial statements that have to be clarified later in a quest, or through contact with the deeper self. Dreams are too connected to the distractions of the unpure self to be relied upon. Only the purity of Vision and knowing that deeper self can be clear. So take your dreams as an indicator that more searching must be done, and not as an end."

We talked for most of the morning. Time and events passed quickly, but my new awareness allowed me to watch most of the events unfold, even as Grandfather spoke. Grandfather explained why the Vision was always a process and never an end. "To me," he said, "the Vision Quest is a most important process, especially to the new apprentice, which we all are until we are very old and wise. Even then, the Vision Quest becomes a friend, a guide that clarifies things that old age distorts. It is a necessity. As food and air are to the physical world, the Vision is critical to spiritual life. With each new quest, more of the primary Vision is realized, each part being vital to the overall understanding. There are no shortcuts to the Vision; it is never a one-time experiencing. For, to transcend fleshly existence to spirit, the Vision Quest becomes the eagle's wings. The first Vision never dies but grows and flourishes through the rest of your life."

The thirst for the Vision Quest has stayed with me all these years. It is a primary source of all my understanding and is vitally important when I need to clarify the obscure. It has become my guiding force and direction and has never failed me even in the most troubled times. It is more than knowing the self or the grand Vision. It is the discovery and rediscovery of the ultimate connection to Creation, and most of all to the Creator. The more I live my Vision, the more I realize that the direst problem today is that people live with no Vision at all. Society provides some superficial experiences similar to the Vision that the masses follow to death, but no man can dictate to another the "right" content of a Vision. We cannot walk another's Vision, but only walk beside him to the top of the mountain. Visions can be similar in direction and theme, but they are never identical, for the Creator speaks to each of us differently, as we are unique. It was once said, "Seek not to follow in the footsteps of the men of old, but seek instead what they sought." The Vision is the beginning, and I am still learning lessons from my first quest.

11

Earth Mother Speaks

Above all else, Grandfather taught the sacredness of the earth. The earth is a guiding force behind all physical realities. She is the mother of all things and the physical manifestation of the Creator. The earth is a temple, a university, where man can learn the lessons of flesh and spirit in their purest forms. The earth is also a place where all truth is manifest, a crucible where one can check the validity of what he believes to be true. The earth, Grandfather taught, is a living being, the sum total of all her parts, and all parts are interconnected to the whole, where the whole is its physical consciousness and love of the Creator. We are all part of the Earth Mother, and whatever we do, whatever we take, we are taking and affecting, in reality, part of ourselves. Within the earth resides the consciousness of all things, which is bound together by the spirit-that-moves-in-all-things, that life "force" that connects us to each other and to that sacred "oneness." It is this "oneness" that makes all things brothers and sisters of one flesh, the flesh of Earth Mother.

Rick, Grandfather, and I all learned these truths the only way they could be learned, by living them daily. Words alone could not explain our connection to the earth; even our individual experiences of survival living and asceticism fell far short of providing us with the reality of that sacred "oneness." Only by breathing, sleeping, eating, working and playing the philosophy of earth did the reality become manifest. Only by really living it did it saturate our every action and thought, and fuse with our consciousness and our visions in a meaningful way.

For us, the earth was a grand temple of understanding. Each creature and entity of the earth was a grand teacher of infinite wisdom, as well as a close brother and sister. In reality, we understood and lived the true family of Creation and the Creator. We were at once part and "one" with all things. We understood that we lived within the realms of Creation, and Creation lived within the realms of our existence. There were no inner or outer dimensions; there was just a sacred wholeness found only by entering through the worlds of survival, asceticism, and especially the Vision Quest.

We learned to listen patiently and silently to the voices of Creation and to each nuance and mood of the earth. Each creature became, at once, many things—a source for our survival, a teacher of physical skills, a teacher of spiritual skills. Grandfather taught us to look closely, beyond the apparent, beyond the names, beyond physical actions, to a deeper world of spirit and knowledge. Passing through the doorways of understanding we learned the true life of family ties, realizing in our comprehension of the oneness of life why the ancient ones referred to each other in terms of family and to the elements of Creation as relatives. Reverence for survival, of the natural order, made clear that our lives were connected, as if by an umbilical cord, to that of the earth. Asceticism brought us nearer to the physical teachers of the earth and a sense of "oneness," but it was through the Vision experience that we were transported beyond the flesh to the maternal realm of Earth Spirit.

It was a few years past my first Vision Quest that I first had a grand Vision, the Vision of Earth. Even though I had undertaken a Vision Quest about four times a year since my first experience, I had not yet received what I yearned for: one of the powerful Visions of the ancients. Certainly, I had felt a direct link between myself, Creation, and the Great Spirit, or the spirit-that-moves-in-all-things, but the communications had been vague and general. What I sought so hard was a specific directive, or a powerful understanding. I longed to hear the Creator's voice, unobstructed and clear. I wanted to be a servant, to live a Vision, a truth, beyond the self, and to dedicate myself to it completely. That thirst for pure Vision and communication filled my consciousness every day, directed my every move, moving me ever closer to what I wanted to become.

The Earth Vision did not come during a time of an actual Vision Quest, but during a short hike I was taking into the inner recesses of a large swamp. Sometimes Visions come when least expected, but only to those who have already undertaken many quests. I was moving through the swamp toward its center, where there was an island of high ground. I was hoping to spend the night on the island, collecting herbs and otherwise drinking in the ambiance of the area. As I approached the island, I sat down on a fallen cedar giant to rest, and suddenly the ground surged and contorted beneath me like a moving animal. I fell toward the cedar log, clinging to it like a cork on a wave. Tall cedars groaned as they swayed with each ripple, sounds of sucking and splashing emerged from the swamp, and I instantly realized that I was in the middle of an earthquake. A quake was a near impossibility in the Pine Barrens, but there I was in the middle of one huge rumbling.

The surging of the earth began to slow, and a few feet in front of me the brush on the island began to part. As the earth finally came to rest, the brush formed a long dark tunnel to the island. All was as quiet as before, no damage had been done, except for the tunnel. I should have known that this was no real earthquake, for if I had listened to the birds and watched the movement of animals, nothing had changed as it would have after a quake. I sat for a long time looking around trying to understand why there had been no damage. I could feel the fear deep within me, fear of such awesome power and of the potential of being hurt or swallowed by the earth. I had heard horror stories of what the earth could do when she moved, and I certainly didn't want to become a statistic.

A long time passed before I felt it was safe to get off the log. Cautiously I walked toward the tunnel in the brush, concerned that it might hide some fissure in the crust. I meandered up the tunnel toward the center of the island. Everything looked in place. Even the parted brush remained unharmed, right to the very roots. I tried to come up with a logical explanation, but my heart rejected all of them. Deep inside, I knew that it was more than just a physical occurrence. The intensity of the events around me foretold of a spiritual reality. Once it dawned on me that what had happened was in good part a matter of the spirit and not merely physical, I began to see all around me with a spiritual consciousness. Everything was not as it had been before, it was as if things were out of normal context, flowing in some separate reality. It wasn't anything I could put my finger on or describe, it was just a sense that all was not in sync with physical reality, that the upheaval more than moved earth and parted brush.

As I approached the clearing in the center of the island, I noticed that a few deer were feeding at the distant edge. I slowed my pace but didn't stalk. I wasn't interested in deer as much as unraveling the mystery of the quake and subsequently gathering the herbs for Grandfather. As I walked to the center of the island, the deer remained motionless, watching me but never moving to cover. I sat down in the sun and placed my collecting bags on the mossy earth. It felt good to relax in the sunshine with the soft carpet of moss cool against my flesh. Bird song was vibrant and very close, and insect choruses mingled with the voices of several frogs to create an overwhelming symphony of music and motion. As I looked up from my bags, a deer stepped close to my face and licked me on the nose.

I froze into absolute stillness, the excitement welling up within me to a point where it could barely be managed. Surely, this deer could not have known that I was human, or it wouldn't have been licking my face again and again. Out of reflex, I pushed him away gently, as if he were a pet, but he came back for more. Without thinking, I reached up to scratch him behind the ears, while watching the other deer boldly approach me. It was then that the shock and realization of what I was doing struck me. For a moment I tried to reason out why the deer were so friendly, but the mere process of reasoning seemed to spook the deer. So I abandoned all thought and began to play with them whole-heartedly, running, jumping, and petting as each opportunity presented itself. Birds, squirrel, and rabbits also joined the play, all without any signs of fear. But then, suddenly and without warning, alarm gestures went out, and they were gone in a burst of terrified motion. Something outside the island had frightened them.

I was sad and angry all at once. For the first time, without persistent coaxing, I had played with a number of animals without fear. Now the magic had ended, and the mix of anger and disappointment flooded me. I too could sense a danger coming, just outside the swamp. In a few moments I could hear the roar of engines and tires grinding deep into the dirt. Voices could be heard as the engines fell silent, followed by the crashing of brush as people pushed through the swamp toward the island. I was torn between running and fighting, but I froze where I was, unable to flee, as the first man crashed into the clearing. He was covered with dirt and mud, carrying a case of beer and an axe. Several other people followed, carrying more beer, axes, saws, and food of all sorts. The stench of beer mixed with sweat and fuel filled the air. Cans were opened, garbage strewn everywhere, live trees cut and burned. Within moments the pristine area had been turned into a dump of destruction.

They did not notice me, even when walking nearby. It was as if I wasn't there. I watched them for several hours drinking and partying and paying no attention to the area they were defiling. I know they were all of legal drinking age, but I couldn't understand why they were coming here instead of going to a local bar. A voice broke the confusion, saying, "It is because they need the purity and freedom of the wilderness, but do not know what to do with it when they get here. So they drink and destroy, doing the things that are familiar. To act otherwise would leave them alone and afraid. For if they slowed down and paid attention, stepped outside the noise and confusion, they would have to face the lies of their flesh." I turned to see where the voice was coming from, but there was no one around, not that close anyway. It was a gentle voice, soft, like a whisper, very feminine and very comforting. I yearned to find its origins, but it was all around me at once.

The voice again spoke, as I looked around for its maker. "People have lost their connection to the wilderness but desperately need its power. They have strayed from the earth and all the purity of Creation. Their souls so desperately search to fill the void. At once the earth intrigues and nurtures them, but there is also a fear of the solitude and peace. They hide behind their toys and gadgets, whether of play or of religion, for they need some of their external distraction and reality to hold on to. That way they will never be forced to confront themselves, or the lies of their fleshly lives." The voice continued, "They come to the wilderness as aliens, and like a disease they drive the very animals from the forests. They find freedom here but cannot confront that freedom. They find peace and solitude here, but choose to know it not. They leave behind pockets of destruction and the litter of society as a flag, a monument, that banners their conquering. Yet they can never conquer Creation, for in conquering the wilderness, they must conquer themselves. To conquer themselves, they find themselves, and in that discovery, cannot and will not conquer wilderness."

But how can I reach them? I asked. "Some you can reach, more you cannot," the voice said. "Their fear is too great, their insensitivity too strong. Their belief in external riches far outweighs any promise of spiritual fulfillment. They seek only the instant gratifications of life and will never slow down long enough to look inside themselves, especially deep enough to find the purity of 'oneness.' It is beyond their comprehension." Is there no hope? I asked. "There is hope," the voice continued, "but we must reach them on a level that will affect them the most. We must teach them first, then allow the heart to lead them back to the earth. There is always hope, for in the heart of each person there is the place of connection to the earth. You cannot force this change on them with hatred and violence, only with patience and love." But how can I contain my rage? I asked the voice. "How did you treat your toddler cousin who broke one of your best skulls? With rage and anger?" Of course not, I said. "No," said the voice, "you taught her that it was bad to break that skull, and why. You taught her with love, not rage."

I thought for a long time about what the voice had spoken. That voice had been so alluring, so peaceful, and so nurturing. I decided then that it must be the actual voice of the earth, different than I ever imagined it to be. I walked to the area that the people had trashed, and I picked up all the garbage, then lay down to rest. I had done that so many times before, yet it produced no visible results. The people always returned and trashed the area again. It seemed as if they were content to sleep and play in their own garbage. The voice came again, "They sleep and play in their own garbage here in the wilderness as they do back in their homes. The waste of society is strangling itself. How can you expect them to do differently here?" Will mankind ever learn from his garbage before it is too late? I asked.

The voice did not answer right away, but I could feel the earth's vibration beneath me. "Man does not understand the laws of Creation," she said, "and feels he is above all things and all laws. Modern society wrongly believes that if a society is not living up to modern ways of life, then it is suffering. Modern man does not take into account whether people are happy and content, for he believes that if people are primitive, then they are suffering. Thus modern society tries to change any primitive people and bring them modern farming, industry, and new values. Modern society cares not that its methods are in conflict with the natural laws that the primitive people live by. Eventually, the new society will fall to starvation, disease, or drought. Many will die, as the natural order seeks to reestablish its balance. Man overlooks the real reason why this happens, then blames it on an error in the natural world. He does not look deep enough into the origins of the problem, his meddling. He feels that he can do no wrong and that he is above the laws of balance. That is why he will not learn from his pollution until it is too late.

"There must be prophets and teachers to enlighten the masses and point to a new direction," she said, then fell silent. I lay against the earth in utter despair. I should have confronted the people who had trashed the island, instead of just picking up the garbage and remaining out of sight. I had been afraid of that confrontation, because I knew they would not understand me and would mock my concern, as so many others had done. I could have been violent, but as the earth had said, "There is no wisdom in violence. People shown violence, become violent, and know only violence." I was so frustrated, not knowing what to do or even how to start. I knew that I had a lot to learn before I could do anything, but what was stopping me from trying now? As I hung my head toward the earth, I was jolted awake by the terrified screams of a woman.

As I craned my neck around to find the origin of the sound, a thousand images, all at once, hit me like a cold splash of water. There on the ground, only a few feet in front of me, lay my own mother. She was badly beaten and dying. Blood poured from gaping wounds, and all around her lay rotting garbage, twisted metal, and vile chemicals. I tried desperately to get to her, but I was held fast to the ground. I couldn't move. I heard some-one coming in our direction, and I began to yell for help, but there was no response. The footfalls kept coming as before, un-changed. An older man, wearing a business suit, came walking up the trail toward us, carrying a bucket. As he came close to my mother, he stopped for a moment, looked around sheepishly, then poured the bucket of chemicals all over her. Enraged by his action, I shouted at him to stop. I tried desperately to pull myself from the ground. He paid no attention but kicked my mother hard in the face. Blood poured from her mouth and nose. Cries of pain faintly came from inside her.

I heard other voices coming, and again I screamed for help, but as before there was no response. People began to pass me, some kicked my mother, some bit huge chunks of flesh from her, others busted her legs and arms, and still others threw garbage upon her. In all her pain and suffering, she kept looking at the passing people, loving them, even though they continued to beat her. She desperately tried to touch each, but none paid attention, except to beat her more. More people came up the trail. A never-ending stream of beatings became more violent. Some urinated on her, others smeared feces in her face, and still others injected vile liquids into her veins. She looked toward me, begging, pleading in hoarse whispers for my help, but the ground held me fast. I could see her slowly dying, and still the surges of people continued. No one paid attention, except for a few, who did nothing more than to shake their heads in pity, then walk off. Some never noticed that they stepped on her hands and face.

The masses stopped coming for a moment, and I looked at my mother lying there. Tears filled my eyes, and my body shook with rage, every muscle straining to tear free of my bonds. All the time, my mom watched me without a word. The horror and the pain in her eyes became too much to bear. Footfalls came again, softer this time; fear and panic overwhelmed me. An old Indian came up the trail, and upon seeing my mom, he ran to her, crying. He desperately attempted to bandage the gaping wounds, giving her water and praying the entire time. He seemed so helpless because there was so much damage, and he shook with fear. Suddenly more footfalls were heard coming up the trail. The old one tried to stop the advance, but the people pressed in on him, kicking him, beating him, killing him where he stood. They tore his flesh and limbs and scattered them all about. They ran then to my mother, tore away the bandages, and beat her again unmercifully. She lay in worse condition now than ever, because the old Indian, her only hope, had died trying to save her.

I heard more crowds coming, and the stench of garbage and chemicals preceding their arrival. I flew into a raging panic, snapping my body free from the ground, and ran to the trail before the crowd. I kneeled beside my mom, trying to comfort her, when I was kicked violently to the ground. I arose with a tremendous burst of power, tearing an axe from a man's hands and violently pushing him into the crowd. I swung the axe overhead, threatening anyone who came near me or my mother. Violence raged in my head as I fought back the urge to kill those who hurt my mom. The crowd was shaken to attention as I spoke. I said that from now on, whatever they did to my mom the same fate would befall them, and I cast the axe down and stepped aside. I prayed feverishly to the Creator for help, as the first man walked to my mother. He bent over and bit a huge chunk from her arm. I filled with rage, but a huge chunk of his arm was ripped off, as if bitten away as he had done to my mother. The others, seeing this, ran off in blind panic.

An old Indian walked up the trail, as had the other. He smiled at my mom and then at me, saying, "My heart is filled with thanksgiving that you have been strong enough to help my mother." Your mother? I said. It's my mother lying there. The old one only smiled and said, "She is all of our mothers." With that, my mom looked up, her face changing. It changed to someone I recognized and loved, but it wasn't my mom. She spoke to me in the same voice that had spoken to me before. She said, "I am all mothers and fathers, sisters and brothers, and I am all things of flesh and spirit. You have taught people well and made them understand that what they do to me, they also do to themselves. You have learned that violence breeds violence, and taught them instead with love. You learned to tear away from the barriers of ignorance, even at personal pain, to save me. And in me you have seen your mother, and you love me as you do your own mother. Save me then, grandson, as you would your own mother." With this the old Indian handed me an eagle feather, then both disappeared into the ground.

I came back to consciousness still sitting on the old cedar log in the swamp. I looked around and realized that it must have been some sort of a dream, a very real dream at that. It was then I noticed that I was holding the old eagle feather. I had had a Vision. I was so shaken up, not only from having a powerful Vision, but also from what the Vision had taught me. I ran through the brush to the center of the island and found it as pure and untouched as if no man had been there. It was then that I found the romping deer tracks interspaced with my own. I also noticed blood near the path. I was confused. Surely I hadn't moved from that log. How then could I have also been there in the center island? I understood that the grand Visions could work on both spirit and flesh, but I could not understand how I could be physically in two places at once. These things had to be taken to counsel, and the only counsel I knew was Grandfather.

As I entered camp, Grandfather said matter-of-factly, "So how was your talk with Earth Mother?" Normally a person would be shocked by that statement, but I had learned to accept this and many more things as normal. I related the whole Vision to Grandfather, showing him, finally, the eagle feather. He told me that I needed no help in interpretation, for a true and powerful Vision never needs interpretation. The Vision always speaks to us in a language and reality we understand, where anything unclear is answered in dreams or other Vision Quests. He then finished by saying, "Your Vision is very clear, and you now know the best way to save the earth, but now you must find the Vision of how you will accomplish this. This Vision has also taught you that you can dwell in two places at once, and that the spirit self can take physical form, as you found in your tracks on the center island."

Grandfather said that I had much more to learn before I could follow that Vision fully. I had much more pain to endure, many struggles before I could pull free from my bonds of ignorance. I had to realize that all I could do was watch my mother dying and struggle to get free. What I was doing now was fighting for freedom, fighting to understand, fighting so that I could help her. It was now the most difficult time. I could not give up, for defeat would mean I could never fulfill that Vision of saving the earth. I was more determined than ever to fight the bonds, no matter how much pain or sacrifice.

12

▼▼▼▼▼

The Ceremony

Grandfather stressed custom, tradition, and ceremony as part of our spiritual growth but, I suspect, not as much as he could have. Certainly these things were an important teaching device, but Grandfather taught only the pure ceremony or spiritual tradition. A pure ceremony was one that tested out in the Temples of Creation, for everyone, regardless of beliefs. In essence a pure ceremony, custom, or tradition had to work for everyone and be a proven truth in the natural world. Everything else was the workings of man and his overactive imagination, thus tainted in some way. Man was forever dreaming up ritual to bring him closer to the world of the spirit and the Creator. However, these rituals did not work for everyone, just the select few who originated them. To Grandfather, most customs and rituals were excess baggage that weighted one down, smothering with rote memorization of motion, symbol, and word, rather than enlightening. Most were excessive, many were merely parroted, so even the holy man mouthed the words rather than allowed the words to be as fresh as the first day he had heard them.

Grandfather's first rule to Rick and me regarding any ceremony or ritual was that we know exactly what we were doing, what the ritual was all about, and why. When we recited a prayer or song, it had to be precise. We were not just to read the words but had to feel their essence and meaning, holding each word up to scrutiny in the light of the purity of Creation, before we internalized the whole. Ceremony and ritual, like custom and tradition, were passed on as a direction indicator, never a dictation of belief. We preserved these old ways precisely, learned them, understood them, then modified them to fit our needs, like a model. It is important that the future generations are given the original works, so that they too can modify the original for themselves. The problem comes when what is passed down is a distortion of the original. Then all is lost to the future, and the history of the old ways is forever lost.

Grandfather said, "The customs and rituals of ancient man are but guidelines for future generations. They show where man has gone, and where he is going. They are a teacher, never to be a crutch, and never to enslave. The problem is that we become slaves to the ritual. People begin to worship the ceremony and believe in the shaman rather than in the Great Spirit. The ancient rituals and ceremonies should then be viewed as signposts, and learned, modified, passed down, then abandoned. Rituals are more for the weak of spirit, who need something to cling to, something that makes them feel worthy and holy. For the spiritually attuned, they become excess baggage. There is no need to approach the Creator carrying these things of flesh, mind, and emotion, but to seek him without these crutches.

Nevertheless, there were quite a few rituals and ceremonies that were important to Grandfather and to us. They could not be bypassed but were necessary to our spiritual development. They passed the test of time and truth in the purity of the Temples of Nature, and they became a doorway to our deeper spiritual understanding. Each time these rituals were performed, they pulled us closer to the consciousness that we wished to attain. They were always fresh and new, never redundant, never treated like excess baggage, because they were real and not the typical crutches of man. Most of all, they would work for everyone, regardless of who they were or what they believed. The sweatlodge was one such ceremony. Once all the ritualistic impurities were removed, there was found a basic truth, a pure transcendence into the worlds of spirit.

I was still only seven years old when I first entered the sweatlodge, and the sweatlodge became a baptism into the fusion of ritual and spirit. Certainly we had offered the pipe, during numerous times of thanksgiving and introspection, but that was always light tradition, never a heavy ceremony. For many months, Grandfather had explained the philosophy of the lodge, but we had never even seen one built and had nothing to which we could compare his teachings. It all seemed so alien and complicated to us, but what he was doing was to make sure that we understood all parts of the lodge before we entered its sacred domain. "The sweatlodge," he said, "is the ultimate purification of body, mind, and spirit. Upon entering the heat and blackness of the lodge, you are entering a void, free of all outside distractions. The mind focuses on spiritual things, the body and emotions relax in the steam, and the spirit soars free. It is in the lodge that we enter the domain of spirit, to purify our bodies and thoughts, and to pray. It is here, outside the world of man, that we learn to touch the earth, and dwell in the Great Spirit's love. Here we find renewal and brotherhood with all things. We find the perfect 'oneness.'"

We took several days to build that first sweatlodge, for every part of any sweatlodge has to be perfect. Each sapling had to be taken from a very specific part of the land, with prayers of thanksgiving surrounding each. Different elements had to be selected in certain ways, with certain prayers, and with the utmost thanksgiving. Nothing artificial could be used, as was the case with all things Grandfather built or used. He would use only those things that were pure, manufactured with his own hands and from the raw materials of the wilderness. Shortcuts in anything would not bring the same wisdom as did the skills performed with the slow and natural methods. Any sweatlodge—anything—we built had to be done in a certain specific way. Each entity used, each movement, held deeper philosophical connotations and connections, which would go unrealized if any step was circumvented.

When the lodge itself was completed, we began preparations for our first real ceremony, our first sweatlodge. I had no idea whether our first sweatlodge ritual had Apache origins, or if it was one that Grandfather had learned along the way, but it was very powerful—one I remember vividly to this day.

As the sun set in deep red tones, Rick and I moved fiery stones to the center pit of the lodge, using forked sticks. We prayed each time we placed a stone in the pit, feeling the powerful heat beginning to fill the lodge with each new rock. When we finished, the door was shut, and we stood watching the thin band of light disappear from the horizon as Grandfather prayed and sang. He entered the lodge first and after a long pause, beckoned us to follow. Our hearts pounded with excitement and anticipation. Fear and curiosity also accompanied us as we were enveloped in the darkness. The heat was oppressive, the blackness accented only by the semitransparent glow of red-orange, hot rocks. Thermals of scalding heat arose from the rocks, making them waver and dance. I stayed close to the ground as I secured the door. I shrunk closer still when I sat upon the ground in my appointed position. Fear became stronger as the heat and walls of the lodge began to close in. I felt panic and became claustrophobic. Grandfather's voice broke the silence, saying, "Let go of your fear."

It seemed like we sat there forever, awaiting Grandfather to begin the ceremony. Sweat poured from my body, and my mind felt groggy and faint. I did not know how long the ceremony was going to last, or how long I could hold out, but as the heat grew more oppressive, I let go. It wasn't any conscious effort that caused the release but just something that happened, beyond any physical or mental control. It was as if the lodge had a mind of its own, allowing no fear or tension. My mind expanded beyond the horizons of the lodge, my body and emotions stilled, and my spirit began to emerge. Grandfather began a low, almost inaudible, chant, which seemed to fill the lodge with a sense of magic. My consciousness was carried by his words, away from myself and any imagined discomfort I might have left inside.

Grandfather then placed sacred herbs on the rocks, and the lodge filled with a tremendous fragrance. The odors of burning cedar, sage, and sweetgrass mingled with the heat and tingled the flesh, as well as the mind. As the smoke died down, prayers were sent to the Creator and the earth. Thanks were given to the water, Earth Mother's blood, and the lodge burst with swirling steam. The column of steam billowed from the rocks, mushroomed off the domed ceiling, and gently worked its way to the floor. The steam-ladened heat was even hotter than the dry heat, and more effective. It touched every part of the body. With each splash of water, the temperature of the lodge rose and fell, like some huge earthen heart. So too did our bodies and minds rise and fall, growing closer to the spirit with each surge. Sweat poured profusely from my entire body, as the last shreds of self were lost to the void.

I sat without any clear thought. My mind seemed too hot to think, my body too relaxed to move. The hissing of water on rocks flowed with each wave of Grandfather's hand, causing thicker columns to rise. The rocks partially illuminated the lodge. Faint figures seemed all around; steam took on strange shapes and designs. Grandfather appeared to glow with his own inner warmth, and Rick disappeared altogether. But there were more people in that lodge than just us. I could feel their presence more than I could see them through the steam. It was a feeling from deep inside, a gut feeling, that sensed things beyond what the senses were telling me. I knew that I should never trust what I see, or sense, for what must be trusted is what I understand as reality. I understood that I was not alone in there, regardless of the nothingness of it all.

The lodge, the ceremony, lasted for a long time, the rocks staying hot, and the air hotter still. As the time lengthened, I felt my body floating about, effortlessly, transcending time, place, and distance. I felt alive and awake, my senses pushing beyond the mere physical perimeters and out beyond the horizons. Most of all, I felt a tremendous sense of love, peace, and joy. I also felt a deep sense of gratitude and affection for those who had passed down the lodge to us. I could feel them there, watching, waiting, as if to see that it was all done properly. With this feeling of being watched, I had no other conscious thought or imagery, until I heard Grandfather's voice in song. I had lost time and place, wholly, and now the sweatlodge was coming to an end. As Grandfather sang, I felt a tremendous sense of loss, of disappointment that the lodge was ending. It had been a tremendous feeling to touch all those lives that had come before and to feel the peaceful expansion of self to the horizons of the outer world.

I went back through the door and stepped into the night. The feeling that came over me could never be described in words or pictures. I had never felt so alive, the night had never seemed so bright and beautiful, and I felt a certain sense of total expansion. I could feel the power of the night, the energy from all the living things around me, and a deep connection to the earth. I prayed that I would not lose this feeling of expanded awareness and this sense of wonder and holiness. I walked to the stream, my body still steaming from the heat in the night air, and I slipped beneath the water. With the stars above and the water below, I felt like I was suspended in space yet connected to the earth. I sensed the water connected to all waters of the world and to the skies. I felt so relaxed, so aware, and so alive. I pulled myself up on the bank and lay back on the earth, fusing myself to the ground and feeling the flesh of the earth and my own flesh becoming common ground.

Later that night we listened to Grandfather speak about the sweatlodge. I understood fully, now that I had been baptized into the magic of the lodge. He said, "You have felt the presence of the ancients, the expansion of self, and the peace. You know now what a true ceremony should be, for as you felt the power of this lodge, so too will others, regardless of belief. The sweatlodge speaks to all people in the language of their own beliefs, and it thus becomes a universal truth. So then, use the lodge as a tool, a doorway for physical and spiritual renewal and cleansing, a pathway to expansion, and a vehicle to the worlds of the unseen and eternal. In the lodge, you will find purity from all outside distractions. Without the distractions of man, you will touch the Great Mystery."

When Grandfather passed down a ceremony to us, it had to be precise. I could take many months just to learn the simplest of ceremonies, but the slow learning process was important. Because Grandfather had no real written language, all history and ceremony had to be passed down by word of mouth. Thus, to preserve the purity of a ceremony, every gesture, word, and action had to be precise. There was no room for error, because an error, handed down in future generations, could become a grand distortion. If truths were to be passed along, then they had to be passed along correctly. Even simple parables and stories had to have the same meticulous memorization. It was many years before I could ever run a sweatlodge or hold a pipe in ceremony. Memorizing ceremony was one of the most difficult things we had to do, but it wasn't for ourselves as much as for future generations.

It was not many months after the sweatlodge that I attended another ceremony, equally as important and powerful as the first. It was a teaching ceremony, one we had to learn very well because of its healing properties. The fall had just touched the Pine Barrens with color. Leaf margins were beginning to change, animals moved about with more purpose, and many plants were in seed. The days were still warm, but the nights had a little cool nip. This night was no exception, for even the remaining insects retired their voices early. I thought that we could get a good deal of frost by sunrise, though I was warm and comfortable as I sat near the ceremonial fire, wrapped in a blanket. It was a peaceful and still night, an excellent night for a ceremony. Every leaf and star seemed to speak.

Grandfather stepped into the flickering puddle of firelight. Our eyes were riveted to his every move. He carried no sacred entities but faced the night in just a loin cloth. He lifted his hands to the stars and began to pray, thanking the Great Spirit for a bountiful summer, for good health, and for beautiful lands. All things were honored in Grandfather's prayers, none were forgotten. He sat at the distant edge of the firelight and began to chant. His words echoed through the night, dancing off myriad trees. He prayed again, this time for the power of healing, so that he could give it to a friend. Watching as his outstretched hands covered a clear starry sky, a flash of intense lightning blinded me and hit an old dead tree behind where he sat. The smell of electricity and charred pine drifted over our area in a thick haze, almost choking us. Grandfather remained unmoving like a statue made of stone, not affected by the sound and crash of the lightning as I had been.

I was astonished. I had seen unexplained things and occurrences around Grandfather each day, but none so powerful and vivid. He raised his hands again and began to sing, a song named "The Calling of the Spirits." As he began, the misty smoke began to swirl and take shape, as if something or someone were moving within. Soft, almost inaudible, footfalls could be heard all around me, footfalls not of animals but of people, definitely in moccasins. As I stared out into the blackness, listening to the sounds that mingled with Grandfather's spirit song, images began to appear. All around me, stealthily walked the spirits of the ancients. As they neared the fire, they sat down, some just behind me. I was frightened, trying desperately to get Grandfather's attention, but his eyes were shut tight, and he continued his chant. As the chanting drifted off to an end, so did the spirit entities. Grandfather closed the ceremony.

He spoke, "Grandson. Do not fear the spirits called up in pure ceremony, for they are good, they are here to be your guides. You have seen that this ceremony brings the power of healing, and also the power of the spirit worlds. No sacred things were used to call up this power, only the power of the heart and the power of faith. These spirits, this energy, is always out there. Learn to call it up when you need it, for it is part of the spirit-that-moves-in-all-things, a force that you have at all times. This is not of my power, but the power of faith, and a power to be used to heal a brother later on in this day. Do these things in secrecy so that no man can marvel, for the power must always remain hidden from the view of the unworthy, from the disbelievers."

He continued, "Remember that all things of power, especially those things of a ceremony—words, songs, and chants—have greater power as long as they come from the heart and are delivered with pure faith. Once you begin to walk the spiritual path, the power of the ceremony will teach and guide you, as does the Vision Quest. However, once the ceremony shows you the way, and you no longer need the crutches, then abandon the ceremony. Then, the only time a ceremony becomes necessary for you is when those that surround you need it to see sacredly. Ceremony teaches you the old ways, points the directions, then helps you, for a while, along your way. It is always there if you need it, like an old friend." I asked Grandfather why he used the ceremony tonight, if he had abandoned most. He said, "The ceremony was not for me, Grandson, it was for you. That is the only way you can see into the world where I dwell."

Grandfather walked away into the night, and I was left alone with the fire. I thought for a long time about his words and about ceremony. Why was it that we should learn a ceremony, only to abandon it later? Was there no other way than to commit to memory every ancient action and reaction, every song, and word? Grandfather called to me from the brush, saying, "It is not pointless to learn something that shows you a clear way. Without that teaching, you would fumble for the remainder of your years for answers. Without them we would be forced to repeat the same mistakes of the ancients that went before us. The pointlessness comes when we continue to use these things after they become unnecessary to us." I listened to the night as Grandfather wandered off back to camp. Things at once seemed so clear, yet so complicated. I was in awe of the night's events and the ceremony, but I was frustrated by my inabilities.

In my stubbornness I attempted to try things without ceremony, only to lose in utter frustration. At other times I refused to let ceremony go, resulting in long periods of stagnation. We must never abandon ceremony but use it as a guide, and later as a friend. Ceremony provides a structure for the conscious mind and body to enter a state of spiritual consciousness. Without ceremony we would never transcend the barriers of self. There is a danger, however, of allowing the ceremony to become the end result, where the ceremony is worshipped and the shaman uplifted to an exalted position. We fail to see that ceremony is but a teacher, a direction, and we must transcend this to find the absolute and pure consciousness.

13

▼▼▼▼▼

The Omen

We were deep in the swamp when the night fully closed in around us. It was darker than I could ever remember it being. Winds kept creaking the trees, and all around the outer edge of the swamp, brush moved and rustled. We had sat down to catch our breath before resuming our journey back to camp. Rick was wet from falling out of a tree and into the stream, I was covered with mud from doing the same, but, as usual, Grandfather was dry and comfortable. Being in the swamp at night always conjured up images of demons and spooky things. Rick and I were not quite ten, and very impressionable, especially when it came to ghost stories, horror, and gore. It was bad enough that our minds were overactive in this field, but the old Pineys (those who over time, with age, out of love, had come to know the Pine Barrens and call this place home) kept adding fuel to the fire by telling us their own ghastly tales. Grandfather did not help much either, for he always lived in that mysterious place somewhere between life and spirit and could scare all hell out of us with just one look. It was certainly one of those nights that just reeked of demons and horror.

The night was suddenly broken by the calls of screech owls all around us. The descending screams caused me to fall from the log into the mud and stood my hair on end. Rick remained motionless with fear, while Grandfather caught his breath from laughing. I knew damn well that they were screech owls, but the voices had caught me by surprise and were very close. The owls sounded again, and again, their talking and singing following them out to the far end of the swamp. It was then, in the stillness, that Grandfather made his deadly comment. "To some of the ancients," he said, "the owl was an omen of death. To see an owl at a certain time would foretell of someone's spirit slipping to the other side." I was too scared to ask any questions, for fear that my voice would cause the owls to return. Owls used to intrigue me, but now I didn't care if I saw one again for the rest of my life, especially if I was alone.

Shortly after we reached camp, Grandfather disappeared for the night. Rick and I talked late, trying not to listen to the sounds of night, for fear of hearing an owl. We swore to each other that we would never look for owls again, not even collect their discarded feathers. Owl medicine had become death medicine, and we wanted nothing to do with it at all. Going to the creek to drink and going to relieve ourselves became harrowing experiences that night. We did everything together, real close, for fear of encountering a deadly owl. Neither Rick nor I got much sleep that night, for every noise I heard had to be an owl. I was torn between the world of listening and not listening for owls. Part of me wanted to know when death was about, and the other part didn't want to know.

The next morning, Grandfather, Rick, and I headed into the swamp again to do some exploration. I'm sure that Grandfather knew that something was up, when we kept our heads to the ground and didn't look up into the trees. I was sent into a blind panic by what I thought was an owl pellet, which turned out to be some old and weathered raccoon scat instead. Both Rick and I wandered about in a daze of fear—fear to look up and fear to look down. In moments we were alone, we talked about owls and where they might be. We halfheartedly joked with each other, calling our fear of owls, "owlatosis." It wasn't long, however, before my fear was compounded, when Grandfather separated Rick and me to have us explore opposite ends of the swamp. I was so paralyzed with the possibility of seeing an owl that I began talking to myself and staring straight ahead. I could not look up or down without having the hair on the back of my neck stand on end.

I wandered down into the deepest recesses of the swamp, getting lost in the huge root systems that blanketed the sphagnum ground. I was bending over, looking at a sundew plant when I heard a blood-curdling scream—Rick's scream—and it sounded like he had been hurt bad. I ran toward the area of the scream, crashing through brush and bounding over fallen cedars. It was on one of these bounds that I came face-to-face with a barred owl sitting on a branch. I yelled in panic and ran blindly, crashing into things in my blind fear, and the owl did the same. I ran right into Rick, who was running toward me. We passed each other, stopped, then ran back. We both had seen owls, and we both had assumed that the other was dead, or about to be. We hadn't seen Grandfather standing nearby, giggling and listening to our conversation.

He sat us down, then calmed us down, and said, "I told you the story of owls to show you the foolishness that omens can cause. What I failed to do was to tell you the whole story." He continued, "The entities of nature live a dual life, as we do. Part of them is physical and part of them is spiritual. When the animal is living in the physical body, he is going about his daily business. This can become a teacher for those who observe, but nothing more. If, however, the animal comes to us in the spiritual consciousness, then he becomes an omen, an omen sent by the Creator, or Creation, to foretell something. An owl going about his daily business is no omen, but an owl doing something totally out of context is a communication. The owl becomes the sign of death when a conversation is being held about someone, especially someone near death's door. Then the owl, showing himself out of context, doing something that owls do not normally do, becomes an omen of death."

He burst into a prolonged laughter, regained composure, then said, "Can you imagine how hard it would be to live in the woods and not see owls? Can you see the lunacy that can develop through knowing only half-truths? There are people who spend their whole lives thinking that everything is a sign or an omen, some to an extreme insanity, an insanity that keeps them paralyzed with fear. Omens and signs are very specific and do not happen very often, except when the Creator, or Creation, wants to communicate with us. This usually happens when you haven't spent the time inside yourself to get the answers. It is the Great Spirit's way of telling you to slow down, to pay attention, and to take the time to search your heart. A man, living through his heart and spirit, will never need an omen or sign, except in times of dire need."

What is the difference between a sign and an omen? I asked. "A sign," Grandfather said, "is something asked for. It is a beckoned response from the Creator or from Creation. It answers a question, gives you a direction, or comes in time of need. As with all things sent from the outer world, its meaning is very clear and vivid to the individual, but only to that individual. For it is he who has asked for the sign, and the sign will be his alone. Groups of people may ask for signs, but again it is some sign that they will all see and interpret the same way. Great problems, and even bad medicine, could arise if someone else tries to interpret your sign." Is the asking of a sign enough to bring that sign, and could we use it often? I then asked. "Signs are rarely sent," Grandfather said, "except to those who are worthy. But then, if one is worthy, he is in constant contact with his heart and does not need a sign. Signs should be rarely asked for, for it could show a weakness in faith. Signs should come only through the heart."

Grandfather continued, "The omen is something not asked for

that comes as a powerful warning or answer. As with a sign, an omen's meaning is immediately apparent. If, for instance, you are walking in the woods and see an owl, this is not a warning of death, but simply an owl. If, however, you are speaking about a friend who is dying, and an owl appears out of context, then it is an omen. By out of context I mean that the owl would be doing something that he would not normally do, like appearing very close to you, gesturing, as if to get your attention. This then is an omen. It can also come when you are deep in thought, or confused about things. Again the animal or other entity will show itself out of context, and you will immediately know it as an omen. It is usually sent to you when you are too troubled to go inside and to pay attention to the things around you. It is a gift that could change your life forever."

I thought long and hard about the things of omen and sign, worrying that I would not be able to know them when they happened. I knew how to tell a physical sign of an occurrence in the woods, by being aware of the concentric, emanating rings of motion and sound. By listening to the crows or jays, I could tell where certain predators were located. By listening to everything else, I could know what was happening throughout the woods, but signs and omens were different. They did not deal solely on a physical level of cause and effect, but went deeper, into the realms of spirit. I wondered if I would ever see a sign or omen and know the difference. Grandfather cut off the thought, and said, "When it comes, you will know it, without doubt."

Many months passed after the lessons of the sign and omen. I had thought about them periodically but felt that if I learned to live within my heart, I would never need a sign. I was hiking to an area of the Pine Barrens that I had never been to. It was the site of an old ghost town, and I hoped to find antiques and possibly pottery for my mother. The town was in the woods, but it was very close to a new development that had been built to its north. I kept as secretive as possible, for I wanted no encounters with people. When I was in the wilderness, I was a true scout, avoiding all detection, getting in and out like a ghost. Though this scout game was all in my mind, it was a tremendous way to practice my scout techniques and absolute stealth. As I drew nearer to the old ghost town, I could hear the hammering in the distance, and the sounds of small children at play.

I reached the first foundation by midday and began to scout around all the foundations in the area, attempting to locate the town dump. I tried digging in a few areas, but I came up with nothing but a few old nails and some horseshoes. Periodically I would find a bit of broken New Jersey blue glass but not the piles I had so eagerly sought. It was then that a crow showed up and began calling. It was a strange call, not an alarm call, so I paid no attention. The crow drew closer and closer, trying to get my attention, but I kept looking for bottles. Finally the crow landed a few feet in front of me and began calling wildly while flapping its wings. I looked up in amazement. The bird had certainly caught my eye, and I knew that it must be some sort of sign, but what? I hadn't asked any questions or for any sign!

The crow kept flying off to the east and coming back, screaming. It was almost as if he wanted me to follow. As I walked along the path, the crow kept up his antics, but I felt no answer to any questions. I did notice that there were tire prints from bicycles on the trail, and I knew that I was getting close to civilization. I hesitated to go any farther, but the crow was insistent. I followed some more, but going toward any development, especially on a weekend, was against my moral principles. Just as I was about to turn around and head back into the woods, the crow let out a wild scream, wilder than I had ever heard a crow sound before. As I looked toward him, he had settled on the handlebar of a bicycle. I walked toward it cautiously and quietly, so as to escape detection. There was no one around, no sign of the owner. Could the crow be telling me that I now owned a new bike? But I hated bikes. What was a bike doing out in the woods all by itself, anyway?

The crow flew a few wingbeats away and landed on some disturbed ground, called a few times wildly, and flew off over the treetops. I walked over to the disturbed ground and found that there were several half-buried slabs of concrete strewn around. It was then that I noticed the tracks and heard a small feeble voice calling for help from one of the crevices. I followed the sound and found that two of the slabs covered a well. At the bottom of the well, a small boy was hoarsely crying. Though the well was only seven or eight feet deep, it created a bottleneck with the concrete slabs, and there was no way out. Fortunately the well was dry and the concrete thin. I pried away one of the slabs and easily jumped down to the boy. To my delight he was unhurt and had been in the well for only a few hours.

I boosted him out and climbed out behind him. All tears had stopped, but he was still visibly upset and trembled a little. The sun seemed to warm him and make him feel better. I asked him to go back to his parents and tell them what had happened. I also asked him to have his parents fill in the well so no one else would be hurt. As I went back to digging in the distant foundation, I found a bottle embossed with the flying crow. In the distance I could hear the shovels working and voices laughing as the people filled in the old well. I was excited beyond all words. I had truly experienced a sign and was rewarded with this bottle. I had to tell Grandfather right away.

Grandfather was very proud of me when I told him the story of the crow and the boy. He praised me for not seeking the glory of the rescue afterward, saying, "We do things silently, for our rewards will always follow us silently." He spoke more on the wisdom of sign. "You have experienced your first sign, sent not because something was asked for, but as a messenger from the Creator, and from the crow. Signs can be sent to you from others, as you can send signs. Pay attention to all things out of context that could be giving you a sign. As you have witnessed, you knew the sign then, without question." My fears of not knowing how to tell signs were dispelled forever, and I understood much more of the interconnectedness of all things—the force of life that surges through us all, connecting me to a crow and a small boy on that day that I will always remember as the day of the Crow Sign.

My first real omen came quite unexpectedly while I was exploring the swamps near the main tributary of the Toms River. I was sitting on a large gnarled maple that overhung the water when my mind began drifting. I spotted an old fishing line tangled on a lower root, and I suddenly began to think about my blood grandfather who used to go fishing with me. He was such a kind and gentle soul, so patient, and always smiling. Suddenly, a huge great horned owl alighted on the same branch where I sat. At first I was so amazed that I just sat there, not a thought of doing anything other than marveling at the owl. He just sat there staring at me with his huge eyes, clicking intermittently as owls usually do when disturbed. He gave a half-hearted hoot, then flew off, to the direction of my house. It was then that I realized that he had been an omen. A sickening feeling came over me when I realized that I had been thinking of Grandpa McLaughlin.

I ran home, frightened that the omen was true, praying it was not. I arrived at my house and burst through the front door. My mom was crying and my grandfather was lying on the couch. Shortly after, my dad came home, his face in anguish, his body shaking, as he hugged my mom. He looked at me in disbelief. "You were supposed to be camping all week," he said. "Why are you home?" I told him that I just had a feeling that Mom needed me, so I rushed home. He didn't pursue it any further, other than to rush me out of the room and back to the woods. I was upset and crying when Grandfather found me. "Take heart, Grandson," he said. "Death is only a waste in the white man's world. Your grandfather is in a much better place, at home with the Creator. Do not mourn him, for someday we all must follow him. His work here was finished, and we all must go when the Creator calls. Mourn him not, but learn from him, remember him, and he will never really die. The owl omen brought you to your mother when she needed you the most, and your grandfather sent him. You see, he is still with you even after physical death."

It was more than a year after the owl omen of death appeared to me that I received another omen. All through that year I had assumed that all omens were bad medicine, especially after my first encounter. I was in isolation, surviving alone on a small hill near our sacred area. I wasn't quite on a Vision Quest, for I had the use of all comforts and was in a full survival situation. It was more like a self-imposed asceticism, a time to think deeply and clearly. I was quite comfortable, spending most of my time relaxing, praying, or just contemplating. These camps of introspection helped clarify so much. It gave me time from my skills and Grandfather's teachings to reflect on what I had learned, and to go deep within, getting in touch with my spiritual self. It was a lazy time, the rest was profound, the days long and soothing. Life seemed so easy, yet so intense. It was truly a world apart from all else. It was pure reality.

I must have fallen asleep, for I was suddenly awakened from a strange dream. I was shaking all over and very upset. I had vividly dreamed of a pure-white coyote, scarred from many battles, lying beside a pond. The coyote looked strong and healthy, but a cloud of agony hung over its head. Suddenly, the belly of the coyote rolled, and she gave birth to many little coyotes. This was strange, I thought, for it was definitely a male coyote. The pups were snow-white, like the parent, but had black spots here and there. Unlike the parent, they were unscarred. The white coyote took care of them, nurtured and played with them. At times the old coyote could not play, for the cloud about him seemed to suffocate him. None of the little ones removed the cloud, though some tried. Suddenly the little coyotes began biting at the coyote, tearing hunks of flesh from its body as they tried to kill him.

The old coyote dragged himself away and hid. He nurtured himself back to strength, growing stronger, until the veil of pain lifted from his head. The little ones quarreled amongst themselves, tempers fumed, and they attempted to do what the old coyote had done. Suddenly, an eagle alighted on a rock near them and said, "You lack the scars of the old coyote, you lack the time, and you must rid yourself of the black spots." With that I came awake. My whole body ached, and my head pounded with pain. I wandered to the stream to bathe, thinking of the dream and how ludicrous it had been. I was thinking about telling Grandfather of the dream when a pure-white coyote came to the distant stream's edge to drink. It looked at me knowingly, then vanished. Back at my camp I began to feel better, regaining my sense of reality. As I sat down to eat, a bald eagle circled overhead, slowly descending to and alighting upon an old pine tree at the edge of my camp area. He looked at me for a long time but remained silent. As he dove from the branch and circled above me, I knew that he must be some kind of omen, but I could not understand the meaning.

I broke the silence and solitude of my camp and went to find Grandfather. This was too important, too complicated, not to find out the meaning immediately. I could always return to my asceticism and quietude. It took most of the day to locate Grandfather, and the dream and omen grew more powerful in my heart. I told Grandfather the whole story, and he sat back, in silence, for a long time. He said, "It is not good for anyone to interpret your omen and dream, for it is yours alone. However, you must live this dream some day, you must be torn by those coyotes, before you can rid yourself of the cloud. This omen is neither good nor bad, just a warning of things to come." I thought long and hard of what Grandfather had said, but I did not know what the dream and omens had to do with my life. What I knew was that I needed another Vision Quest to clarify things.

I decided to quest the following week, feeling that the dream was a guiding force and warning me to do so. I felt as if the little coyotes were all the things that needed to be worked out in the quest, and I had to quest as close to the dream, and the omen, as possible. I chose a very arid area by an ancient trail. The area had recently burned over. The land and vegetation were blackened with charred death. There was not a living thing in the area, just the scars of the hot fire. I sat in a small clearing on a pile of sand and charcoaled bark. The area looked dead, devastated. As the sun rose in the sky and began to bake the landscape, I began to think that my choice of areas wasn't the best. It was not yet noon, and the sun was already eating my flesh. I felt a tremendous sense of death and destruction all around me, and it put me in a morbid frame of mind. I had a funny feeling that it was going to be a difficult quest.

Despite the intense heat and burning sun, I had a rather easy day. My mind closed down early, and I could see deeply, clearly into myself. I looked out on the charred landscape and felt a deep sense of loss. Not a year before, I had camped in this forest, and it had been so lush and beautiful. Now all was lost. I knew how important the fires were to keeping the Pine Barrens piney, but such a hot burn caused deep wounds. I felt a certain sense of hopelessness to it all, like I was living on a land of the dead. It was then that I noticed a tiny green plant growing just a few feet in front of me. It was a little pine, just beginning to sprout. As I looked closer, the entire ground was covered, as far as the eye could see. The forest was on its way back to life, all around me, yet all I chose to see when I first arrived was the char. I ended my quest with that profound lesson, and the omen of the little pine tree.

The quest had taught me many things. It taught me that I should not concentrate on the bad, but should seek instead the good. It also taught me that life can spring from the most blackened death, that there is always hope even when all seems hopeless. It had taught me that there can be tremendous life, especially after such bad medicine. Possibly that was the lesson of the pup coyotes tearing apart their father. Sometimes it takes destruction to bring to life new growth, just as the skin of a snake turns pale and leathery before being shed. Most of all the quest taught me the lesson that there was no true bad medicine if we can learn to grow from the lessons of life. I finally got my first good omen, the little pine growing in the ashes of destruction.

14

The Eternal Cave

Grandfather spoke the wisdom of many of his Vision Quests, telling us just enough of his Visions to teach us, but never revealing totally any Vision. Visions are very personal and should never be fully revealed to anyone. The impact of the Vision and its signs, omens, and nuances are only understood by the one seeking. Visions are a personal guiding force, to be shared in part but never fully to anyone, for no man can fully understand another man's Vision. Imparting the wisdom of a personal Vision is as a guiding force to others and leads to a deeper understanding of that person and his quest. It gives the listener a clue to what guides the one with Vision and to his purpose in life. Many times, Grandfather would draw our attention to a special place, a place of the spirit, where all searchers should stop on their way to total Vision. The cave was just such a place, one I heard of many times, and I began to seek it for its wisdom. Though it was never said, I could feel the draw in Grandfather's voice and could tell that it was important to him that I go to the cave someday to quest. Many years later I was on my way.

It loomed out of the darkness like a doorway to some mystical cathedral. I knew it well, even before my eyes first feasted upon its beauty. I heard of it time and time again, in myriad stories told by Grandfather, alluded to in light conversation, or ancient parables. My heart thirsted for this cave, driving me since the first day I ever heard its name. Now many years later and six hundred grueling miles across unknown lands brought me face to face with this vision of rock. It was a journey of a thousand lifetimes that took me here, a difficult journey, not only of flesh but also of the spirit. The journey was part of the quest, like an ancient rite of passage that tested the searcher to see if he was worthy to receive the wisdom of the cave. My mind and flesh were weak and dizzy from the relentless journey. I slept a profound and deep dreamless sleep outside its huge, breathing opening. A strange feel of fear laced with reverence followed me to the unconscious sleep. I vaguely remember dreaming of Grandfather and his quest for this same eternal cave as I lay asleep by the cave's orifice.

I was very young when I first heard its name. The night was very dark and the camp fire's flicker barely illuminated the camp. Shadows danced about, creating strange images behind the brush and trees. Faces seemed to appear from the treetops, casting an icy chill over this otherwise hot summer night. Grandfather spoke in a low monotone. His words were accented by the play of firelight on his face and the slow graceful movements of his hands. The cave, with no time, came into focus as he spoke of spiritual things, leading us to a greater understanding of the world beyond senses, a world only the soul and the heart can reach. I could tell it was hard, very hard, for him to put into common words that which is beyond all symbols and beyond even the most vivid imagination. He spoke of his younger days and his quest to seek the world of the spirit through the Vision. The cave was foremost on his mind, for this night, like the cave, seemed timeless and eternal, described in the same terms as the cave.

He too was very young when he first heard of the cave, and I suspect it had the same impact on him then as it did to me now. It isn't something you soon forget, for the ramifications of even hearing its name grow strong with each spiritual step, even before its surging confines are penetrated by the soul. He spoke of his quest for the cave, how it grew stronger and more compelling, especially after each Vision Quest. The cave always seemed to hold the answers to many questions, even to those not yet formed. His first visit to the cave was when he was a young man. The story of that first visit he revealed to us this night. He had searched through many Vision Quests, each leading him closer to what he had to learn from the cave, and each quest being important to his overall understanding of what secrets the cave held.

Without the initial seeking there could be no understanding. It was a rite of passage, paying one's dues, to prove oneself worthy of what the cave had to teach. He warned us that to each the cave speaks differently, though the lessons are always profound and the searcher is forever changed, transformed to a new plane of understanding and unity with all things of Creation and of the Creator. To those who are unworthy, the cave remains mute and unmoving, driving the pseudospiritualist from its depths with a thousand screaming voices, as if its sacred sanctity were defiled by the unworthy trespasser. We took the warning to heart. His words rang in my ears to the very day I faced its mouth alone. He too had worried that he was unworthy as he had approached the mouth, intimidated by the gaping darkness and the power of the wall that contained the passage.

At first the whole area felt so powerful and oppressive that he felt insignificant, the agelessness of the ancient rocks mocking the frailty of his flesh. He felt as if he would be thrown from the entrance and cast off the cliff to his death. The feeling quickly evaporated as if the cave had searched his heart and accepted him, drawing him almost unconsciously to the dark door. He had no control over his body or legs. They moved toward the door with a mind of their own, slowly, carefully, each step blessing the earth as if a prayer, to a point where he felt he was floating. He soon slipped into the doorway and eternal darkness; all thought was cleared from his head and he could not think; his body became weightless, floating through the darkness, drifting through bodies of heat, then cold, then humidity, drawn closer to the cave's throbbing heart.

The darkness of the door was quickly passed like penetrating an icy veil. At first it was like passing through a mirage of a normal cave, a thin, almost transparent painting through which he easily walked. This must have been the dimension of time and space set aside for curious onlookers and wanderers, set up as a facade to guard the real inner secrets. Suddenly the cave walls transformed into myriad holes, some large enough for a man to walk through, others smaller, where a man would have to slide through on his belly, and others so small he could barely look through, not unlike the eye of a needle. The cave seemed to him to pulsate and tremble, as if a living creature. A distant soft rumbling from deep within the cave vibrated him to the core. Strange movements, pockets of heat, then humid chill brushed against him as he searched the cave. Often he heard the faint murmurings of someone talking or chanting. The cave was thick with spirits.

This was where he would end the story of the eternal cave. He would say only that each hole was a part of the overall vision. Each opening was of things of the past, of possible pasts, and of pasts never lived. There were also holes for all the possible futures, those that will happen, those that could happen, and those that never will. Doorways within doorways, holes within holes, leading to a labyrinth of overlapping worlds, each dependent on the other as the branches of a tree are dependent on its roots. The cave, he said, is a vision of timelessness and eternity, of all paths taken and untaken, of all the paths of man and nature, good and bad, leading to all the possible futures, and to those paths abandoned or passed by. He told us that we must someday seek our own Vision in the cave to understand what it had to teach. He warned, however, that it would fill us with fear, regret, but also hope, and change our lives forever, forever, and I awoke to the abyss of night and the breathing opening of the cave.

I began my preparations to enter the cave. All the stories and myths swirled in my head, and fear overtook me with an uncontrolled trembling. I did not feel worthy. As I made a circle of small stones to mark the place of my quest, I passed in and out of thought, in and out of dream and reality, and worry over my unworthiness washed over me. Resolving myself to the fact that I had been guided here, though in a haphazard way, I was here for a reason, not curiosity. Pass or fail I would at least try to enter the cave and not let the fear drive me away. My hopes were to sit in absolute silence and prayer at the cave's entrance, fasting for four days, then enter the cave on the day of the fifth sun. Though I felt deep inside that I should enter the cave right away, my mind delayed the entrance. I reasoned that I would be more worthy after a quest of fasting silence, but actually what I was doing was putting off the inevitable. I did not want to find out, just yet, whether I was worthy or not.

I sat watching the sun break the horizon and cast the dark landscape into stark reality. The land appeared desolate and sparse, primitive, as if it had just emerged from the ice age. Hardly a sound of bird or beast could be heard. Only the tiny scurry of footfalls. Life here is not seen in magnificent terms; one has to look close. It is a world of insects and mice, of reptiles and small birds that can live within the sand and craggy rock jungle. I lost all thought of time and place as I studied the landscape, plants, and animals. I followed tiny tracks with my eyes as they flowed around stone and bush in a labyrinth of lacey trails and etchings. Sound was distorted along with distance; time seemed to stand still; only the grain-by-grain degrading of tracks by the weather marked any rhythm of time. I felt alone and vulnerable. The agelessness of the rocks mocked my flesh and I felt insignificant. I prayed for strength, my body sore with fatigue and my mind surging with senselessness.

The day was hot. The dry winds felt as if they were passing through my body, threatening to tear the flesh from my bones. Thirst was intense. My lips were dried and cracked, my eyes burned, and my head pounded with the pain of hot sun and constant squinting. The sun tore through my tan and burned my body again. My shoulders, nose, and lips felt as if hot coals had scorched them. The pain was overshadowed only by my fear and the drive to complete the quest. I wanted desperately to sleep but I was afraid that something, some sign, would pass unnoticed. My mind reeled again with doubts and demons, surging into nothingness, then back again to the pounding reality of consciousness. I slumped over in sleep, only to shake myself awake time and time again; intermittent relief of dream, then the pain of reality again. I drifted off again, only to awaken in total darkness. I was in the cave.

I don't even pretend to know how it happened. Some things are better left unexplained, but I was there. My fear was intense, body trembling uncontrollably with each pounding beat of my heart. Sweat poured from my body as I reached out and touched the damp walls. I could feel the totality of the darkness. The pungent rock mixed with the thick but cool humidity, choking but soothing my burned and battered body. I had expected my entrance to be much like Grandfather's, but expectations distort what is real and concentrate on the lie of what should be. I dropped all expectations and cleared my head, leaning against the cool walls for relief. My mind raced over all the whys, faltered, and fell into a deep sleep. No dreams penetrated my world in this sleep and my body finally relaxed.

I was jolted awake by the echo of bats squeaking. A cold spot passed by, dragging a silken cobweb across my naked thigh, and I could sense some presence other than myself. Faintly I could hear the distant rhythmic rumblings of the cave. Voices and laughter drifted on the faint whispers of breeze, though I could not decide whether they were reality or the echoes of my thinking. Fear rampaged freely. I felt trapped, smothered in the blackness. I did not know the way out. I desperately felt the cave floor for tracks, but dirt was scarce, with only rocks and bat feces to mark any traces. There were no tracks. The fear intensified, and I could hear the echo of my scream ricocheting off a thousand walls and hollows. Whether by plan or design I was here, and I accepted that reality, for that was all I had. I had to be here in this reality, not distorted in some dream of how things should have been. My fear eased and I felt relief again.

I sat immobilized, afraid to move, trying to remember how I had gotten here. I remembered a dream of walking through the cave's door but with no detail as to when or how. My eyes ached, opened wide to penetrate the darkness, strained from the abyss of nothingness. I closed them for relief, but the monotony of darkness continued. Opening my eyes again I began to notice faint outlines of the cave, growing lighter every moment, but no light source could be found. It was as if the walls of the cave were glowing with their own inner light, much like the cool light of phosphorescent fungus or fireflies. The walls of the cave seemed to pulsate with that light. Pastel colors appeared on rocks and stalactites. Shapes, shadows, and textures began to move, flicker as if in firelight. I could feel the movement of a spirit other than mine. The primal rumblings of the cave grew stronger, and I could sense the voices outside my thoughts.

Slowly I arose, my body stiff and cold from the cave floor. I felt an inner draw to follow a large passage before me. I began walking, stumbling at first, and approached the mouth of the passage. There, as a guardian of the entrance, stood a huge boulder with a flat top. It stood solitary, stalagmites reaching around it to guard its pocked walls. To me it was an altar. I placed an offering of tobacco, and I prayed with the intensity of a warrior about to face a battle of no return. The fear of dying dissipated, and I felt strong, my mind clear and eager. It was as if I had stepped out of my old self, the self of another dimension, and walked into clarity. The pull on my soul to travel the passage increased its force, and I went. At first I walked softly so as not to trip, but I soon lost consciousness of my lower body, to a point where I was no longer walking but floating, weightless.

The monotonous walls of the passage gave way to crude lines, shapes, and etchings in the rock, soon growing stronger in design to that of primitive cave paintings, the likes of which I had seen at various times in my life. There were pictures of strange beasts and those not so strange, of hunting parties and weapons, of camps and of other symbols. I was fascinated because they looked so fresh and new. Even the collage of hand prints that were placed on the wall were as fresh as if they were made a few moments earlier. It appeared that time had stood still and not ravaged these old paintings. A grunting call of a humanlike voice lifted my attention to a distant tunnel wall where the light of a flickering fire danced. Reflected on the wall were the shadows of people sitting, moving, and talking. Their heads and bodies were grotesque in proportion. The outline of animal skins could be seen loosely flung across shoulder or around waist. Primitive spears and atlatls were leaning on the wall, where a torch burned. I shook my head in disbelief, and they were gone. Only the echoing voices lingered.

I ran around the corner of the tunnel to the origin of the fire. Only an ancient pile of ash and charred rocks marked its probable place, all else was gone. I thought, with all that had happened, my imagination was playing tricks on me, but it was difficult to explain away the old fire location. Passing it off as some sort of fatigued hallucination, I followed my heart further, down a labyrinth of tunnels, until I reached a huge cavernous hall. It was as Grandfather had described, myriad holes of all shapes and sizes, found all over the cavern. Looking back, so I could retrace my steps, I saw that the tunnel I came from was one of the larger ones. I got a sense that I had just, in some way, come from the past, though I couldn't explain why. It is something instinctive, something known, without any rational explanation. Ahead of me lay several large tunnels, which eventually came together into a room just like the one I was in now.

I was pulled once again to one of the tunnels, and I began to slowly walk down its corridor, the draw on my unconscious growing stronger as I entered its hallway. The walls were lavished with a series of small holes, some lighted from within and others dark. My curiosity was so overwhelmed that I had to stop and look through one of the holes, though for the life of me I didn't know why. As soon as I pulled myself up to the hole to look, there was a flash and an explosion. The hole was transformed into one smoke-and-dust-filled mass. As the dust began to clear, I could make out the smoldering skeleton of a building, twisted metal, and the wreckage of some kind of truck. Strewn about the ground were various bits of wreckage, barbed wire, old guns with bayonets, and some helmets not unlike the ones worn during the First World War. There too lay the broken and bloody bodies of men, torn apart and scattered like the debris. Faint cries and screams came from the distance. There was another explosion, and I dropped back into the cave.

I was shaken up, trembling and sweaty, as if I had just emerged from some nightmare. But it was no nightmare. It was real and very powerful. I not only saw the explosions, the torn bodies, and twisted metal, but I also could smell the burned blood and death. I wondered about the origins of the cave, what it was all about, and searched my inner self for answers. I ran back toward the origin of the tunnel and peered into another hole. An Indian village here was burning and in ruin. Warriors lay dead alongside cavalry men; women and old ones lay burned, twisted, and bloody. Little children were strewn about, their faces contorted with their final pain, and the stench of death was everywhere. I was sickened at the senselessness and pain of it all. My mind reeled in distortions and disbelief, and I collapsed to the floor of the cave, showered by my own vomit.

I knew then that I was in the tunnel of the past, more recent than the primal cave of my origin, but still a long way to go to my reality of now. I wandered up the cave toward the second cavern, where all the tunnels converged, still sickened by what I had witnessed. I began passing through clouds of choking steam. The pungency of astringent chemicals burned my throat and eyes, and I could clearly smell the burning coals and automobile exhaust. Farther still the stench of civilization gave way and the tunnel cleared. Curiosity overwhelmed me again, and I peered through another hole. A city this time reeled before me like an old black-and-white movie. I could see the city shrouded in the cloak of pollution, hear the roar of hurry, see the saddened faces of the masses, crime, rape, and starving children. Everywhere there was the rushing chaos, people in silent pain, desperate, searching, lost in the sterility of uncaring masses. I could take no more and ran from the hole's reality.

I had to sit down for a while, for I was shaken to the core. Certainly I had seen the cities before in my own reality, I knew the scene of the First World War and the slaughter of the Native American peoples. But the cave made them clear and real. I was there and had experienced it beyond the books and the imagination. I felt as if I could not go on, and I wondered if there was any good in this tunnel. I arose from the floor and quickly peered through an old crack in the wall, and my spirit rejoiced. A pristine scene of a forest stretched before me, cool and refreshing, full of song and ribboned with a gentle little creek. The symphony of bird song stopped, abruptly, as if someone were coming. The stream surged forth with an oily sludge. Dead fish floated, and the plants framing the waters turned brown, wilted, and died. A roar of an engine shattered the silence, trees began falling everwhere, the whirr of chain saws gave way to the dusty approach of a bulldozer. I cried out in pain and turned from the crack. I could hear the faint crying of children in the distant caverns.

I stumbled on, more shaken than I had ever been in my life, sick in body and mind. At the place where all the tunnels converged, I rested, my body exhausted with emotion, my head unable to assimilate all the things I had seen. As I sat, I got a feeling about all the tunnels and a feeling for time, place, and destination. I could sense that each of the tunnels was of various peoples of the earth, all converging on this one main hall of time, place, and humanity. In my subconscious I could feel all the streams of life coming together into one faceless culture, one huge blind society, all thundering blindly in one direction. There were screams, crying, and whispers in many languages I did not understand flooding my ears, and the roars and stench of this time and place overwhelmed me. Man had come together here, the global consciousness fusing into this ever-widening tunnel, leading to the grand hall. It was something I knew but was never taught, something strange but real, removed from what the divine destiny of man should have been.

I walked on, hoping beyond all hope that there was some glimmer of good in this place. All the holes in this larger section of tunnel were dark or had just a faint glimmer of light, much like a tiny candle illuminating a dark room. As I gazed at all the tiny holes, I had an overwhelming sense of peace. I felt as if these were answers, these were directions that men had tried, but they had failed. Some still held light and hope for a new direction, a new consciousness. Nearing the larger room I was drawn to a tiny hole, and I peered in, hoping to touch the purity of this direction. There before me kneeled Grandfather, his face younger than I had ever known it. His body trembled, and tears ran down his face. He was standing in the main hall that lay ahead. He was gazing down a large tunnel, but he was there in another time and place, not where I stood. He glanced up toward me, and with a pained smile he pointed at me, then motioned toward the tunnel that lay before him, beckoning me to look. Slowly, his image went out of focus, then disappeared. The wailing of my voice, calling his name, echoed from countless walls and holes.

I backed away from the tunnel, upset but fascinated. Somehow, in some strange, unexplainable way, I had touched Grandfather's Vision; our worlds and times had become fused in the fissure of a rock. The sense of loss, of missing him, welled up in my heart, and I slumped to the floor sobbing. There were so many questions about life I had failed to ask him, before he changed worlds, so many new questions, and no one there to guide me. I felt so alone, so vulnerable, and my mind ached for the rapture and simplicity of my childhood. Even though I understood the essence of the cave internally, there were still so many unanswered questions. All I had was my own intuition to lead my heart, and I did not know if I was missing the greater lessons or even looking in the right holes for answers. I felt as if I were running out of time here, and there was no answer yet to the hopelessness of the cave. I yearned for Grandfather's wisdom and guidance, but I knew that I had to forge my own trail, my own Vision.

Instinctively, I knew what I had to do. Grandfather wanted me in the large room to look down the tunnel where he had looked, so many lifetimes ago. I dreaded going into the cavern, instinctively fearing to experience the same pain and sorrow I had seen in Grandfather. My memory flashed back to the many times Grandfather had spoken about the cave. I remember the pain and remorse in his voice, but I also remember the essence of hope. So often he alluded to my time to come in the cave. How it would bring me to the valley of hopelessness and utter despair and eventually to bravery and to my own sense of hope. He said that it would also teach me commitment and dedication to things higher than self. But to understand the cave fully, I would have to rise above my own fears and limitations and face the ultimate corridor of things yet to come. That is where I stood now, paralyzed in fear but determined to follow Grandfather's wishes.

I let go of my fear, feeling that to face pain or even death was a small price to pay for what wisdom lay ahead. I had prepared myself far too many years and traveled too far to be turned away. I began walking toward the main cavern that lay ahead, stepping softly and carefully so as not to stumble. Strewn on the floor were bits of garbage, twisted metal, spent rifle cartridges, stains of chemicals, and pieces of bones and skulls. The stench of rotted flesh mingled with that of caustic chemicals, overshadowed only by the din and distant drunken laughter. The closer I got to the main hall, the more the stench increased and the litter grew, until I had to pick my way through a labyrinth of garbage to move ahead. My eyes watered with the stinging of chemicals, making it difficult to see or even to breathe. Still I pressed on, passing decaying forest litter and the persistent and increasing sound of people crying and wailing, and their obsessive insane laughter.

I stood for a long moment at the end of the corridor, gazing into the cathedral-like hall that lay before me. There was no debris on the ground, or stench in the air, and no sound of voices. Only the low droning rumble of the cave could be heard. The cavern seemed new, freshly chiseled from the rock, with the smell of fresh dirt heavy in the air. Despite the newness of the cave, I could sense an ancient anticipation, as if something were about to happen, ominous and draining to my mind and spirit, manifesting itself in my trembling flesh. I got the feeling of now, the immediate, of things that were happening outside these walls, in the physical world of modern time and space. I stood on the brink of time, in the temple of now, watching the future begin to unfold, etching itself on the distant walls. I walked across the massive floor of the cavern, heading to the distant pocked and eroded walls. One of the distant openings, though fresh and shallow, was so much larger than the others.

The earthen floor of the cavern rippled out from where I walked, like concentric rings on a quiet pond. Suddenly the floor surged and the earth tore away, like a veil, revealing a miniature version of civilization as it now was. I stood in the center, gazing down upon the world. The people and their movements below took no notice of me. I was invisible. I watched people hurry to work, the traffic jams, and factories spewing smoke and vapor. I saw forests falling to the whirring of saws and the earth being slashed by heavy equipment and gashed by dirt bikes. I could hear the cries of children, the drunken laughter of people, and the masses wandering aimlessly as if affected by some mind-altering drug. Everywhere there was despair that seemed to grow with the mountains of garbage that lay outside the city limits. I could sense the hopelessness of it all, the absolute desperation, and ultimately the searching. People seemed afraid to touch or even talk to each other. They were afraid to face the grand questions of life and living and also were very content to rush aimlessly so as to avoid finding that their lives lacked purpose and dedication to things other than their superficial selves. I could feel no spiritual commitment in many of them; others made only halfhearted attempts to seek the things beyond the physical realms. Life here was running on shallow physical and mental energy with no depth, and no spirit.

The floor flickered once again, rippled, then returned to solid rock and earth. I felt a certain disgust for what I had just witnessed. My lofty position, like the unnoticed soaring of a hawk, showed me how utterly hopeless it all was. How many people worked only for themselves at a physical level, paying no attention to what their actions would have on future generations, and caring more for instant physical gratification than for the eternity of spiritual rapture. I felt that if people would only slow down long enough to catch their breath, they would have time to look deeper into their lives. They would eventually ask questions about their direction, the direction of mankind, and what life was all about. They would also see the hopelessness and the shallowness of the path they were taking. Their search would eventually lead them to the paths of the spirit, to the Creator, and to the real meaning of life. Instead, what little searching there was led to the forgetfulness of alcohol, drugs, games, or TV. Thus there could be no confrontation of self, and possibly no hope or change of direction.

Feeling an emptiness, the hollowness of it all, I walked to the distant wall. I knew now that each mark, each crack, dent, and pock was the diggings of the future and all the possible futures of mankind. I was frightened at what I would find, especially at the biggest opening, where I had seen Grandfather gazing. Knowing what I knew about the actions of man, I could only imagine the grim destiny that lay ahead. Looking at the overall wall, with all its little dents and scrapes as compared to the huge orifice of man's direction, all seemed so hopeless. My mind raced with my heart as I neared the wall and touched its skin. I grew sick again, feeling the emptiness and despair overwhelm me. Could there be no hope? Is man digging his grave as this orifice is being dug? To me there seemed no other direction. Everything was being pulled toward this hole, sucked in. To change direction would be like swimming against a strong tide, stalling the inevitable disaster. Could this end have been what Grandfather wanted me to see? Was this to make me give up hope of ever trying to change things, or was there more to the cave's teaching?

I turned away, to go back from where I came, but I could not move. I was frozen in place, full of fear and fatigue, terrorized by what lay ahead in the future. Anger at my fear welled up from deep inside, and I grew brave again. Anger can be a tremendous motivator and, like fear, can be turned inside out for good. All that is left after the metamorphosis of anger is the energy that fed the anger, which can then be channeled to other things. I faced the wall again, with renewed strength, now more determined than ever to find the answers to the cave. I thought about expectations and how they can cripple pure experience with their prejudices. Possibly I had been looking at the wall all wrong. My fear could be unfounded, created by my own analysis of reality and my personal definition of fear. I knew whatever lay ahead I could handle, I would have to handle. I had unwavering faith that the Creator had led me here and that he would not send me anything I could not understand or deal with.

I looked into one of the medium-size pockmarks nearest to the ominous large opening. It led nowhere, dead-ending at solid rock. I thought I heard voices coming from inside, but they were distant, more of mind than of the cave. Even if I could have heard them clearly, they were in a frenzied state of argument, anger, and high tension. It seemed strange that this was the only hole I gazed into that did not reveal its secrets, so I looked again. This time the rock appeared as a hazy veil that soon evaporated. There before me was a large group of men and women heading toward a distant battle. Many people I knew were there, some I had only read about in newspapers and magazines. Native Americans, environmentalists, theologians and religious leaders, all heading to the distant battle. All of them were active environmentalists involved in saving the earth and its people. The only problem was that they weren't getting anywhere. As soon as someone got going, he would stop to argue with another about policy or to dispute another's trail or tactics. All the while the distant battle raged, they fought amongst themselves, making hardly any progress.

As I slipped back from the hole I wasn't surprised or shocked at what I had seen. I had witnessed this sort of thing many times before. I had seen good environmental groups floundering in lack of leadership, where all wanted to be leaders and none followers. I had also seen huge amounts of energy expended on criticizing or fighting other such groups or individuals. At these times the battle to save the earth was forgotten, and the immediate fight was taken up with only a token of energy spent on the major battle. It was much the same way with the great religions. More energy was being expended fighting and denouncing each other than on the greater issues of world peace, hunger, and spirituality. Any time something was done, it wasn't done for the overall good, but for propaganda and superiority over the other groups. When running toward a battle, certainly there will be warriors bumping into each other, but their main goal is to win that battle. Petty differences are laid aside, along with arguments and prejudices, until the battle is won. The greater battle to save the earth was failing because the old battle tactic of divide and conquer was being used.

The enemy was a fierce fighter, not only in destroying the earth because of ignorance and greed, but it was also defeating the defending warriors with the mental warfare of power, greed, and glory of the individual. I could clearly see the stupidity in all of this. If only they could learn to fight together, their battle would be easier. It is the unity of thought, of overall consciousness, of purpose, and of love that are the greatest weapons. So close they were, yet so far. Their energy was drained on the different beliefs of others that fought with them. Their infighting would not only cost them the battle but also their visions. They were in a no-win situation unless they pulled together. My lesson in all of this was very clear. No matter what path I traveled or what lance I used, I should never criticize a fellow warrior. I should be involved only in the greater fight and not waste energy on who is right or wrong. I must rise above the trivial prejudices and the power struggle, and be more like the ancient ones. They accorded each man the right to his own beliefs and never forced their beliefs on anyone else.

I walked a little closer to the large hole and peered into another pock. There sat a group of men and women around a large table. I suspected that they were corporate executives of some sort because of what issues they were discussing. They spoke of developing an area of forest owned by a community. The land had been left to the community to be kept natural, but these people were talking about buying off officials and getting the land status changed. The only person concerned about the land was arguing with the others. His battle was brought to an end when he was told that one small piece of land did not matter and that there were plenty of other lands. He was also threatened with losing his job and enticed with the fat profits that could be had. The issue was settled on the promise that the one small tract of land would not make any difference to the overall national ecology. The picture burst into thousands of similar pictures from all over the world, all with people discussing the same thing but different lands.

I backed away from the pock, frustrated over the events I had just witnessed. Were we selling the lives of our grandchildren for immediate profits? Could we be so blind not to see that these people were not the only ones destroying lands? In my mind and heart, all land mattered, no matter how insignificant. Living so close to the destruction of the earth and its creatures, one piece of land does matter. One piece of land could tip the ecological balance toward total destruction. Instead of fighting over what lands should be developed, we should be fighting over what lands should be reclaimed. We should begin to tip the balance the other way. It was clearly the ignorance and greed of these people that were killing their grandchildren. We have got to stop being a society of people that kills their grandchildren to feed their children. I knew that re-education could be the only answer to this deadly ignorance. To me, what you don't know can hurt you, and all people should know the laws of Creation.

I had witnessed two grand events leading to the cavern of man's destiny, one caused by ignorance and the other caused by prejudice. I did not want to see others. I walked bravely to the largest cavern, the passage of man's future, prepared to face the worst possibilities. What I witnessed far exceeded my expectations and preparations. The huge chiseled hole stank of chemicals and rotted flesh again. All about me lay dying vegetation, people, and animals. The air was thick with smoke, dust, and vaporous chemicals, which blackened the sun. Children cried, starvation was everywhere, fighting and killing over food and water was common. Streams ran as thick as oil, flies and rats ate the flesh of those dead or dying. All around was pain and destruction. Areas of the earth appeared bombed, destroyed; life as I knew it did not exist anymore. But there was still the greed, the power struggles, the killing, the prejudices, and the hatred. Man here still did not know the laws of Creation or survival.

Over in the distance, barely visible through the smoke and vapor, stood a small group of people looking over the final chapter of civilization. They were of this time and place but removed from it in a way. They were carrying ancient weapons and wearing the torn remnants of modern clothing, heading off to the distant mountains to live. They were the dawn of the new humanity, abandoning the old ways of death and seeking a new life in the last ramparts of nature. As they turned toward the hills, one old man looked back, held his hands aloft and prayed. An eagle circled and called over his head, drifting off to the distant mountains like an omen. The old one, without question, followed. The killing and dying continued all around me. The earth erupted and swallowed the remains of man in gaping fissures that ran across the land. The land now looked as it did before the dawn of man, primitive and mystical. All traces of the cancer of man were gone; except for the small band of people, the earth had purged itself.

I ran from the hole, gasping, sobbing, and collapsed to the floor. My mind swooned with the carnage I had just seen. Were these the only answers to the healing of the earth? Was the cost of all these lives the price we had to pay for the sins of our grandparents? Were the ancient skills only passed down and remembered to survive this day? Was there no other way? So many questions mingled with so much despair flooded my body and mind. My spirit sickened and my emotions were out of control. I could not think at all. Everything seemed so hopeless, people so helpless, so ignorant. It was the greed and ignorance that brought us to this place, the hatred, the wars, the prejudices. I was angry at no man but in a rage over humanity and its actions. Most of all I realized that if mankind was guided by his spirit rather than by his flesh, we would never have to face this day. I arose from the ground, shaking and weak, and headed back to the grand cavern of the now.

I stood at the entrance to man's destiny for a long time, trying desperately to compose my thought and body. I prayed out loud, sobbing as I called upon the Creator. "Is there no other way?" I shouted. "Is there no other way?" My voice echoed off caverns, walls, and corridors, my aloneness caving in on me with the oppressive silence. Nothing spoke, no answers came, all was still as if the Creator and Creation had turned its back on me, refusing to answer. "Is this why you brought me here?" I wailed. "To show me the hopelessness of it all?" Again, silence. I hung my head, and there on the floor at my feet was an arrowhead, freshly knapped from fire-treated chert (quartz). My heart jumped because it was on the floor of here and now. It also showed a certain artistry and love, a deep understanding of the ancient ways. It held hope. I turned and looked into a small scratch on the wall near the cavern of man's destiny. There I sat, asleep at the main entrance of the cave, in my Vision Quest circle, just as it was when I had left.

I awoke in my circle to a brilliant dawn. I was angry, for it had all been but a dream. My body ached with fatigue and still trembled with the events of the nightmare still swirling in my head. I drifted in and out of sleep and reality, trying desperately to focus on the Vision, trying again to get ready to face the cave. I stood up and began to walk from my circle toward the cave's door, feeling that the dream was telling me to enter the cave now. That is when I noticed another set of footprints leading to the door, then many days later, back again. They were mine. A sharp pain in my right hand penetrated all the other pain, blood ran from my closed fist. As I opened my hand, there lay the arrowhead that I had collected from the cave's floor. I sat down, shaking, trying to get ahold of my emotions and thoughts, attempting to make sense out of the dream or reality I had just lived through. The tracks on the ground were definitely mine, but I didn't remember ever walking to the door or back again. The age difference in the tracks was four days, but I felt that I had only awakened from a night's sleep. Even the tracks from my first day's travel were aged several days. I had been gone, certainly, but I did not know how or where. All the evidence pointed to the cave.

I sat for a long time, praying and meditating rather than trying to think or sort out events. I remembered Grandfather telling me that the cave would distort time and reality, but I never realized how much. Dream or reality, the cave had been a very powerful teacher. In a strong way, the vision in the cave had been very negative, but I had faced negativity and bad medicine before but always turned them into very powerful lessons. Negativity can be as powerful a teacher as the positive. The cave had shown me what could and would happen if mankind did not change his ways. It had shown me the desperation and destruction of the future, of all things, and the little chance of changing that destiny. But it also gave me hope, in the form of an arrowhead, and determination to do whatever I could do to change that destiny. I would fight for that change, like a warrior, never giving up until death released my spirit. No matter how small my voice or how little impact I had on the overall consciousness, I would try to the very end. I fell to sleep, exhausted beyond exhaustion.

I awoke to darkness again, but this time not the darkness of the cave. The stars burned holes in the abyss of endless sky and silhouetted the craggy rocks into weird forms and sculptings. I felt a presence again, just like I had felt when I had first entered the cave. I was frightened and disoriented. I stood up abruptly to make sure I was not having another dream, and to fight, if necessary. I was now a warrior for the earth and was not going to be intimidated by any dream or reality. I knew my path, the cave had spoken, all else could only be messengers from the dark side of medicine. I heard the echo of a distant voice coming from the mouth of the cave, calling to me from the entrance. I picked up a large stick and slowly walked to the cave. My reluctance was hardly that of a warrior. The blackness of the cave seemed to suck me in, soon overwhelming me with its silence and blackness. As I looked back, the rocks by the door seemed to move, then from behind them stepped a man.

I could see only his outline accented by the distant sky. He was definitely Native American, tall and wiry, loin cloth and feathered braid barely visible. He carried with him a long lance that was strung with feathers from its sharpened tip to its base. I knew instantly that he was a warrior, and judging from his lance and dress, he was ancient. I felt so frail and insignificant standing there, facing such a splendid and powerful warrior. I would fight him, however, if he came any closer. He stood for a moment looking toward me, then without a word planted his lance in the ground and sat upon a rock, still facing me. He called my name and said, "Grandson, a true warrior is always the last to pick up the lance or go to battle. His battles are fought with the lance of love and understanding. His enemies are prejudice, greed, and bad medicine, and the biggest battles are always fought within himself. So, do not go out upon the earth to battle unseen demons of the physical world, for your hatred will be like theirs. Instead, go out as a true warrior, with love and understanding." He arose slowly, picked up his lance, and disappeared behind the rock. "You are not yet ready, Grandson. I have spoken." His voice rang through the caverns, then trailed off to silence.

I went back to the Vision area and sat down, watching the dawn slowly edge out the darkness. Many questions swam in my head, yet there were many more answers. Yes, the cave had taught me to be a warrior, to never give up hope, and to fight to the end. It taught me that each little scratch in the wall made a significance, a small change, but still a change. It taught me that no matter how long or tough the battle, I should keep trying and working with those who are fighting the same battle. And now it taught me the true essence of a warrior, a code to fight and live by. I turned my head skyward to pray, only to see the trail of vapor from a jet slashing through the cloudwork. Anger welled up inside my chest, but suddenly I understood, and I prayed for those who rushed by in the skies, pitying them for never knowing the dawn of this cave, but I swore that someday I would teach them reality.

I stayed in the area of the cave for several more days, hoping that the cave would reveal more. It remained silent and unyielding. Instinctively, I knew that I had learned all I could from the cave for now. I had many more horizons to face and much to learn before I would face it again. I tried to formulate a battle plan for doing my part to save the earth, but everything seemed so complicated, so difficult. I had no power, my voice was weak at best, and who would listen to a bum anyway? Upset at not knowing what to do, I left the area and headed back across the country to the distant Pine Barrens. As I walked the ridges, I spotted a flash of sunlight being reflected from the desert far below. Thrilled that it might be a camper, I headed to its origin. A few miles later I found that the reflection was from the bottom of an aluminum beer can that had lain there for quite some time. I cursed its existence, picked it up, and put it into my bag. Suddenly, the desert looked purer, brighter, and more alive. I had found another answer: start out slowly, doing whatever I could do, even if it was just to pick up a lone beer can in a vast expanse of purity. Sometimes the greatest wars are won with just a little effort.

15

The Spirits

It had been a long and very strenuous day, and now that darkness was upon Grandfather, Rick and me, we were more than ready for sleep. We were on our way to one of our winter campsites, far to the south of the medicine cabin, and we only had a few days to complete our journey. Winter had a firm hold on the landscape, though temperatures during the day were still above freezing. The heavy sand trails we had walked were still very soft, and we sank deep, restricting our movement and tiring us more than usual. We had traveled since dawn and had not stopped moving until we built the temporary camp. There had been no time to hunt or forage, and water along the route was nonexistent. It was these trips that tested our endurance, especially of the relentless cold and fatigue. Though we loved to push ourselves to the limit, this particular trek was beyond what we had expected. To make matters worse, we had left all our heavy outer clothing back at the cabin, to further test our skill in a moving survival. The true test of a skilled survivalist was one who could stay very comfortable while traveling quickly. Unfortunately, we had only been into the skills of survival and body control for a few years, and it wasn't that easy for us yet.

As I crawled into the debris hut, the temperatures were already plunging well below freezing, but the air was dead still. Foraging animal sounds echoed through the forest and lulled me into a deep sleep. The thirst and hunger had no hold on me, and I was snug and warm in the warm womb of the hut. In a matter of minutes my mind raced through the events of the day, only to be cut short by a deep and profound sleep. Living the free and wild life of survival, close to the nurturing power of the earth, always produces such a deep and restful sleep, a sleep that few could ever know while living with all the cares and duties of modern society. Sleeping in the womb of Creation, surrounded by purity of air, land, and spirit, the sleeping mind remains uncluttered. The natural sleep of wilderness is always far superior to the sleep I experience in controlled, sterile environments of houses.

Sometime during the night, I had a vivid dream. It stood out from all the others because it had seemed so real, so urgent. I first had images of walking along the trail that we were to take the next day. The landscapes I passed were very clear, the travel was easy, and the day was far warmer than it had been on the previous day. I could see every detail of the landscape and of Grandfather's and Rick's presence there. I then dreamed of approaching the stream, one that we usually drank from, and the first we would pass since the beginning of the journey. I could feel the rush of emotion and relief as I drew close to the edge of the water. I could feel the anticipation of my thirst being quenched after such a long and hard journey. The stream produced images of pristine beauty, a soothing energy, and a gift of life from the Creator.

As I bent over to drink, I was taken aback by the image of an old Indian reflected in the stream's surface. I looked up across the water, and there stood the same Indian looking back at me. He looked very old, older than Grandfather, yet he still stood very straight, strong, and regal. He waved his hand, palm down, across his chest in greeting, then sternly spoke his warning. "Do not drink from this water, from this day forth. You must also deliver this warning to your grandchildren, and their grandchildren to come." With that he motioned upstream and said, "They have poisoned the stream for all things. Do not be deceived by the clarity of the water." Before I could ask any questions, he vanished, and I fell back into a deep dreamless sleep.

As I awoke the next morning, the dream stayed with me, but I would not tell Grandfather. I knew that some dreams were important, but most were merely imagination and logical static. I did not want to take the chance in making a fool out of myself, no matter how important the dream still seemed. We cleaned up the camp area, returning the area to as it had been. It was important for a good survivalist and scout to leave an area undisturbed, or better than it had been. That was the mark of a caretaker and necessary for the balance of things, no matter how long it took to restore order. The time was well worth the effort, but in no time we were back on the trail again, heading south.

The day grew warm fast, far warmer than it had been the day before. The clarity of dawn caused the surrounding forest to stand out in bold relief, and travel became easier. It was exactly as I had dreamed, and the urgency I felt during the dream began to intensify. As we drew closer to the stream, I wanted to tell Grandfather of the dream, but still I felt reluctant and let it pass. I walked toward the stream as I had seen in my dream and began to kneel beside the water. Rick and Grandfather did the same. As I looked at the clarity of the water, I realized what a fool I had been to think that there was something wrong with the water. It looked so clear, pristine, and beautiful. As I cupped my hands to drink, the image of the old Indian appeared momentarily on the surface, just as in the dream. Without thinking, I yelled to Grandfather and Rick, with urgency, "Don't drink the water!"

Rick stopped for a moment, then ignored me, raising his hands to his mouth to drink. I dove for him and knocked him back from the edge, water flying everywhere. He came back at me quickly, and we wrestled in a rage. Grandfather quickly broke up the fight, settled us down, then asked me what it was all about. Reluctantly I told him about the dream, giving great detail of the events, how they were the same today, and the old Indian's face reflected again in the surface of the water. I told him that I didn't want to tell him because I thought it had been my imagination. Rick readily agreed and went back to the water to drink. Grandfather held him back, and said, "First we will look upstream." Rick reluctantly agreed, gave me a dirty look, and muttered to me as I passed. "Great imagination!"

We began to walk upstream, looking closely at the vegetation in and out of the water. Rick kept saying that there was nothing wrong with the water, but now Grandfather said, emphatically, "The water is sick; the color of the plants is wrong!" We continued up the stream to where it intersected an old dirt road. There, thrown all over the road, were barrels. Some were toppled and leaking; all of them were rank with the odors of chemicals, and several had the poison symbol of skull and crossbones emblazoned across them. Grandfather said, in a disgusted voice, "Your spirit was right. This water is no longer good to drink, for you or for your grandchildren. All will die who drink here." I was amazed, for not only had the dream been real, but also Grandfather had mentioned a spirit. I was excited and honored, for the mystery of the spirits seemed so far out of my reach. Now I had a real communication with the "outer world."

I withheld all of my questions, allowing the events of the day to filter into my mind fully. I wanted to be sure that I knew what I wanted to ask, for where the spirits were concerned, Grandfather was very short with answers. We set camp by the second stream, and by the night fire Grandfather began to speak without being prodded. "There is a separate spiritual reality," he said, "of things of the unseen and eternal. There is a world of spirit that dwells just outside the Creator. The spirit world exists next to our own, and their wisdom transcends all barriers. They can teach us things we could not know through our physical senses or logical mind. They protect us, guide us, and teach us to heal others. They are a link to the past, and all the possible futures. To them, to their world, all is known, and now they communicate with you in your dreams and Visions."

I knew that all of Creation was a duality, part flesh and part spirit. I knew that man had to learn to deal equally in that dual reality to become whole. I had learned to transcend the physical realms and enter the universe of spirit through the void of the veils. I understood that things existed on both a physical and spiritual level, and I was beginning to see the spirit in all things. What intrigued me now was that Grandfather had spoken of a spiritual world greater than just the spirit of things existing in this time and place. It was a world rich in spirits that did not have fleshly footholds in our physical reality. Such was the old Indian who had warned me of the bad water. The excitement of it all was that there was far more existing out there than just the spiritual entities of Creation, and we could communicate with that world freely.

Grandfather continued, "Modern man will never know the spirits of Creation, for he has no faith. Knowing the spiritual side of all things becomes a doorway to knowing all of the spiritual worlds. Rarely does a spirit manifest itself in flesh, but a spirit comes to us in dreams and Visions. However, there are as many bad, or evil, spirits as there are good spirits, and only your heart can know the difference. Evil ones can affect all parts of man's mind and body, bring sickness or death, and cause wars and destruction. That evil can come as fear, hatred, rage, or wearing many other faces, for the evil spirits feed on man's negativity. Evil must never be fought with rage or hatred, for that will only make it stronger. You must never fear the evil ones, for your fear will consume and destroy you. Instead, fight the evil spirits with love and compassion, for those are our greatest weapons."

That day my world expanded beyond my wildest expectations. I was concerned and frightened about the possibility of evil spirits, but that could not dampen my enthusiasm about this grand new dimension. I now understood the powerful connection I had to the spirit world through my dream. All doubt was erased, for I had learned things from the dream that I could not have known, and the spirit had saved my life. That day became my doorway to a world of tremendous power and knowledge, a world that could only be known through the power and the purity of wilderness, guided by Grandfather.

The spirit of the old Indian that came to me in my dream stayed in my mind for a long time. Every time I bent to drink water, I looked for his face in the stream, but he never came back. Time began to remove him from my consciousness as I repeatedly tried and failed to contact him. The frustration of repeated failure began to make me feel as if I was not worthy of a spiritual communication, and I thought I was doing something wrong. I also felt that the spirit belonged to Grandfather and only came by to warn me out of duty to him. Whatever the reasons were for the spirit guide's absence, I felt unworthy, and I desperately needed to quest to clear my mind, to reorient myself to my spiritual path, and to find out what was keeping me from the spiritual world.

I decided to put myself in a dangerous place for my quest. That way my senses would stay alert and transcend the mental barriers more quickly. There were no places more dangerous than on the barren lip of the dump, where the largest and fiercest packs of dogs lived. I not only had to be alert but also continuously invisible to everything. This would easily keep me on the edge of the abyss for four days. The essence of danger also added a tremendous excitement and depth to the quest. There, I could also punish myself with the fear for being unworthy of a spirit guide, a fact that I left out when telling Grandfather of my plans. Reluctantly he nodded permission, though I could tell that he knew something was not right with my soul. I guess that my enthusiasm overshadowed all else. But looking back, I knew he knew the whole story, and he had to let me go and face my fears.

I stalked all the way to the dump, taking great care not to make a sound or leave a scent. I had taken a long sweatlodge and washed myself with sweetfern leaves so as not to allow my scent to lead the dogs to my area. The lip I had chosen was barren of all trees and very steep. Though the dogs could not easily climb to the top of the mound, they could pin me there for weeks, if they found me. To reach the mound I had to cross the lower portion of the dump, then quietly dig foot- and handholds in the steep walls of the mound to reach the top. Grandfather had said that this mound reminded him of a small mesa, though it was made by a front-end loader. It took hours to dig enough holes quietly, and it was almost light when I reached the top. Cautiously and quietly I set up my quest area, then sat down to watch my first sunrise.

As the sun broke the horizon, I could see the elusive shapes and shadows of dogs moving at the far end of the dump. They were on their way back to their hides, finishing with the night's foraging and hunting. The sight of them sent a chill down my spine, causing me to shiver, a shiver that created enough noise to stop the distant dogs in their tracks. They seemed to thrive on fear, especially mine. Fortunately enough, they continued on their way when they heard no other sound. They looked around but never up to the top of the mesa, for only birds would go there, and they could not easily catch birds. I knew that the only events that could give me away were sound, motion, or scent, and I was taking great care to minimize all of them. The shiver had been an unconscious mistake, but a mistake I would not repeat.

As the sun rose high and the heat began to pump from the dump's floor, the lip of the dump became a frying pan. I felt like I was on an anvil, and the sun was a hammer, pounding my flesh into submission. The heat was oppressive, but the stench of rotten garbage was worse. At times it grew so vile I thought I was going to choke and vomit, but any cough or sound would alert the dogs. I began to grow dizzy, unable to sit up for very long without feeling sick to my stomach. My eyes could not take the intense light from the white sands, and I was forced to look down at my burned legs, or keep my eyes closed for long periods of time. This only heightened the dizziness. By high noon the heat and stench were intolerable, but now came the biting flies. I did not dare move fast to slap them but had to move slowly, as their bites burned holes in my flesh. I prayed so hard for a breeze to blow away the heat, the stench, and especially the flies.

Thirst grew intense, more painful than I could ever remember. I could not drink, for I dared not lift the jug. It would only give away my location to the dogs, so I had to wait until nightfall as planned. Anyway, there was no shade, and the water was burning hot, hot as the top of the mesa. Birds came frequently to rest atop the lip. Those who saw me gave out alarm calls that came dangerously close to alarming the dogs. Fortunately, I sat motionless, and the alarm calls were short-lived. With each sound my heart surged, only to fall back again to the sickening dizziness. By midafternoon, I could hold back no more and quietly vomited all over myself, as I tried desperately to quiet the retching and the falling vomit with my hands. I lay down and stayed in a semiconscious stupor for the rest of the day, too sick to think, as the sun and flies continued to beat my body and mind. I felt isolated, yet a spectacle, a fool, for all the entities of Creation to see.

I regained consciousness at dusk, though the moon was rising almost full and illuminating the whole dumpscape, as if I were looking out on the surface of the moon. The piles of garbage became obscure, appearing as huge craters; the dogs appeared as marauding ants. The night was full of the sounds of insects, growling dogs, and grating teeth puncturing garbage. The smell of the dump had all but disappeared with an oncoming night breeze; dampness soothed my burned and bitten skin. It wasn't long, however, before I began to shiver in the night air, and the mosquitoes took over where the flies left off. The water remained warm, though it had a bitter taste, probably from the thick dump air. Soon after taking a drink, I felt sick to my stomach again and began to vomit uncontrollably, muffling my face this time in the ground.

Whether by the sound of retching, my motions, or the smell of sweat and vomit, the dogs suddenly knew I was there. I could hear them growling from below; the sounds of claws scratching and sliding on the walls of the mesa became louder. I froze with my face buried in the ground, afraid to move. After a long wait, I slowly lifted my head from the ground and peered over the lip. The dogs were all around the base, some trying desperately, but in vain, to run up the walls. There was no doubt that they knew that I was there, and one way or another they were going to get to me, even if they had to wait me out. Thoughts of having been teased for several days by the dogs just a few weeks before, filled my head and terrified me. I desperately tried to think of a way to get out of the dump, but my thoughts were clouded and distorted by my fear. I felt so alone, so afraid, and so very vulnerable. I knew that the dogs could hold out longer than I could, and the fear of dying violently cut deep into my soul. I cried, and the dogs howled.

I stood for the first time all day and nearly fell off the edge with dizziness. I looked down on the dogs in the moonlight. They seemed so big and mean, so determined to get to me. I wiped the tears from my eyes and began to shake, not with fear or chills but with anger. Suddenly, in a fit of rage and fear, I lifted my staff from the ground and walked to the edge of the lip. I was determined to jump down to the dogs and die fighting like a warrior, not cowering atop this mesa. I had given up all hope, I had lost everything, including my self-respect, for being such a fool, and now I became the most vicious animal on earth. I remember what Grandfather had once said: "A man who has lost everything is the most feared enemy." Now I had become that animal, and I stepped to the lip, ready to jump. At the last moment a hand grabbed me firmly by the shoulder, yanking me back to the ground at the center of my quest circle. I stared up into the face of the old Indian.

Before I could say a word, he said, "Sit for a moment and think about what you are doing. Fear and rage are not good companions to clear thought or action." But where did you come from, I asked? "I came because I was needed," he said. "I only come when I'm needed, especially when you are in danger, or when you must be warned. I come only to protect you, and at no other time. I am a guardian," said the old Indian. But it was because I couldn't find you that I came to this Vision Quest, I said. I felt that I was unworthy, and I wanted to punish myself. "You must look beyond the learned perceptions of your mind," he said. "When you first saw me, it was a time of warning. If you had been aware of the time I had come, you would have understood that I was there as a guardian, not a playmate." The dogs continued to howl from below, and I grew worried again. In desperation, because I thought he was about to leave, I asked him to help me get out of the dump. He simply said, "The wisdom you seek is in the sun you have known all day long," and he vanished, leaving me more alone and afraid than before.

I awoke with a start, my face still upon the earth. It took me a while to sort dream from reality. Had the whole thing been a dream or did the dogs really know I was up on the mesa? Wearily, I looked over the edge of the lip, and the dogs were still all around the base. Somewhere I lost consciousness to sleep, but at what point? My staff still remained in its original place, and there were no footprints proving that I had stood at all. I was perplexed and disoriented, unable to piece together the sequences of consciousness. I could not even trust the spirit, for I could have hallucinated the whole thing through my fear and fatigue. Some of the messages he had given me seemed so vague, and ridiculous, but I could not take the chance of denying the information. Grandfather had told me to obey the directions of all the spirits I trusted, and I trusted that old Indian spirit, ever since he saved my life.

At first I cursed that old Indian. I needed a tangible plan of escape, not some coyote riddle. Then as I picked the warm jug of water up to drink, the answer came to me. The same laws of Creation that had tortured me all day long would also torture the dogs. The sun broke the horizon in a fiery ball, pumping the dump floor into choking heat. By noon there were only a few dogs left, and by early afternoon all were gone. I jumped from the top of the mesa and walked from the dump. There was not a dog in sight. From that day on, I have allowed my life to be guided by the wisdom of the spirit world, through countless dreams and Visions. I have fought the bad medicine spirits, though they have entered my life with their sickness, pain, and distortions. Good or bad, I have learned that all spirits are teachers, directing, protecting, and educating me in the wisdom of the outer worlds, and of the things unseen and eternal. They have truly expanded my world and my inner consciousness.

16

The Healing

As long as I can remember, Grandfather was a tremendous healer and herbalist. He would visit many old friends throughout the Pine Barrens and supply them with various herbs and remedies to preserve their health, alleviate injury, or heal their sickness. He also was a psychiatrist of sorts, listening patiently to anyone and delivering helpful advice. He was a healer of body, mind, and spirit in a very real sense. He was always such a caring and patient person, sometimes traveling many miles out of his way to visit a sick friend. In essence, he followed the traditions of his ancestors, fulfilling his destiny as shaman and medicine man, as his Vision foretold. He had a tremendous command of the uses of the plant people, using herbs to cure illnesses that doctors and modern medicines had given up on. He struck a balance and harmony in people, spreading good health, peace, love, and joy wherever he would go. His ability to help people overcome all illness bordered on the miraculous.

We accompanied Grandfather on his journeys of healing whenever possible. He would use us to gather his fresh herbs, shortly after he decided what herbs the patient would need. We also helped him make and mix various herbal medications and assisted in the administration. That way, we too learned to become herbalists, from start to finish. We observed his analysis of the patient. He explained to us what he needed and why, and helped us blend and mix the herbs. He then taught us how to give the herbs to the patient at what time and how frequently. The teachings went far beyond the basic use of herbs and into complicated mixtures of primary plants and catalysts. We knew which plants were toxic yet medicinal, and how to remove that toxicity through the introduction of other plants. We learned the best way there was to learn, through doing many times in real situations year after year.

Most of all we became aware that Grandfather's mere presence would do wonders for the patient, uplifting his spirits more than any medication. We also observed his touch. That touch was his trademark, for he could touch a patient and know exactly what was wrong, calm him down, and begin the healing process. He had a saintlike manner about him that seemed to fill the room with some undefined, glowing energy. Whenever he helped someone, he seemed to be the happiest, the most at peace, no matter how far he had come or how tired he had been. He was always so full of love and compassion for the sick, the lost, and the searching. To many, he was the last resort, even to the desperate nonbelievers. When all else was exhausted, all doctors, hospitals, and modern medications had failed, they then called Grandfather. Deep inside, they knew that he could do what others had failed to achieve—miracles through his ancient remedies.

We had accompanied Grandfather for many years of herbal healing excursions, when an event occurred that would forever change my life and my perceptions of the power of healing. It took place when Rick and I were just approaching our teens. By then our abilities and knowledge of the healing herbs was quite considerable. We knew, intimately, many herbs, remedies, and mixtures so well that Grandfather would send us out to take care of some of his people when he was busy with others. I was getting good at diagnosis and what herbs were needed, but I lacked something that Grandfather seemed to innately possess. I could administer the same herbs, in the same way as Grandfather, yet he would get effective results immediately, where I would get very slow and erratic results.

We were relaxing at Grandfather's camp one evening when the stillness was shattered by a rather distraught voice calling Grandfather's name. At first I thought it was from the spirit world, but with the subsequent brush-rustling and footfalls, I knew that the caller was of flesh. Grandfather sent us to fetch the person and lead him back to camp. I could tell that Grandfather knew exactly who he was and why he was coming, even before we heard his voice the first time. Grandfather had an uncanny ability to know of things long before they occurred, for he lived the duality constantly and religiously. He was always connected to things outside the realms of senses, always listening to the distant voices, and always fused to the greater consciousness. He seemed to be a direct link to the "force," the spirit-that-moves-in-all-things, and was "one" with all things, flesh and spirit.

We slipped through the swamp, down the deer trail, and to the old sand road, following the voice to its origin. We found an older gentleman who had been wandering back and forth along the trail calling Grandfather's name and trying to locate his camp. Neither Rick nor I had ever seen him before. He was wearing clothing and shoes that told he was from a town and not living in the woods like the people of the pines. We led him back to camp and introduced him to Grandfather. Grandfather seemed to know who he was and why he was there. As Grandfather spoke, the man was visibly amazed at how much Grandfather knew of his situation and plight.

The man's mother was dying and in a coma. She had been to doctors for many years and had spent considerable time on medication for cancer. The cancer now affected her entire body, and she was close to death. Apparently she had been hospitalized for quite some time and fell into the coma there. Her last request was that she die at home, and she was subsequently moved there the day before. The doctors said that she only had a few hours to live and was failing fast. The priest had already given her the last rites, and the family was waiting at bedside for her to die. Apparently the man had heard about Grandfather from an old Piney chicken farmer and now had come to find him. Though the family did not believe in herbal medicines or the old ways, Grandfather was the last resort, and the man was willing to try anything to save his mother. His voice and actions seemed desperate yet still contained a paradoxical disbelief in Grandfather's ability to do anything. Before we left, he asked Grandfather not to tell the family that he was an herbalist or to show any mystical abilities. This would only upset the family.

We left camp and traveled to town. We were brought to the house, and the man told his family that Grandfather was an old friend of his mother's and wanted to see her alone. With reluctance the family left the room, but the man stayed, refusing to leave. Grandfather turned to me and whispered, "Get me a glass of water for the old woman." But what about the herbs, I asked? Grandfather said hoarsely, "Do as you're told." I went to the kitchen to get a glass of water. I could not see what good water was going to do, or how he was going to get her to drink it, as she was deep in a coma. I returned quickly and handed Grandfather the water. He winked at me and with a half smile, whispered, "This is for the man's benefit, not his mother's." With that, Grandfather slowly slipped a hand under the old woman's neck and lifted her forward. Her body was frail, skin covering bones and not much else. Her lifeless gray color foretold the closeness of death. With the other hand, he placed his finger in the water, then transferred a drop to her lips. With that he laid her back down, placing one hand on her head, the other on her stomach. The man sat by, mute and motionless, a solemn, agonized expression on his face.

The room was lit only with a small lamp in the corner, casting the bed into deep shadows of grayness. I watched Grandfather slowly bow his head in prayer, his hands still firmly planted on her lifeless body. Suddenly, I saw Grandfather's body begin to vibrate slightly, almost imperceptibly. In the dim room I could see his hands, as if they glowed, and I had to shake my head to make sure that I wasn't seeing things. At that moment, like a dull flash the old woman's body glowed also, as if illuminated from within, then her body fell back into the original shadow. Grandfather slowly removed his hands, and the old woman groaned. Her skin now looked white, not the dull, transparent gray that it had been moments before. The old woman then began to stir a bit, obviously coming out the coma. The man jumped to his feet, staring in utter disbelief.

Grandfather looked at him and said, "I go now. Do not tell anyone what you have witnessed here." The man began to speak, but Grandfather cut him short, saying, "Do not be amazed at what you have seen here, for the ancient herbs are sometimes more powerful than your modern ways." The man began to profusely thank Grandfather, but again Grandfather cut him short. "There is no need to thank me," he said, "for I have done nothing. I am just a bridge for the force of Creation." With that, the man fell silent, and Grandfather said, confidently, "She will walk within the hour but have no recollection of what has taken place. She will be restored to her full health within seven suns." Without another word, Grandfather left the house. The man stared at me and I at him, both of us in utter disbelief. As I left the house, I heard the old woman call her son's name, and the family rushed by me. I cried like a baby, for I was certain that I had witnessed a full miracle.

I followed Grandfather back to camp. Not a word was exchanged. My mind was filled with more questions than I had ever had. How could a glass of water make a person well, what was the strange glow I had seen in Grandfather's hands, and what kind of medicine did he use? These were just a few of the most pressing questions. I had heard of faith healing, but I knew faith healing had more to do with a person's faith than with the healer. In essence, a faith healer is nothing more than a catalyst for the patient to focus upon. The patient is so convinced of the faith healer's power that it sets the patient into self-imposed recovery. It is the patient who heals himself, through faith. Grandfather had healed someone who was in a coma, for a family that did not believe in things of the unseen and eternal. How could he have possibly accomplished this healing, for there was no herb and no faith? My mind overflowed, and I was overwhelmed with the rapture of it all. I had borne witness to the impossible.

I sat at camp, staring into the fire in silence. I watched Grandfather moving about camp as if nothing out of the ordinary had happened this night. I held him in awe; my heart felt like I was in the presence of a deity. He glanced toward me and searched me with his eyes, and I could feel them reading my soul. He said, "Do not hold me above all else, for I have done nothing. I am but a bridge for the force of Creation to flow from, and I do nothing that any man, who knows the truth, cannot do." He continued, "The water was not the healer. The water was a crutch for the man to feed upon, while I directed the spirit-that-moves-in-all-things to heal the woman. The water was merely a camouflage for those who witnessed but did not believe. It was not my power that healed the old woman, but the power of Creation's life force surging through me. You too must learn that all the tools and remedies of man are but mere camouflages, crutches for those who do not believe. You must learn to control and use this life force, for that is the only healing."

Given the experience I had with the power of the healing herbs, and the power of the veils, I still could not fully understand all that Grandfather was saying. How could it be possible to become a bridge to the life force, and what was that force? How could someone direct and control something that is intangible and unseen, or not fully understood? How, too, could someone direct this force to do a specific healing, especially to something as powerful as a body full with cancer and coma, as had been the old woman? Certainly, I knew of the duality of Creation and the spirit world. I also knew invisibility and the void, and I could feel the spirit-that-moves-in-all-things creating a certain "oneness" in me at times, but how could I put it to use? At best, the whole mystical process seemed as a distant, impossible dream, something for those more worthy than myself.

Many days had passed since the healing, but I had not ventured further questions. New questions were never asked until the old answers were understood and lived fully. More answers came, however, the day we walked past the house where Grandfather had done the healing. As we passed the front of the house, I spotted the old woman seated in a rocking chair, knitting. Grandfather looked toward her, smiled, and asked, "How are you feeling?" I thought that the old woman would be quiet and timid, since she had never formally met Grandfather. Without hesitation she jumped from the rocking chair, easily walked down the steps, and approached Grandfather. All traces of illness and coma were gone. It was hard to believe that this spry old gal was the same woman who had lain in death only a few days before. She reached out and touched Grandfather's hand lovingly and said, sincerely, "Thank you. They told me what you had done." With that she cried, gazed for a moment at Grandfather's face, then solemnly walked back to the porch.

We headed back to the woods and moved Grandfather's camp to a new place. He just said, "They know now, and I must not be found. Those who really need me will find me." "Why don't you take credit for what you have done?" I asked. "Because it was not me who has done this healing; it is the life force. I am nothing more than a bridge and a man, not to be admired or worshipped. The Creator is all that should be worshipped, for it is only through the Great Spirit that we can heal. It is never from our doing, only through our faith, but modern man can only see the bridge, not the healer. Man must learn that all miracles come from the Creator and not man. Every day there are miracles for those who are aware through faith and believe. All men can become bridges, if they give up all else to learn."

"How do we become bridges, Grandfather?" I asked. "There

is only one way to the Creator, and that is through the purity of Creation, without the distractions or laws of man," Grandfather said. "But where do I start?" I asked. "Through dedication to finding the path of truth. Through time, aloneness, and asceticism, in the purity of wilderness, and through the Vision Quest. It is a long and hard path. There are no shortcuts, for man must live and die, be born and reborn, in purity of wilderness and spirit, many times, before he can become that bridge. This path is not for modern man, for modern man seeks things far too quickly. That is why the society of man has so many spiritual frauds who perpetuate the lies of life. Mankind feels that with some miracle or one Vision, he becomes a healer, a sage, and a prophet, and needs not look further. He is like a child who has seen yet never understands and has given in to the fad of spirituality. He plays many games with the spirit world and has no fear of that world, because he does not know its power. Beware of these instant healers and seers, these self-proclaimed prophets, for they will ultimately destroy themselves, and those who follow. I warn you: there is no shortcut. You must be reborn in the purity of wilderness or perish as a false prophet."

I was frightened and concerned about his words and warnings. "How are we to know when we have spent enough time?" I asked. "When you become that sacred 'oneness,' and the force of Creation freely flows through you. When you have bled and died, forsaken all things, know the timelessness of long periods of asceticism and countless quests, then and only then will you be worthy of the bridge. But take care when you have these things, for there are those who will call you 'Grandfather' and 'brother' only to steal your skills, your spiritual teachings, and your time, and proclaim themselves as healers, prophets, and teachers, without knowing the truth of asceticism and struggle that you have known. They will steal from you, deceive themselves and others, and denounce you, as they have done to me. Their lust for quickly gained power will destroy them. They become dangerous, for they distort the purity of the message that time and experience can only clarify."

I felt bound up inside. Was Grandfather referring to me stealing his skills? Was he trying to tell me in a roundabout way that I was unworthy, or was it warning me of things to come? I certainly knew the power of the spirit world and what it was capable of doing. I had also seen the power of the life force, and in no way did I even feel close to knowing that power or anything else. I would never call myself a prophet, healer, or teacher without first living and dying in wilderness. I was so mixed up, so full of pain from not knowing if I was even worthy to seek that which Grandfather had spoken, far less to try to hold myself up as anything but a searcher. I asked Grandfather to guide me on a Vision Quest so that I could know my path, so that I could understand what I had to do and know the purity of Grandfather's words.

For several weeks I prepared myself for the Vision Quest, a quest that I would come to call "the healing." The preparations were different than I had ever experienced with any quest, in that I had to continuously seek the void through aloneness and the sweatlodge. I prayed continuously, in and out of the Pine Barrens, my mind constantly thinking of that quest to the exclusion of all else. As time drew closer to the day I was to leave on the quest, people began to think that I was ignoring them or not paying attention to the events around me. I was so preoccupied that I even forgot to fully live in the moment. Though it was dangerous to dwell in the future or have any expectations of what was to come, I found myself there quite a bit. I began developing time warps, where I would have no recollection of walking down trails until I would arrive at camp.

Grandfather led me to the quest area he had chosen, a few hours before dawn. It was in the center of a huge swamp, near Eaden Lake, on a small dome of earth that sat high and dry from the surrounding area. It was very open, not at all like the confined areas I had sought out in the past for quest areas. The tall cedars stood like pillars on all sides, creating a temple. Being there and seeing the cedars reaching to the starry sky made me feel even closer to the Creator. Grandfather spoke for the first time since leaving the silence of camp, saying, "You must go beyond what the quests have been in the past and find the path to the 'healing force.' You must be pure in thoughts, spirit, and reason, to approach this path. You will never find it if your ego or greed go with you. You must accept what that path teaches and resolve yourself to follow that path, even at the sacrifice of all things. If you choose to follow that path, you must dedicate yourself to its challenges, its pain, and its self-sacrifice. Once you decide to go, there can be no turning back, for a man who abandons his Vision is living death." With those words, he turned and left me alone on the island.

The events of the first three days that followed were very strange, in that absolutely nothing out of the ordinary happened. Even on the quests where I felt no real Vision, I at least was given some personal insight. What was really strange about this quest was that I had a very powerful feeling that I was being closely watched. I felt that even my thoughts and emotions were under severe scrutiny, much like living under a microscope. At times I grew very paranoid, other times I felt giddy, but rarely did I sleep or stop praying. I wanted this Vision more than anything else, not for its powers but for its answers and directions. I had felt so lost lately that any insight, direction, or truth would be a tremendous relief. With the absolute emptiness of each passing day, I prayed, danced, and pushed harder and harder for that ultimate answer. On the approaching morning of the fourth and final sunrise, I was more desperate than I had ever been. I wanted this Vision more than life, and now my hopes were fading with the advancing dawn.

Out of my mind with the fear of failure, I scrambled to the edge of the island and grabbed my bag. I took out my flint knife and headed back to the center of the island. I knew that a few tribes would scarify, inflicting intense pain on themselves during the Vision Quest, and though Grandfather had never spoken of this, I was desperate to try anything to show my worthiness. I held a chest muscle in my left hand and drew the sharp blade to the skin. Just as I was about to gouge a huge cut into my chest, a clap of intense thunder rocked the island, then rumbled deeply across the clear sky. I shook with fear and dropped the blade to the ground. Regaining my composure I picked the blade up again, feeling that the thunder had been a freak happening. Again, as soon as the blade neared the skin, the thunder roared, and the blade dropped back to the ground. I knew without a doubt that I had been warned.

I felt now that the quest was not a loss, that I had been watched over and protected, and had communicated with the Lord of Creation. I was satisfied that it was not yet time for me to understand the wisdom Grandfather had passed on to me. A deep sense of peace and hope flooded my every thought, and I felt close to all things. As my mind drifted to the soft fissure of light that marked the dawn, I could feel a deep vibration within me. Then suddenly I realized that the very island was vibrating. Looking down in amazement, I saw the strange light gather beneath me, then surge like a shock through my body. Thunder rolled in the sky and the light glowed in my hands as it had in Grandfather's. I could feel a deep connection to the earth and her energy, and the energy of all things near me. I stared at my palms in utter disbelief for a long while, completely oblivious to the rising sun and the stir of waking Creation.

It was then that I heard a voice in the distance, and at once it was all around me. The voice told me many things, and the voice directed me onto the "path of no return." Most of all, the voice told me to ask Grandfather for further guidance, and as the sun rose, the voice disappeared to the sound of a coyote's howl. I ran to Grandfather and told him of the Vision. Grandfather then warned me that, from this day on, I should never reveal a Vision, fully, to anyone, including him. I should always hold something back, for Visions are for the individual, and sharing whole

Visions weakens that Vision. Sharing an entire Vision would also be a violation of trust between the questor and the spirit world, for the intimacy must always be protected. So I told Grandfather the most important parts of the Vision, and that the voice had told me that he would be a guide to that path.

Grandfather listened very patiently, then spoke. "I wish this path on no one, for the path is difficult, at times painful, and always lonely. Search your heart and know that this is what you want more than life. Know that this path will mean hardship, asceticism, loneliness, and the abandoning of all that modern society teaches. Know that you will lose friends, and that you will never return to where you have been. Know that once you choose to walk this path, you will walk it forever, or perish. Decide if you are willing to dedicate the rest of your life to this path, and know that there is no room on this path for you. The you that you are dies, and you become a bridge to be used by the Creator and Creation. You, your wants and needs, must always become second to that path, for you cannot serve the path and yourself."

I looked Grandfather directly in the eye, and he smiled. There was no need for an answer, for we both knew. A long sweatlodge followed, as did a baptism into the realm of the path. His teaching began immediately, and I could feel the awe of it all. I did not know if I would ever complete the path, but I was going to try and never give up until death. Certainly I knew that I would make many mistakes along the way that would make me stumble, but I was determined to pick myself back up and continue on. I knew that each mistake would be a test, a trial, and I dedicated myself from that day on to make it to the end. Grandfather and I grew closer than ever before, and we began to speak a common tongue on all levels of our existence. That day my life began.

17

■▾■▾■

Crystal Vision

Grandfather had been gone for several weeks, and I never felt so alone in my life. The ten years I had spent learning from him had seemed forever, and now all was so empty. Not only had he become my teacher and spiritual Grandfather but also my best friend, the only one I could ever talk to, especially about spiritual things. Now he was gone forever. His Vision complete, he had gone to rejoin his people. No one I knew understood the essence of Creation, the skills, or the asceticism and rapture of pure wilderness. Everyone outside the Pine Barrens seemed to be caught up in the rush of society, chasing goals, accumulating things, or imprisoned in the many social games. What little spiritual searching there was seemed to be trapped in some faddish hippy movements, or in a few cosmic masturbators who sought power, but who had little knowledge of spiritual things. Whatever was out there, I wanted no part of its insanity. I resolved myself to live in the wilderness for the rest of my life as Grandfather had done. I would wander this country from one end to the other, practicing my skills and following the spiritual path. Most of all I would stay away from people, their rush, and the distractions of society's fleshly, materialistic existence.

For many weeks I had thought about the journey I was about to undertake. In a few weeks I would be leaving the Pine Barrens and heading west, or at least that was my plan. I wanted to practice my survival skills in every possible environment. I wanted to track in different soils and push my awareness skills to the limits of every landscape. Most of all, I wanted the long periods of asceticism and aloneness in the purity of wilderness that was so necessary for spiritual growth. It would be sad to leave the Pine Barrens, but that was only temporary, for I knew deep inside that I would someday come back to this place of my spiritual birth. Before I left, however, I wanted to take one last Vision Quest here. The clarity of the quest would then be my new beginning and my guiding force for the first part of my journey. It would also bring me close again to Grandfather and the spirits, and for a short time I would not feel so alone.

As the days of preparation for the Vision Quest slipped by, I grew lonelier and more helpless than I had ever felt in my life. Certainly there is a huge gap between being alone and loneliness, but there was an emptiness within me that the spiritual connection to Creation could not fill. I had no one to teach me. I felt like a child not yet ready to strike out on my own. I longed for Grandfather's love and wisdom. The night before I was to leave for the quest area, I began to feel the oppression of loneliness more than I ever had. It was then that I decided to take with me all the sacred things that Grandfather had ever given to me. That way I would not feel as lonely or lost during my last days here. I ran back to my house and gathered up all the medicine bundles, feathers, and skulls that had spiritual significance. I could feel their power soothing me as I carried them back to camp.

This quest would be different from all the others, for it would be my longest Vision Quest yet. I had decided, for many reasons, to quest for forty days. I had always held Jesus above all else, and I knew that he had spent forty days in the wilderness, where he was tempted by Satan. This was one of Christianity's most powerful Vision Quests, and much of the Bible was directed by

Visions. I wanted to duplicate that time, not to be like Christ, but to understand the vast dedication required to spend that much time questing. It was the first of four forty-day quests I would take in the next decade, and still one of the most powerful of all my Visions. Grandfather, too, had frequently quested for many days, once for more than two months, and he always spoke of that intensity. This time, this last quest before my journey, had to be powerful and endless.

I left my camp area long before dawn of the first day and headed to the quest area I had picked out. The area I had chosen was very near the medicine cabin. A small creek ran nearby, and I could have fresh water every day. This area was special to me for many reasons. It had been so much a part of my life. It was here that I learned my first pipe ceremony, and my first sweatlodge. It was near to where I had my first Vision Quest, the medicine cabin, and the first place Grandfather began to teach me of spiritual things. Grandfather and I always considered this place sacred, a place where surely the Great Spirit would come to visit. We had buried a medicine bundle in the ground at the water's edge, and it was there on the mossy bank that I chose for the area of my quest. We had always called this area Medicine Creek, and it was perfect for what I had to do.

I carefully set the four medicine staffs to mark each of the directions. Each staff had taken years to make, carefully and with much prayer. They marked many sweatlodges, ceremonies, and past Vision Quests, and were sacred to Grandfather. Every time I looked upon them, my mind drifted to spiritual things, to past times, and to the awesome power of Creation's force. Near each of the staffs, I laid sacred pipes, crystals, drums, feathers, rattles, beadwork, quillwork pouches, bags, bundles, skulls, and necklaces that we had used in past ceremonies or healings, and that were given to me by Grandfather. It was sunrise when I finished placing all the sacred things around the circle. I felt a deep peace, and a closeness to Grandfather once again. All these things had deep meaning to me and were very powerful in their own right.

They marked my progress through the path and had become necessary tools for that path.

A sacred entity is not just an artistic assemblage of wood, stone, bone, and feather that symbolizes some sacred action. It is a power unto itself, not only for the power of the things contained in it and for the power of the people who put it together, but also for the power in its own right. It transcends the power of its makers and begins to take on its own personal power, becoming affected by all things and charged with surrounding power. Modern man does not realize the potential danger in collecting artifacts. These entities, if used in the wrong way, by believer or nonbeliever alike, can cause serious problems, even death. There is a tremendous power in everything, especially sacred things. I felt secure, protected, and energized by the circle of power that surrounded me in my quest, and I was now more than ready to begin.

Time passed quickly and the first several days fused together in a blur, defined only by the slashes I had placed on the time pole. Many things happened on these days, tremendous insights filled me, time wore me down, loneliness and fatigue destroyed my thoughts, only to build me up again with more insights and wisdom. Yet nothing of visionary quality came. I had learned to be very patient with the quest, for even the most humble times contained great insights into life and deeper meanings than were immediately apparent. What bothered me was that I had now surpassed all other quests in time spent, yet nothing had happened, and I was growing concerned. Possibly, I thought, I should have taken this quest at another time and place. Then, on the twenty-fifth day, all was changed.

I had awakened that day to the sound of arguing. It was not yet sunrise, but the earth was illuminated by soft light. I would not leave my area to trace the argument, for I was determined to stay confined until the fortieth day passed. I felt that any distraction was only an attempt by the spirits of bad medicine to distract me from the quest, so I stayed put. I knew that I was too far back in the woods and too far from any trail for anyone else to be here, especially this early in the morning. It was still too dark and people are generally afraid of the dark, especially dark wilderness. I knew that the arguing had to be from the spirit realm and not of flesh, but the sounds intensified, and other sounds of civilization joined in. Tires screeched, horns blasted, people yelled and talked loudly, engines and factories roared, and all natural sounds were drowned out. Still I held my ground and would not move.

Then, at the edge of the morning shadows, a figure emerged, wrapped in a dark blanket. He motioned to me to follow him to the other side of the creek, and I immediately arose without question and followed. Reaching the other side of the creek, I suddenly realized that I had left my quest area, and I began to question the origin of the spirit. Looking back, I saw myself still sitting in the quest area, sleeping. I had been taught to move out of my body and had done so many times before, but I was never led by a spirit. The fear of spiritual harm and unprotected travel began to fill me, but my heart knew that the spirit was a messenger and I should not fear. I continued to follow him, picking up my pace so I could catch up, yet still I stayed behind him as I used to walk with Grandfather. It was a show of respect for the spirit's power.

We traveled through the woods, passed the medicine cabin, and went toward the outer edge of the Pine Barrens. Emerging from the thicket, I saw bulldozers plowing up the earth, men cutting trees and brush, and other men widening a creek. A huge sign stood by the paved road, depicting this as a site of a nuclear generating station. The area they were destroying was one of Grandfather's favorite herbal collection areas and a tremendous place for all manner of animals. I knew it well as a child, but now it looked like a huge barren wasteland—the earth cut and bleeding, trees dying, and the creek uprooted from its natural bed. All wildlife were gone. The area was now silent and sterile, except for the drone of bulldozers and the chatter of man.

I turned to the spirit, who now stood beside me, and asked it if anything could be done to stop the insanity. Didn't these people realize what they were doing to the earth, the animals, and to their grandchildren? Without a word, the spirit pointed to a group of people gathered in front of the construction gate. They chanted and carried signs, protesting the building of the plant. Others walked the nearby streets, carrying petitions, preaching, and talking to other people. Many people were joining the protest, but the bulldozers continued to roll, trees continued to be cut. I could not believe that with all the intelligent people protesting, all the names on petitions, and the threat of killing future children and grandchildren that the people running the construction would not stop.

The spirit moved me to a huge construction office trailer, where a large group of people had gathered. Everyone was dressed for business, phones were ringing, and the chatter grew almost deafening. There was a man arguing with another, who was seated behind a large desk: These were the same voices I had heard in the quest area. The young man was trying to convince the other that he would have to give up the construction. He definitely was concerned about the protesters and all the bad publicity. The older man ordered the younger man to face the protesters, lie to them if necessary about the need for this plant and how safe it was. There was too much money tied up in it already, and much more to be made, and a few protesters should not stand in the way. "The government is on the side of the construction," he said, "and we'll have the police break them up if necessary. People have short memories and will forget about it once the plant is built."

Suddenly, I found myself back in the quest area. The dark shadow of spirit then spoke to me for the first time, saying, "As you know from your own experience, and by watching the results of this day, protesting and signing petitions do not work. If they do work, then the victory is only temporary. Money and power will always win out over the masses. There is not yet a powerful consciousness binding people, and until people are fused in one spiritual mind, all protest becomes pointless." He continued, "The only way we can bind people into that collective consciousness is to re-educate. People must be led back to the common ground of wilderness, touch the old ways, then make new decisions based on the laws of Creation. People must be joined in the wilderness consciousness, for it is this same consciousness that causes one bird to veer from the flock and the rest to follow. Re-education must come before change."

How could re-education possibly work? I asked. "If you were to take the man behind the desk out in wilderness," he said, "and have him live close to Earth Mother once again, then all would be changed in his heart. For a man who has touched the purity of wilderness can no longer destroy his mother. He must be led back to that wilderness, for he cannot be changed by the protests or petitions. He must first find his roots and realize that money and power are but flesh and lies; only the spirit is truth." But what can I do? I asked. "It is not yet time for me to reveal that truth to you," the spirit said. With those words, he vanished into the shadows, and I suddenly awoke to the rising sun.

I spent the next several days trying to sort through all that the spirit had revealed to me. I could understand the need for re-education and getting people back to the earth, but I had no idea of how it could be done. Generally, people lived far from the earth. Even when they entered the wilderness, they were still removed, connected back to civilization by that invisible umbilical cord called a backpack. They were encapsulated and insulated from the earth's energy by heavy clothing and shoes, with a consciousness forever seeking that death they call comfort, security, and safety. I could not see how anyone could be re-educated in wilderness, especially those who had no lust for the wild places at all. The task of teaching effectively seemed so impossible, with even more impossible odds against getting people to a point where they could be taught. It would be impossible to find a teacher anyway, and I certainly would never give up the freedom and spirit of wilderness to teach. Who would listen to me anyway? There was a certain hopelessness in it all, and I finally gave up thinking about it altogether. As far as I was concerned, it was someone else's problem.

Days slipped by faster than before, blurring into a sublime bliss that I had never before felt. I was like an old tree stump that had stood there for years rooted to the ground and watching over all. Animals began to pay no attention to me, as if I were a part of the landscape. Many passed within inches of where I sat, and birds sometimes rested momentarily on my head. I felt so much a part of the earth, and surrounded by all my medicine objects and in this special place, I felt safe and secure. I knew that I could easily spend the remainder of my life here, free from all the outside distractions. I grew more determined than ever to follow the spiritual path, always being an ascetic living in purity. For me, there could be nothing else. I wanted to wander the rest of my life.

On the thirty-eighth day my life turned miserable. The bliss that I had known was now replaced by a restlessness. Hunger began to affect me badly; at times I felt very weak and dizzy. The cool of the nights and the rainy days were hard to tolerate; my energy was low and my metabolism could no longer keep up with the heat demands. My reality existed someplace in the space between awake and dreaming. All thoughts were badly distorted and I began to feel disoriented most of the time. Loneliness crept in, causing me a great deal of anguish. I began to question my own motives and reasons for living in wilderness, even the validity of my path. I needed to talk to Grandfather so very badly. I knew that he could make sense out of all of this and help clarify my path once again.

By sunset, the pain of loneliness had grown oppressive, almost intolerable. It was then that I decided to break the tradition of the way I lived the quest and smoke the pipe, granted that some traditions allowed the pipe to be smoked in the quest area, as well as allowing many other things. But my personal way of seeking the visionary experience was as unencumbered with external or spiritual things as possible. I knew in the past that I was easily distracted by such things. This I knew would bring me close to Grandfather and fill me with its powerful energy. As I reached for the pipe, a small voice cried out. "You don't need that," it said with conviction. I pulled back from the pipe quickly, glancing around to find the origin of the voice. There was nothing to be found. Only the animals moved outside my circle, and the voices of insects filled the air. I reached for the pipe again, feeling that I had imagined the voice, when again the voice said, "Please, you don't need that, for you have all that you need inside of you." This time I followed the voice with my eyes and found that it was coming from a cluster of sacred crystals I had put at the base of my northern staff.

I looked closely at the larger of the crystals, and in the dimness of dusk, I could clearly make out a face. It was an old and weathered face with piercing eyes that seemed to contain the knowledge of the universe. I looked at it for a long time, in utter astonishment, and the crystal looked back at me, silently. I fumbled for words as I asked it what it had meant by my not needing the pipe. It quickly and lovingly answered, "You need no sacred external things. Sacred things are but triggers to your consciousness, outward expressions of inward realities. Sacred objects are powerful in and of themselves, but at best they are tools to carry you to spiritual consciousness. They are a camouflage for the masses, a trigger for young spiritual searchers, and are a crutch for those who refuse to let them go. Once you have used a spiritual object and understand its power, you must learn to get to that power from within, rather than with an external crutch."

Blasphemy! I said angrily. "Look at me," said the crystal. "I am a sacred object that helps you detect imperfections in the body, mind, and spirit of people. My power can help correct those problems, but I am a self-limiting crutch for you. Why do you need me, when you can find that same power from within? You must learn to wean yourself from these sacred objects and go in purity, unencumbered by any external objects, as the laws of Creation teach you to do. These objects you will always hold in reverence, but as your power grows and you learn to tap these same powers from within, there is no need for the excess baggage. You travel lighter, both in body and spirit. To cling to any sacred object or ritual will only retard your growth and limit you to the crutch. Without the crutch, you will then become powerless. That is why your Grandfather rarely used these things, except when you were around, or when someone needed that crutch or camouflage. He knew that his power came from within, and he was powerful enough not to need the external reminder." But what should I do with all these things? I asked. There was no answer; the voice and the face had now disappeared.

I understood what the crystal had taught, for Grandfather had not used many sacred things except around me. He always traveled so very light and free of baggage, as the wilderness dictated. He was able to find that power within himself and his power became limitless, for there were no self-limiting external crutches. I knew then that I would have to leave all my sacred things at home or give them away, so others could grow and pass them on. With that thought, I felt lighter and unrestricted, ready to undertake my journey, purely. Somehow I slipped out of a dreamlike stupor and into the intensity of the night. Stars seemed to burn in the sky, and the landscape seemed illuminated from within. I glanced back at the crystal, then at all the other sacred things. I could still feel their power, but now I could feel them moving within me also, and I was ready to give them up fully, accepting the challenge of finding the power within my own consciousness.

The dawn of the fortieth day brought a tremendous insight. I would not leave the Pine Barrens just yet. I felt a need to spend at least a year or more in its purity. I had to test my skills here first, without tools or clothing, so I could face what lay outside this wilderness with confidence. Here I would begin my journey, my life's quest, and push myself to the limits of purity. As I was about to leave the area, I felt the presence of Grandfather, and I knew that I had made the right choice.

18

The False Gods
of the Flesh

As I've wandered, I've become a keen observer of people, as well as animals, plants, and the other entities of Creation. It began by studying footprints and walks of people that I encountered at the edge of wilderness areas. I would carefully watch their actions, then check their prints when they moved on. This way I could push my tracking ability into the world of man, which I did since man has been one of the most dangerous and devastating influences on the earth. I also pushed my scout skills by entering the camps of men, observing their actions closely, then leaving without being detected. At times I became an animal, existing just outside their realm of perception. I observed them as I would anything else, closely and carefully weighing their every action and reaction. Eventually I learned to tell more from man's tracks than from anything else I tracked. I could tell moods, thoughts, actions, diseases, strengths, and weaknesses, and it wasn't long before I grew very proficient at reading emotions and even thoughts.

Eventually my observations carried me outside the realms of wilderness and the various campers, backpackers, and outdoor enthusiasts, and into man's home territory. I sat beside roadways watching expressions and observed the behavior of children and adults at work and play, always keeping myself invisible to everyone. I became very good at entering the world of man and staying out of sight. Several times I entered the world of larger cities and used the various buildings and alcoves as a sort of rock jungle of hiding places, at times living with the hobos and homeless to learn of their survival skills. Wherever I went, I observed closely and keenly. Just by the way a person tied his shoes, by his body English, his actions, and so many other nuances, did I learn about people, and about life in society. Many times I would get so close that I could pick up conversations, games, and actions that might have otherwise gone unobserved. I came to know a lot more about mankind than he knew of himself.

After years of careful observing, I was well satisfied that I wanted nothing to do with man or society. Everything was so sterilized, safe, secure, and fake. Every day was a game, and there were games within games. I remembered what society had taught me when I was younger, and what my friends had been taught, how children were placed on well-worn paths to chase elusive goals, directed by external shoulds. I watched how people became slaves to those goals, and how they destroyed their inner yearnings to become what society wanted them to become. I saw people doing jobs that they hated, chaining themselves to money, power, fame, and external treasures. I saw people living lives that they hated, rushing to work frowning, working, rushing home, watching TV, then doing it all over again. Play became parties, bars and nightclubs, watching sports, and a little outdoor recreation, and they always returned to the same old rut, and the play also became ruts.

I could feel the general desperation of society, yet they accepted their prison in silence, afraid to slow down and question, afraid to face the reality of themselves, and what they truly wanted in life. I felt that if people slowed down long enough, they might be forced to confront themselves, to realize that there might be more outside the fleshly and boring repetition of life. Wherever I went, I saw drug abuse, alcoholics, people running from each other and themselves. I saw through the games people played, the masks of happiness that they wore over pain. I saw children and adults living in security and comfort, longing, lusting after adventure, excitement, and rapture, yet not knowing where to find it. I saw many drifting in and out of religions, following gurus, and engaging in intense searching, desperately trying to quench their thirst for the spiritual realities, yet never being satisfied. These were the most desperate, for they knew that there must be more to life than just physical existence and were willing to try anything to find that more, their hopeless desperation growing with each failed attempt with the various spiritual fads.

The American Dream was failing the masses and the world, fooling those who perpetuated that lie. Yet society still teaches its children to find purpose and happiness in externals, the false gods of the flesh. Society teaches its children to seek fame, fortune, and power in such things as bigger houses, flashier cars, grander titles, and larger bank accounts. I learned through the wisdom of Creation that man works for only four things in life: peace, love, joy, and purpose; and these things cannot be found in external things and possessions. They can only be found within. Modern society tries to force its beliefs on the world, blindly assuming that societies with few possessions are primitive, yet never stopping to ask itself if these people they call primitive are happy. Instead it forces its beliefs on them and so the lie continues to be perpetuated. Modern man seems never to slow down long enough to search his soul. He cannot stop chasing the goal, and the tyranny of both the chase and its elusive end thwart his quest for fulfillment.

Those who have made it to the "top," who have achieved that ultimate goal, seem the most unhappy. In their eyes is an emptiness, a frustration, and a mediocrity of spirit. Upon reaching the goal, they find no happiness, and so they must press on to higher goals. Thus begins a cycle of desperate searching.

That is why most seek the thrill of drugs, drink, and wild existence, for they can not handle the emptiness or face the fact that they have never lived at all. They realize that they have wasted their lives. They do not know their families, their friends, or the intensity, excitement, adventure, and rapture of life. They know that there is no love, joy, peace, or real purpose in what they are doing, and they do not know how to find love, joy, peace, and purpose. Yet they still rush, and they still drive their children toward the false gods of the flesh, until there is emptiness in everyone's eyes.

Mankind, society, needs to face itself. People need to slow down and take stock of the goals they are chasing, of the rushing, and of what they are really working for in life. They must find out what the real treasures of life are, and find them within themselves, instead of rushing toward death never really living at all. Society needs the Vision Quest, to search out the other, greater part of life, that of the spirit. Mankind must reach inside and find the ultimate peace, the boundless joy, the rapture of perfect love, and the grand purpose. For the longer man denies the reality of these things and perpetuates the false gods of the flesh, the surer he can be that the earth will seek its own purification, to reestablish the balance of the natural order. Then man will witness the fire in the skies and an earth that will no longer support his gluttonous life-styles. That is when all the true children of the earth will have to start over, out of the rubble of man-made hell. We must then seek and build a world of Vision. It is not too late.

19

▼▼▼▼

The Dedication

I had wandered for nearly ten years in and out of wilderness and all over the country. I had searched the wild places, tracked from Canada to Mexico, pushed my awareness and scout skills to the limits, and most of all followed the path of spirit. I had quested more times than I could ever remember, always seeking the limits of Grandfather's teaching. Yet with all that I had accomplished, and all the Visions I had sought, there was still an emptiness inside of me, a deep yearning that cannot be described, like some part of me was missing. So often I would see a grand part of nature and run to tell someone, anyone, but no one was ever there to share it with. Again, I was where I had been before, alone, searching, with no one to talk to, no one to share things with. I don't know what prompted me that day to come out of the woods, exactly at that time and in that way, but that day changed my life forever. I fell in love.

Judy was always so special. She took away all the loneliness, and I could share my life and my Visions with her. I also fell in love with her children, for they were so open, so thirsting for the deeper things in life. Soon I found that there was no way I could live without her, so we were married under that ancient tree. Judy and I had a dream, to pay off her debts and move back into the wilderness. We wanted to raise the kids close to the earth, start another family, and live off our land in close harmony with Creation. There was never a doubt in either of our minds that this was what we should do, and the kids, Paul and Kelly, were thrilled. We planned and dreamed for months as we worked diligently toward that goal. I had no place in society and found it hard to cope, or even to communicate with people I didn't know. Judy helped me through the hard times, working, while I did odd jobs around the neighborhood.

Suddenly, a chain of events turned our lives around. A number of publishers wanted me to write a book about my life. They had heard about many of the police cases in which I had tracked criminals through the wilderness, and they thought a book would be of great value. I was dead set against the idea, for I considered a book to be a form of prison, a responsibility that would only tie me down and keep me from going back to the purity of wilderness with my family. Judy felt otherwise. Through long talks and her form of mild coercion, she convinced me that a book would show many people that my life was not a folly as well as help to preserve Grandfather's teachings. I couldn't see what good a book like that would do, but my defenses eventually collapsed, and I signed on with a publisher. I promised myself, however, that after it was written, we would go to the Canadian Rockies and away from society.

Reader's Digest picked up on my manuscript, *The Tracker*, and wanted to reprint it in their condensed book section. I could see no harm in allowing it to be published there, especially since it was to come out the following month in book form anyway. Several weeks later, I was camping alone in the Pine Barrens to get away from things when the magazine editor called Judy. They wanted some sort of epilogue, to tell people what "The Tracker" was doing now. At the time, I had run a few classes in wilderness skills for close friends, which prompted Judy to tell the editors that I had a small tracking and wilderness survival training school. I knew nothing of this phone call, that is, until it was too late. Not much later came a knock at my front door. There stood the postmaster, with bags and bags of mail. I had no idea where the people had gotten my address or what they wanted, but the mail filled most of the living room.

I opened a few and found, to my horror, that people were asking me how they could register for my school. A number of them had referred to the end of the article in the magazine. I opened the magazine for the first time and was shocked to find that at the end there was a small epilogue talking about the school. It didn't take me long to realize where they had gotten the information. Judy and I had a tremendous fight that night. She tried to convince me to run a school; I was dead set against the idea. No way was I going to give up my dream of living out the rest of my life in the wilderness. I refused to be tied down to anything in society, and a school would do just that. For days, Judy, my family, and a few close friends presented their case. They reasoned that the old ways would be lost, that people needed the school, and that I could use it to save the earth. The more they tried to convince me, the more I resisted, until the subject was completely dropped.

Within the next month, two grand things happened in my life. First of all, my book came out, and most important, our baby was born. I was beside myself with joy and wonder. More than ever I had to get back to the wilderness, especially for my new son's sake. I went to the woods to pray that day, to give thanks to the Creator for my son, my wife, and my kids and ask Him to direct our lives toward the wilderness. It was then that I remembered what Grandfather had once asked me to do: In the moon of purification, January, after my son's birth, I was to bring him into the Pine Barrens to give thanks. Grandfather always could foretell the future; I can remember no prophecy that he spoke that did not come true. I was to take little Tommy to Medicine Creek, to the sacred grounds, where I was to raise my pipe in thanksgiving as Grandfather once requested so very long ago.

I remember vividly that cold and clear January day. I drove to the Pine Barrens with little Tommy and my pipe, so happy, so at peace, and so excited to be going back to the purity of wilderness. I had not seen the sacred area for nearly a decade and was thrilled to be headed back, especially with my baby. I parked the car, bundled little Tom up in one arm, carried the pipe in the other, and wandered down the trail to the sacred area, deep in prayer. My heart truly soared with the eagles, that is, until I rounded the bend in the trail that led to Medicine Creek. I was stopped dead in my tracks, and my spirit trembled with sickness, for there, as far as the eye could see, was a sea of garbage. The area had been plowed for development and abandoned, and had now become an illegal dump site. Piles of garbage and chemicals were strewn all around, the stream was glazed with oils, and what few trees were left had been burned.

I had to lay my baby down on that pile of garbage, for no earth showed through anywhere. Trembling and crying, I raised my pipe to the Creator. I now knew why Grandfather had asked me to bring my baby here. He knew that it would forever change my life and begin my living Vision, which I had for so long denied. I realized at that moment that my own son would never taste the wilderness I had once known. I saw the results of a society that gives no thought to the survival of its grandchildren. I was more shaken than I had ever been in my life. I felt even more helpless than the baby lying at my feet. It was then that I saw the place where I had taken my first forty-day Vision Quest, and it rushed over me like fire in the pines. I raised my pipe again and swore to the Creator that I would no longer run, that I would give up everything else in my life to save what was left of the wilderness. Someone had to have the guts to fight, and give up all else, for the grandchildren. I could no longer go back to the wilderness, for I had to now teach, re-educate, so that my own child could run free and wild as I once did.

• • •

I remember Grandfather's words. "Tell me something you are dedicated to in life," he said, "and a true test of that dedication is, Would you die for it?" I dedicated myself to that Vision of long ago, and the purpose for the rest of my life is to teach the old ways. There can no longer be any room for me, for the Vision is the most important, and I would gladly die for that Vision.

There is no going back to the purity of wilderness for me, or for Judy. We are in this Vision together, and the Vision is strong, consuming. Slowly, now, with me, and all the other schools and environmental and spiritual groups out there, there is coming a fusing of consciousness. I pray that we can all work together to change society's direction. Instead of wasting energy criticizing and fighting with each other I'm hoping we learn to cooperate in order to fight the bigger battles before it is too late.

Certainly it has been a difficult path to travel, running the school and following the Vision. I have fallen from the path so many times. I have succumbed to the distractions of society, only to be yanked back to the Vision. I have hurt people in trying to deal with the pressures of society and the school, and all too often neglected my friends and family. My obsession with the Vision sometimes excludes all else, and I have made many grave mistakes. As with all things, I will probably make many more, but living this Vision has been one of the grandest quests of my life. But I cannot take the credit for this Vision, for it is also Grandfather's Vision. The real credit, for the living Vision, must go to Judy, and to her, I dedicate this book. Judy has had to give up the most for this Vision. She has caught me when I have fallen, forgiven me for the unforgivable, guided every facet of the school and the books, and has been a buffer between me and the world outside my Vision. Without her, this Vision would not have been possible. Without her, my life would be impossible.

I often ask people to ask themselves truthfully: Are you happy? Is your life full of intensity, adventure, excitement, and rapture? Are you filled with peace, love, joy, and purpose? If not, then you need Vision.